THE GREAT DAYS OF
DERBY COUNTY

THE GREAT DAYS OF DERBY COUNTY

Edited by Anton Rippon
Research by Pip Southall

The Breedon Books
Publishing Company
Derby

First published in Great Britain by
The Breedon Books Publishing Company Limited
44 Friar Gate, Derby, DE1 1DA
1993

ISBN 1 873626 58 4

Printed and bound by Hillmans Printers, Frome, Somerset.
Covers printed by BDC Printing Services Limited of Derby.

Contents

Dedication

This book is dedicated to the memory of Jack
Stamps, Tim Ward and Ken Oxford, three of a
rare breed. They were fine footballers who
served their club so well and then continued to
be fervent supporters long after they had
retired.

Introduction

ALL football followers have special memories of their club, the great afternoons, the breathtaking nights when their team scored a triumph which lived on in their minds long after the result had been consigned to the history books. Derby County, it seems, have had more than their fair share of such occasions and *The Great Days of Derby County* sets out to recall many of them, mostly through the eyes of the contemporary reporters who brought their own view to supporters.

Of course, the choice of the 90-odd matches to appear here is entirely subjective and whilst there can be no argument over some — the 1946 FA Cup Final, the defeat of Benfica in the European Cup, the night when Chelsea were knocked out of the League Cup, for instance — it is certain that other people will wonder why this match is included or that game is not. Indeed, their own special memory of the Rams may be missing, but an attempt has been made to capture all the memorable times and all the significant moments, too, so that throughout the book runs the thread of Derby County's history

as milestones are reached, records set, great players and club servants introduced.

So apart from the classic victories, we also have the debuts of players like Steve Bloomer, Jack Bowers, Tommy Powell and Kevin Hector, the Rams' first game in the Football League, the official opening of the Baseball Ground, the last game before World War Two ended League football for six years and so on.

This means that whilst the Rams won the overwhelming majority of the games featured, not every one ended in a Derby victory. But who, for instance, could rule out the FA Cup thriller against Aston Villa as recently as February 1992, which the Rams lost by the odd goal in seven but which was one of the more memorable nights in the club's history.

Inevitably, Brian Clough's time at the Baseball Ground provides many of the matches recalled, but there are games from every era. So sit back and enjoy again some of the great days in Derby County's history.

Anton Rippon
Derby
August 1993

Acknowledgements

THE match reports included in this book have been drawn largely from the columns of the *Derby Evening Telegraph* and its predecessor, the *Derby Daily Telegraph*, and so acknowledgements must be made to the various reporters who, over the years, have brought the affairs of Derby County to readers. They include Frank Nicklin, Wilf Shaw, George Edwards and, for the last 20 years or so, Gerald Mortimer. Prior to World War Two, it was the fashion not to identify the journalist, but again the *Evening Telegraph* provided the basis for this work.

An enormous debt is also owed to Raymonds Photographers of Derby, particularly to Les Parkin, who readily agreed to provide many of the photographs of matches post-1959. Inevitably,

publication of several books on the Rams over the years has meant that finding new photographs for this latest work has proved difficult. The *Derby Evening Telegraph* have always been very helpful, but like any source their material is not unlimited and so Raymonds' major contribution this time has meant that many previously unpublished pictures can be included. Other photographs have been supplied by Empics of Nottingham, the Hulton-Deutsch Picture Library of London and Colorsport of London. Gary Holman and Chris Kendall, two avid collectors of Derby County memorabilia, also provided photographs for some of the earlier matches. Former Rams players Tommy Powell and John Bowers have also been extremely helpful.

Mighty Villa Are Beaten — And The Rams Have Arrived

Saturday, 14 November 1885

Derby County 2   **Aston Villa 0**

FOR Derby County, this was a sort of coming-of-age. Still a fledgling club — the Rams had been formed just over a year earlier — this victory over Aston Villa in the second round of the FA Cup established them amongst the country's leading clubs.

When Derby were formed in 1884, as an offshoot of Derbyshire County Cricket Club, Aston Villa were already ten years old. And when Villa came to the County Ground in 1885, they had plenty of Cup experience and were to win the trophy two years later. At Derby, they fielded two England internationals, Arthur Brown and Howard Vaughton, and were led by their great captain, Archie Hunter.

The Rams, meanwhile, were a team comprised mainly of local club players, the exception being Benjamin Ward Spilsbury. An Old Reptonian and Cambridge soccer Blue, Spilsbury had enjoyed the distinction of scoring Derby County's first-ever goal — against Blackburn Olympic in September 1884 — and had made his England debut in February 1885, scoring against Ireland at Manchester. In March 1886, he would score four against the Irish in Belfast.

Other Rams players included Haydn Morley, son of one of the club's founders, George Bakewell from Derby Midland, and Lewis Cooper from Darley Dale. There were also Albert Williamson from Sawley Rangers and George Evans from Derby St Luke's.

Derby had lost their first-ever FA Cup tie 7-0, going down to Walsall Town in November 1884 when they were without Spilsbury and J.B.T.Chevallier, who had played in four FA Cup Finals for the Old Etonians. In the following season's first round, however, the Rams beat Birmingham St George's 3-0 on a waterlogged County Ground pitch. Now came Aston Villa, who had beaten Derby 4-2 in a friendly game earlier in the season.

On a dull and threatening day, the teams ran out to find the extra accommodation which had been erected well patronised, and the pitch slightly greasy. The Rams defended the Nottingham Road goal. Villa, meanwhile, had their backs to the Rifle Range goal.

Villa had come out of the hat first but, for a financial consideration, agreed to switch the game to Derby in the belief that they would still win easily. How wrong they were was evident from the first minute as the Rams fairly tore into the attack with Evans and Spilsbury both testing Hobson in the Villa goal.

Having survived the early exchanges, Villa edged their way into the game and first Morley had to clear from Arthur Brown, then Rams' goalkeeper Walter Luntley fisted out a shot from Whateley.

After half an hour, the Rams missed a glorious opportunity to go ahead and 'Jammer' Smith was the culprit. Morley got the ball to away to Evans and he laid on the chance which Smith wasted.

A few minutes later, however, Smith more than made amends. The ball appeared to be going out of play when Hobson fisted it out and it fell at the feet of Smith, who this time made no mistake.

Villa came more into the game in the second half but it was the Rams who scored again. Lewis Cooper sent over a left-wing corner and after Spilsbury had touched the ball on, Evans was on hand to hammer in a shot. Hobson should have held it but allowed the ball to slip out of his grasp and over the line.

Still Villa were not out of it, but the main threat to Derby's lead was the fact that it was getting dark and, in these days before floodlights, more than a few games had been abandoned with only minutes remaining. Fortunately, the daylight held just enough to allow the match to be completed and the Rams might have made it 3-0 in the dying moments when Evans missed after Spilsbury had brought the ball through from his own half.

At the final whistle, hats and umbrellas were thrown into the air and a famous victory was

One day in 1885, the Derby photographers W.W.Winter were called to the County Ground to take this photograph of a Derby County team. Alas, the names of the players have long since been lost but the picture gives an indication of how those early footballers looked and dressed. The picture was taken at the rear of the cricket pavilion and some of the spectators at those first Rams matches would have watched from here.

won. The *Derby Evening Telegraph* said: 'Luntley served his side splendidly between the posts, evincing coolness and judgement. Evans played a dashing game at centre-forward and Smith and Cooper fairly outdodged the Aston backs. Spilsbury occasionally was brilliant, but not constantly so. Of the back divisions, Wharmby, Morley and Williamson, worked extremely hard.'

In the next round, the Rams lost 4-2 to Small Heath Alliance — later Birmingham City — at Coventry Road. But their victory over Villa was hugely significant. After this,

the Rams had no difficulty in arranging a top-class fixture list and when the Football League was founded three years later, Derby County were one of the founder-members.

Derby County: Luntley; Morley, Williamson, G.Cooper, Flowers, Wharmby, Bakewell, Spilsbury, Evans, Smith, L.Cooper.
Aston Villa: Hobson; Jones, Riddell, J.Burton, Price, Whateley, Arthur Brown, Hunter, Albert Brown, Vaughton, Davis.
Referee: J.Piggott (Derby)   *Att: 5,000*

A Great Rams Fight-back In Their First League Game

Saturday, 8 September 1888

Bolton Wanderers 3   Derby County 6

FOUR years after Derby County were founded, the Rams took their place as founder members of the Football League. In the 1880s, some of the leading football clubs were becoming increasingly concerned that Cup football alone would not pay their way.

Early exits from the FA Cup and the local knockout competitions, and the fact that the hitherto prestigious friendly games between top sides were not now the draw they were, meant that clubs had to look for other means of increasing their income. Professionalism had not long been legalised and clubs needed bigger attendances and regular fixtures to ensure financial stability.

Thus, in 1888, the Aston Villa comitteeman William McGregor came up with the idea of a Football League, where each club would play the others twice each, home and away. Several clubs were invited to a meeting at the Anderton Hotel in London on 22 March 1888 and the Rams were represented, although their delegate was there merely as an observer and not to take part, so the name of Derby County does not figure in those first minutes.

However, Derby County's man took a full part in the next meeting, at the Royal Hotel, Manchester, on Tuesday, 17 April 1888, and on that day the Football League was officially formed. Besides the Rams, the other clubs were Accrington, Aston Villa, Blackburn Rovers, Bolton Wanderers, Burnley, Everton, Notts County, Preston North End, Stoke, West Brom and Wolves.

Crewe Alexandra, meanwhile, were trying to recruit other 'rejected' clubs to form a rival league, to be called the Combination, and one of the clubs they targeted was Derby Midland. These were, indeed, great times for local football and another local club, Derby Junction, reached the FA Cup semi-finals in 1888, having knocked out mighty Blackburn Rovers in the sixth round on the Arboretum

Field. Junction, incidentally, lost their semi-final, going down 3-0 to West Brom at Crewe.

On the day that the Football League staged its first series of matches, Derby Midland and Derby Junction attracted a crowd of 1,200 to the Arboretum to see a friendly between the two clubs, whilst on the County Ground, the Rams Reserves were entertaining Burton Swifts in another friendly game.

The Rams' first team, meanwhile, had to travel to Pikes Lane, Bolton, for their opening League game against Bolton Wanderers. The Derby team contained only three players — Albert Williamson, George Bakewell and Lewis Cooper — from the side which had scored such a fine FA Cup victory over Aston Villa three years earlier. In goal was Joe Marshall, who had played cricket for Derbyshire, and the full-backs were Albert Latham, a former Midland player, and Archie Ferguson, who had joined the Rams that summer from Hearts. The half-backs were Williamson, a former Sawley Rangers player, Walter Roulstone, who was also from Sawley, and Isaac Monks, who as a centre-forward had scored a hat-trick in an FA Cup tie against Staveley the previous season.

Derby's forward line comprised Harry Plackett and Lol Plackett, brothers from Long Eaton, Sandy Higgins, a new signing from Kilmarnock, Bakewell, another former Midland player, and Cooper, a versatile footballer from Darley Dale.

Derby County made a sensational start to their Football League career. Within five minutes, the 3,000 crowd saw Bolton take a 2-0 lead and soon Derby were trailing by three goals before staging a remarkable fight-back to draw level and then take a 4-3 lead by half-time.

In the second half, according to the *Derby Daily Telegraph*, 'the County played up wonderfully well, and quite nonplussed the Wanderers'. They extended their lead with two more goals and ended their first League game in triumphant fashion. Alas, no local report carried descriptions of the goals but we do know that Lol Plackett, Bakewell and Cooper each scored twice.

When the 22-match League programme ended in February, Derby were tenth and so had to seek re-election. Their League career

Derby County in 1889. Back row (left to right): Chatterton, Williamson, Latham, A.Goodall, Dakin (trainer), Ferguson, Roulstone, Bulmer (umpire). Front row: Bakewell, Higgins, J.Goodall, Holmes, Cooper, Milarvie.

Pike's Lane, Bolton, where the Rams played their first game in the Football League.

had thus begun and in the coming years, Derby County made some impact on the running of the competition. In 1893 they were so hard up that they made the first moves towards imposing the maxiumum wage for players, and even before World War One the Rams were campaigning for the four-up-and-four-down approach to promotion and relegation.

Bolton Wanderers: Harrison; Robinson, Mitchell, Roberts, Weir, Bullough, Davenport, Milne, Coupar, Barbour, Broughton.

Derby County: Marshall; Latham, Ferguson, Williamson, Roulstone, Monks, H.Plackett, L.Plackett, Higgins, Bakewell, Cooper.

Att: 3,000.

Derby County in 1890-91. Back row (left to right): Holloway (umpire), Chalmers, Hopkins, A.Goodall, Haddow, Ferguson, Roulstone, Bulmer (umpire). Front row: Bakewell, McLachlan, J.Goodall, Holmes, Nelson.

Five Goals For McMillan In Rams' Record Win

Saturday, 10 January 1891

Derby County 9   Wolverhampton W 0

WHEN Wolverhampton Wanderers visited the County Ground, Derby, for their penultimate game of the 1890-91 season, they were looking for a victory which would keep their tenuous hold on the Football League championship race. Wolves' hopes were heightened by the fact that they had beaten Derby 5-1 at Molineux earlier in the season and the Rams were now struggling to avoid finishing bottom of the table.

Yet no one could have dreamt that Derby would rattle up their biggest-ever win in League football and inflict upon Wolves their heaviest League defeat.

For one man it would prove a particularly memorable day. Forward Johnny McMillan, who the Rams had signed from the Edinburgh club, St Bernards, the previous close season, scored five of Derby's goals in only his seventh League game. Over half a century later his son, Stuart, would manage the Rams to the only FA Cup Final victory in their history.

These were the formative years of the Football League which still had only one division and comprised 12 clubs. Thus, the season drew to an early close and Wolves had got through their matches particularly quickly. They still had hopes of the title, but challengers Everton, Preston and Notts County had games in hand and, as it turned out, it was Everton who lifted the championship.

Derby were without full-back Archie Ferguson and forward Lewis Cooper, both of whom had been regulars that season, but the Rams had to risk outside-right George Bakewell, who was suffering from a leg injury. Wolverhampton, meanwhile, were without regular defender Charlie Mason, the first Wolves player to appear in an international match when he played for England in 1888. He was replaced by Arthur Lowder, another veteran and former England player, who was on the verge of retiring.

The Rams kicked-off on a beautiful day — blue sky but extremely frosty — and on a pitch that was rock-hard due to the sub-zero temperature they were soon into the attack with Sam Holmes whipping a shot just wide of Wolves' post. Then Chalmers went close before Derby took a deserved lead.

McMillan got the ball out to Holmes, who centred beautifully for John Goodall to take it round a Wolves defender and shoot past England goalkeeper Billy Rose.

It was all Derby. Chalmers and Holmes might have made it 2-0 midway through the first half before Bakewell curled in another teasing cross and McMillan was on hand to score the Rams' second. Then it was John Goodall's turn to shave the woodwork before McMillan tested Rose again. His first attempt was saved, but the Wolves 'keeper had no earthly chance with a McMillan shot that fairly screamed past him. Before half-time, Derby were 4-0 ahead and again McMillan was the scorer.

After the interval, McMillan completed his hat-trick by scoring a fifth for the Rams and after John Goodall had won a corner, Walter Roulstone made it 6-0. Holmes added a seventh and before the final whistle, McMillan got his name on the score-sheet twice more, both the result of Bakewell's crosses.

The crowd had seen nine goals and yet there could have been so many more. As the *Derby Daily Telegraph* commented: 'There was only one team in it from the start and the Wanderers have probably never suffered a more decisive defeat. It establishes a League record for the season and will probably do the County an infinite amount of good.

'The whole team played a thoroughly good game and made rings round their opponents. John Goodall was in his best form and dribbled, shot and passed in good style. McLachlan played a fine game and there was no stopping McMillan when in front of goal. He was always well up without being offside and popped centres through without giving Rose a chance.'

Wolves went on to finish fourth that season, losing their final match 6-2 at Aston Villa. The Rams, meanwhile, lost 4-2 at home to Burnley, beat Sunderland 3-1 at home and then lost 5-1 at Roker Park to end the season in 11th place, three points ahead of bottom club West Brom. John Goodall was their leading scorer with 13 goals, although he missed out as the Rams ran riot against Wolves.

Derby County: Bunyan; Roberts, A.Goodall, Walker, Chalmers, Roulstone, Bakewell, McLachlan, J.Goodall, Holmes, McMillan.
Wolverhampton Wanderers: Rose; Baugh, Brodie, Fletcher, Allen, Lowder, Wykes, Booth, Thomson, Wood, Bowdler.
Referee: Mr A.Hughes (Sheffield)

Att: 3,000

On 21 January 1899, Derby County equalled this win with a 9-0 victory over Sheffield Wednesday in a First Division match at the Baseball Ground. Steve Bloomer scored six for the Rams that day.

Steve Bloomer's Debut — The Start Of A Magnificent Career

Saturday, 3 September 1892

Stoke 1   Derby County 3

WHEN Derby County's secretary forgot to register Ernest Hickinbottom, Sam Mills and Ernie McLachlan for the start of the 1892-93 season, it let in a young lad from the Reserves for his League debut for the Rams. Steve Bloomer made his bow at Stoke's Victoria Ground and thus began a career which would write him into the history books as arguably Derby's greatest ever player.

Although born in Cradley Heath in January 1874, Bloomer came to Derby as a youngster and between 1880 and 1886 attended St James' School, near to what later became the Baseball Ground. He then worked in a local foundry and played football for Derby Swifts in the Derbyshire Minor League, once scoring 14 goals in a single game.

He moved to Tutbury Hawthorn and it was from them that Derby County signed Bloomer as an amateur and in his first game for the Rams Reserves he scored four goals against Darley Dale. In April 1892, he signed professional forms for 7s 6d (38p) per week and on the opening day of the following season found himself lining up at inside-right next to the great John Goodall, an England international signed from Preston North End in May 1889.

The Rams had finished the previous season tenth out of 14 clubs in the Football League — the Second Division was not formed until 1892-93 — whilst Stoke ended it next to the bottom, having just rejoined the competition after one season as a non-League club.

Despite the presence of John Goodall, the Rams were weakened by the absence of the ineligible players and that of John's brother, Archie Goodall, a rumbustuous character who was under suspension for the whole of September following 'misconduct at Sheffield' at the end of the previous season

(although in 1891-92, the Rams did not meet any Sheffield club in a senior competitive match that season).

Despite the lowly status of the two teams the previous season, this first game of the new campaign attracted a crowd of 5,000 — reasonable for that era — and the Rams took 1,000 supporters on an excursion train run by the North Staffordshire Railway. They found the weather fine and the pitch 'in capital condition'.

When the teams ran out, there was some surprise at the appearance of young Steve Bloomer, who was 'pale, thin, ghost-like, almost ill-looking', according to one observer. Certainly, the Stoke fans began to laugh at him and in his first few moments as a Derby County first-teamer, the man who was to become a Rams legend had to endure some jeers and cat-calls.

But with John Goodall to look after him, to nurse him through those difficult first moments, Steve Bloomer settled down and the crowd were soon thrilling to his obvious skills. Said Bloomer later: "John Goodall really helped me. He told me once, 'Go on yourself, lad, and shoot.'

"The very fact that one of his reputation and ability told me to do what I myself might have thought cheeky for a greenhorn, gave me the confidence I needed."

The Rams took an early lead, when Goodall got the ball out to Fred Ekins and the former New Brompton player crossed for Johnny McMillan to score 'an easy goal' after only three minutes.

Despite dominating the first half, the Rams arrived at the interval still only 1-0 ahead but in the second period they went 3-0 up, through another McMillan goal and one from Goodall. Jack Robinson was in no way to blame for Stoke's late goal, which was arguably the best of the game.

The *Derby Daily Telegraph* reported: 'The success of the team cannot but afford the utmost satisfaction to the County's numerous friends and supporters. To beat Stoke on their own ground, and in such style, was an event that even the most sanguine dared hardly look forward to, and the individual efforts of the players are deserving of the highest praise. The forwards showed remarkable form.'

Steve Bloomer, wearing his England cap. He won 21 altogether and his 28 goals were an England record until 1956.

For Steve Bloomer it was a satisfactory beginning. His first senior goal for the Rams came from the penalty spot against West Brom towards the end of that month. It was the first of 332 goals for Derby from the man who was to become the club's leading scorer for 13 successive seasons.

Derby County: Robinson; Methven, Staley, Cox, Garden, Roulstone, Ekins, Bloomer, J.Goodall, Rose, McMillan.

Att: 5,000

Derby County in 1895. Back row (left to right): Methven, A.Staley (trainer), Leiper. Middle row: W.D.Clark (secretary), Cox, A.Goodall, Robinson, Kinsey, Staley. Front row: J.Goodall, Paul, Miller, Stevenson, McQueen. On ground: Bloomer, McMillan.

The Rams Survive In A Test Match Thriller

Saturday, 27 April 1895

Derby County 2   Notts County 1

ALTHOUGH the later half of the 1890s was a relatively successful time for Derby County, with high placings in the First Division and plenty of good Cup runs, there was one season when the Rams came perilously close to losing their status.

After finishing third in 1893-94, the Rams suffered an inexplicable slump in their fortunes the following season. They began it with an 8-0 defeat at the hands of Sunderland at Roker Park, won only one of their first ten games and suffered some other big defeats like a 6-0 hammering at Bolton and a 4-0 reverse at Villa Park.

The defeat at Roker was the famous 'game of three halves'. The Rams were 3-0 at half-time when the delayed referee arrived. John Goodall elected to begin again with the proper match official and Sunderland duly scored another eight.

Derby finished the season 15th out of 16 clubs and were thus required to take part in the 'Test Match' play-off series which also involved bottom club Liverpool, 14th-placed Stoke, and Bury, Notts County and Newton Heath (later Manchester United), the top three clubs in the Second Division.

The Rams, as next-to-bottom club, were due to play Second Division runners-up Notts County and the game was scheduled for the Leicester Fosse ground at Walnut Street (now known as Filbert Street, home of Leicester City).

It was to be one of the most nail-biting encounters in the Rams' history, as the *Derby Daily Telegraph* reported: 'Today, Derby County were called upon to pass through an ordeal, the like of which they have never previously been destined to experience.'

In all matches between the clubs since the Rams were formed in 1884, Derby had emerged victorious with 16 wins and two draws in 26 matches, scoring 78 goals to Notts' 48.

The *Telegraph* commented: 'Fate decreed that they should meet their old rivals, Notts County, and this was generally regretted on the part of the supporters of both clubs on account of the great friendship which has existed between the clubs for some times past.'

Rams goalkeeper Jack Robinson, who went on to play for England and then rocked the club with a transfer request. After a controversial move to New Brighton Tower FC, he joined Southampton and was later reported to the FA for allegedly trying to poach Steve Bloomer for the Saints.

There were 8,000 fans present, braving a miserably cold day on which torrential rain had reduced the Leicester pitch to a quagmire. Derby lost the toss and kicked-off into a strong wind.

After only a few moments they were struck a serious blow when John Goodall began limping heavily. The Rams had taken a gamble in allowing Goodall to play, for he had been suffering from a muscle strain and played 'only as the result of a thorough examination by a medical gentleman.' Now it appeared that the doctor's optimism had been ill-founded.

Yet the Rams dominated the first half and McMillan and Bloomer both went close before Notts County goalkeeper George Toone brought off a magnificent save from McMillan. For that, though, the Rams arrived at half-time without a goal to show for all their efforts.

Early in the second half, Bloomer had the ball over the line but his effort was disallowed for offside. John Goodall was now little more than a passenger and when Notts took the lead, it seemed that Derby were indeed doomed to Second Division football.

The goal came from Fred Fletcher, who had played for the Rams earlier that season. Goalkeeper Jack Robinson got to Fletcher's shot but could not stop his stinging drive, high into the top corner.

But Derby fought back: Archie Goodall moved up front, the Rams forced three corners in quick succession, and then John Paul, a former Hibs player, hit a post. Notts thought they had scored to put the result beyond doubt, but they, too fell foul of an offside decision.

There were only seven minutes remaining when the Rams drew level. A corner was cleared only as far as Jimmy Methven, whose hopeful 30-yarder hit McMillan on the back and fell to the feet of Steve Bloomer, who needed no second chance.

Still the Rams stormed forward and won four more corners. There were only 30 seconds remaining when Jack Cox sent over a perfect flag-kick and McMillan hammered home the winner. The Rams were still in Division One.

Those last few moments had certainly been breathtaking. The daughter of a Derby director fainted in the excitement and one club official gripped his watch so tightly that he broke the timepiece.

Derby County: Robinson; Methven, Leiper, Cox, A.Goodall, Staley, Francis, Bloomer, J.Goodall, McMillan, Paul.
Notts County: Toone; Stotherd, Hendry, Bramley, Calderhead, Shelton, Chadburn, Allsopp, Allan, Sissons, Fletcher.
Referee: A.West (Lincoln) *Att: 8,000*

The Baseball Ground in 1895, looking from the Normanton End. The high fencing on the right was to stop baseballs flying out of the ground.

The Rams Move Home To The Baseball Ground

Saturday 14 September 1895

Derby County 2   Sunderland 0

WHEN Derby County were formed as an offshoot of Derbyshire CCC in 1884, it was natural that they should play their home games at the County Ground on Nottingham Road. Indeed, this splendid piece of turf had such a reputation that several important matches were staged there including the 1886 FA Cup Final replay between Blackburn Rovers and West Brom, the 1895 England-Ireland international and several semi-finals.

But the Derby Recreation Company, who owned leased the County Ground and Racecourse from Derby Corporation, made life difficult for Derby County and whenever there was horse racing at Derby, the Rams had to alter their fixtures. The plum friendly game against the famous Corinthians had been postponed on Easter Monday 1895 because the ground was wanted for another purpose.

The Rams had fulfilled a few home games at the sports ground which Sir Francis Ley had laid out near his factory in the Pear Tree area of the town. It was a 12-acre site and part of it contained a modest stadium to stage baseball. The local industrialist had become attracted to the game whilst on business trips to the United States and Derby County had a team which won the English Baseball Cup in 1897, with Steve Bloomer at second base.

The Rams had first played a League game at the Baseball Ground on 19 March 1892, when Sunderland were the visitors, and again on 12 November 1893, when they entertained Burnley.

In April 1895, a packed meeting at the Derwent Hotel heard the Rams committee agree to a permanent move to the Baseball Ground. Sir Francis Ley had already spent £7,000 on improvements and was prepared to spend another £500 on adding six yards to the Normanton Side (where 'A', 'B' and 'C' Stands are now situated) and five yards to the Railway Side (now site of the Pop Side and Toyota Stand), as well as moving stands from the County Ground to increase the Baseball Ground's capacity from 5,000 to some 20,000.

On 14 September 1895, Derby County

stepped out at the Baseball Ground for the first time as permanent users of the ground. Sunderland were certainly a major attraction, League champions three seasons out of the last four and fielding several internationals. Considering that the Rams had only narrowly avoided relegation the previous season, it was not surprising that the *Derby Daily Telegraph* gave them little hope:

Steve Bloomer, who marked the official opening of the Baseball Ground with both goals against Sunderland.

'It was hardly football weather when Derby County made their first appearance on their new ground, the sun shining brightly and the elements favouring spectators far more than players. It was a clever piece of work on behalf of the committee to have such a great attraction for the opening match. . . .for Sunderland have such a big reputation in Derby that a big attendance was a foregone conclusion. Sunderland have nearly always

been too good for Derby County in former years, for out of 11 matches they have previously played, the County have won only one. Sunderland, on the other hand, have won no less than nine. The goal aggregate previous to this season was 40 goals to 10 in favour of the northern representatives.'

Included in those defeats for Derby were scores of 5-1, 7-1, 5-0 and, of course, 8-0 only 12 months earlier. Yet the Rams put all that behind them to mark their first game at the Baseball Ground with a magnificent victory over one of the leading sides in the land.

After the big crowd had been entertained by a brass band 'playing a number of pleasing selections', Sunderland kicked-off at 3.30pm and for the first 45 minutes it was mostly Derby who dominated with Bloomer twice bringing brilliant saves from Scottish international goalkeeper Teddy Doig and Archie Goodall shooting over the bar when well placed.

Fifteen minutes into the second half, however, the Rams took the lead. Hugh McQueen, the former Liverpool winger, hammered in a fierce shot which Doig could only parry. John Goodall and Bloomer both raced in and it was Bloomer who got the finishing touch. Even then the ball was scooped back into play, but the referee signalled a goal.

Bloomer went close again and when Sunderland managed an attack, they found the Rams' rearguard more than equal to the task. Then, just on time, Bloomer made it 2-0 with a brilliant goal.

It was a happy start and as the season unfolded, so the Rams played better and better. Eventually they finished runners-up to Aston Villa and reached the FA Cup semi-finals. Despite later tales of a gipsy curse, the move to the Baseball Ground heralded a successful period in the Rams history.

Derby County: Robinson; Methven, Leiper, Cox, A.Goodall, Kinsey, J.Goodall, Bloomer, Miller, McMillan, McQueen.
Sunderland: Doig; Gow, McNeil, Dunlop, McCreadie, Johnston, Gillespie, Wilson, Campbell, J.Hannah, Scott.
Referee: Mr Norris (Birmingham)
Att: 10,000

The Rams team which took them to the 1898 FA Cup Final. Standing at back (left to right): Methven, A.Latham (trainer). Standing at middle: J.H.Richardson (honorary secretary), Fryer, Leiper, J.Reilly (director), H.Newbould (secretary). Seated, second row: Cox, A.Goodall, Turmer. Seated, front row: J.Goodall, Bloomer, Boag, Stephenson, McQueen.

Stand-in Boag's Hat-Trick Cup Triumph

Wednesday 2 March 1898

Liverpool 1   Derby County 5

DERBY County's overall FA Cup record for the first few years of their existence was none too impressive. But by the end of the 1890s, the Rams were becoming something of a 'Cup team' with consecutive appearances in the semi-finals, in 1896 and 1897. In 1897-98, they went one stage further and reached the Final for the first time. And there was no greater performance on the way than the hammering of Liverpool at Anfield in the quarter-finals.

Liverpool were a relatively new club, formed only five years earlier by some disaffected members of Everton FC, a club whose home ground was originally Anfield and who moved to Goodison Park only after the Merseyside split. Liverpool, meanwhile, wasted no time in establishing themselves and after a season in the Lancashire League, where they won a league and cup double, they were elected to the Football League and stormed away with the Second Division title. Relegation quickly followed but they were soon back and towards the end of the decade were rising up the table.

In 1896-97, Liverpool joined the Rams in the FA Cup semi-finals, where Derby lost to Everton and Liverpool went down to Aston Villa. Now the sides were on collision course as they tried again. Derby had reached the quarter-finals by beating Aston Villa and Wolves. Liverpool had enjoyed a slightly easier passage with wins over Hucknall St John's and Second Division Newton Heath (later to become Manchester United) after a replay.

Derby County came out of the hat first and at the Baseball Ground on 26 February, a crowd 15,000 saw Jimmy Stevenson's goal earn the Rams a 1-1 draw. So, four days later, Derby travelled to Liverpool for the Wednesday afternoon replay.

The Rams made three changes: Steve Bloomer came into the side in place of Paul, with John Goodall moving to outside-right; and at centre-forward, the former East Stirlingshire player John Boag was called up after Liverpool objected to the inclusion of Alex Maconnachie, another Scottish player, who had allegedly taken part in an 'illegal contest' at Hamilton, soon after signing for the Rams in the close season.

Boag, a well-built but not very skilful player, had been scoring goals in the Reserves — and he was now about to make his mark on this Cup campaign.

The Rams had a former Liverpool player, Hugh McQueen, on their left wing, whilst in goal for the Merseysiders was Harry Storer, a product of local football with Ripley Town and Derby Midland. He had been on the Rams books, but never played in their first team before having League experience with Woolwich Arsenal. Storer also played cricket for Derbyshire, his brother William appeared for Derbyshire and England and his son, also Harry, would play for and manage the Rams in later years, as well as also being a Derbyshire cricketer. The *Derby Daily Telegraph* said later: 'Despite the heavy score

against him, Storer did well.'

There was some controversy after the Midland Railway refused to run a special train to Liverpool, although they did agree to charge only a single fare for the return journey provided that 50 or more fans took up the offer. When the service train pulled out of Derby at 8.15am, there were some 150 Derby supporters on board.

After the Rams players had lunched at the Alexandra Hotel in Liverpool, the replay kicked-off at 3.30pm. Liverpool won the toss and Derby kicked into a strong wind, with the sun in their eyes.

The opening stages see-sawed either way, with McCartney hitting the woodwork for Liverpool before the Rams took the lead after 25 minutes, when Boag hit home a brilliant goal from Stevenson's centre. Five minutes later, Bloomer made it 2-0 from John Goodall's pass, but before half-time, Liverpool had pulled a goal back through Becton, who scored from the penalty spot after Archie Goodall had handled.

Three minutes into the second half, Boag restored the Rams' two-goal lead after McQueen had headed on Archie Goodall's pass. Good work between John Goodall and McQueen laid on a fourth goal for Bloomer and then Boag completed his hat-trick with 15 minutes remaining and hundreds of Liverpool fans already pouring out of the ground.

When the Rams party arrived at Derby Midland Station at 10pm, they found some 4,000 fans waiting to greet them.

In the semi-final, the Rams beat Everton 3-1 at Molineux to reach their first FA Cup Final, which they lost 3-1 to Nottingham Forest at the Crystal Palace. The following year the Rams reached another Final, only to lose again, this time 4-1 to Sheffield United. Their Cup pedigree, though, was established.

Liverpool: Storer; Goldie, Dunlop, McCartney, McQue, Cleghorn, Cunliffe, Finnerhan, Hartley, Becton, Bradshaw.
Derby County: Fryer; Staley, Leiper, Cox, A.Goodall, Turner, Bloomer, J.Goodall, Boag, Stevenson, McQueen.

Att: 10,000.

Bloomer's Hat-Trick Puts Derby In The Semi-Finals

Wednesday 27 February 1902

Derby County 6   **Portsmouth 3**

AFTER their appearance in the 1899 FA Cup Final, Derby County had two poor seasons in the competition before enjoying another good run in the 1901-02 campaign. In early rounds they knocked out Blackburn Rovers (2-0) and Lincoln City (3-1), all five of their goals coming from Ben Warren, a 22-year-old wing-half from Newhall who had been tried to great effect in the forward line.

In the third round, Derby were drawn to meet Portsmouth at Fratton Park, where the Rams were happy to earn a goalless draw against one of the giants of the Southern League, then still a competition probably equal to the Football League, and against a team containing four internationals — Edgar Chadwick and Daniel Cunliffe (both England), Bob Marshall (Scotland) and Matt Reilly (Ireland).

The replay at the Baseball Ground was the Rams' first home game since 11 January and despite the Wednesday afternoon kick-off, there was a crowd of 17,836, Derby's biggest of the season after the Boxing Day clash with Newcastle, when there were 20,000 present.

The crowd was swelled by men from many local factories — including the Midland Railway works and Handyside's foundry — which closed at noon to allow their workers to attend the big game. Also in the crowd were players from Aston Villa, Nottingham Forest and West Brom, all of whom had rushed to the Baseball Ground after training. There were few Pompey fans in the crowd, however, for no special trip had been organised from the naval town.

Despite the close nature of the first game, the replay was one-way traffic in the opening moments and within eight minutes, the Rams were 2-0 ahead.

First there was a scrimmage near the Portsmouth goal, from which Bloomer extracted the ball and fed Warren, who hammered his shot past Reilly from close range. Then Boag exchanged passes with Dick Wombwell, a utility forward who had been signed from Ilkeston Town.

After 15 minutes, Warren added a third goal for the Rams, the ball slipping through Reilly's hands when the Irish international goalkeeper really should have saved the day.

Portsmouth, though, battled back and reduced the deficit to two goals through Smith, who pounced on a loose ball to beat Fryer. The Rams goalkeeper, 'with the sun shining brilliantly in his eyes', saved well from Corrin and Cunliffe and then MacAuley, who had only the Cromford giant to beat.

After half-time, the Rams resumed in the same mood and after 55 minutes Bloomer, 'who had just had one of his hot cannons', beat Reilly all ends up with a fierce left-foot shot. Goodall then let the ball run to Bloomer and he added his side's fifth to put the result apparently well beyond doubt.

Still the frantic scoring continued, however, and suddenly the Rams looked to be in for a nail-biting finish. Jimmy Methven up-ended Smith in the box and Chadwick hit home the resultant penalty. And it was 5-3 when Cunliffe hit an unstoppable shot past Fryer.

All Pompey hopes of a sensational fight-back disappeared, however, when Bloomer completed his hat-trick three minutes from time, rising at the far post to head home George Davis's centre.

The victory earned Derby County a semi-final tie against Sheffield United, who had also won a replay, against Newcastle United.

The semi-final took three games to resolve: Ben Warren scored the Rams' goal in a 1-1 draw at The Hawthorns; Wombwell was the Derby scorer when the replay was drawn 1-1 at Molineux; and at the City Ground, the Rams failed to find the net at all, going down 1-0 to the eventual Cup winners.

Ben Warren's contribution had been eight goals in seven Cup ties — remarkably, he managed only four in 22 League matches that season — and midway through the following season he reverted to wing-half. In that position, Warren won his first England cap in 1905-06 and was capped 13 times as a Rams player before being transferred to Chelsea in

Rams goalkeeper Jack Fryer clears the ball downfield during the first game at Fratton Park.

Derby County defenders move downfield after clearing another Pompey raid.

August 1908 and altogether played in 19 consecutive internationals at right-half. Alas, he met a sad end. Certified insane, after a period in the Derbyshire Lunatic Asylum, he died in his native Newhall in January 1917, aged only 38.

Derby County: Fryer; Methven, Morris, Raisbeck, A.Goodall, Leckie, Wombwell, Bloomer, Boag, Warren, Davis.

Portsmouth: Reilly; Wilkie, Turner, Stringfellow, Chadwick, Blyth, Marshall, Cunliffe, MacAuley, W.Smith, Corrin.

Referee: J.Adams (Birmingham)

Att: 17,836.

Alf 'Snobby' Bentley, whose four goals sank Leeds City.

Derby County, 1908. Back row (left to right): A.Latham (trainer), Nicholas, Scattergood, Atkin, Maskrey, Bevan. Middle row: J.Methven (manager), Barlow, Hall, Richards, Davis. Front row: Thompson, Garry, Bentley, Beauchop, Barnes.

'Snobby' Bentley's Four Goals At Elland Road

Saturday 19 September 1908

Leeds City 2   **Derby County 5**

AFTER Steve Bloomer left Derby County for Middlesbrough in March 1906 — a transfer which shocked Rams fans — the club had to find someone who could continue to supply regular goals. And as Bloomer was an England international who had been the Rams' leading League scorer for 13 consecutive seasons — even in the one that he moved from the Baseball Ground — that was always going to be a tall order.

But Derby did find another prolific scorer, a man who would break Bloomer's record for a season, not once but twice. He was also a man who came from a fairly unglamorous source for such a star player, for Alf 'Snobby' Bentley hailed from Alfreton.

The Derbyshire town had, of course, provided several fine players for the Rams including winger Jack Davis, who was capped for England. But Bentley probably outshone them all with his goalscoring.

He was one of Jimmy Methven's first signings for the Rams, joining the club in December 1906, and made his League debut in a goalless home draw against Woolwich Arsenal just before Christmas the following season. By the end of the season he had scored four goals in 11 games, but Derby were relegated along with Stoke.

Most of Bentley's goals, then, were scored in the Second Division, but for all that he made a major contribution to the Rams story, setting a new record in 1907-08 with 27 goals and extending that with 30 in 1909-10. Not bad for a player who cost only £50.

Bentley scored five hat-tricks for the Rams during his career. And a further three times he hit four goals in a game, two of those feats coming against Leeds City. The first club to suffer in this way, though, were Barnsley in September 1907. Then Bentley scored four against Leeds in October that year. Less than 12 months later, Derby visited Elland Road and again Bentley savaged them with four goals.

The Rams had finished sixth the previous season and were looking to improve on that and gain promotion in 1908-09. They began in unconvincing fashion with a 1-1 draw at Oldham and a 2-0 defeat at Burnley. Derby then got their season back on the rails with home victories over Clapton Orient and, in midweek, Wolves.

There then followed a Saturday afternoon game against Leeds City and there were some 20,000 people at Elland Road on a beautiful late summer's day. Despite their 6-1 win over Leeds at the Baseball Ground the previous season, the Rams might have felt apprehensive, for their previous visit to Elland Road, in February 1908, had resulted in a 5-1 defeat for Derby County.

Now the Rams were practically at full strength, although new signing George Thompson, a former Sheffield United winger, was missing through injury.

Derby's Welsh international full-back Charlie Morris won the toss but any advantage was slight and the Rams were soon pegged back with Roger, McLeod and Croot going close. Derby replied when Bevan's trickery took him past two defenders but Bentley hit his pass over the bar.

Then City's White conceded a corner after 21 minutes and from Davies' flag-kick, Aitken got the ball to Hall, whose shot took Naisby by surprise. Leeds soon drew level again when a miskick by Nicholas let in McLeod and his shot was turned against an upright by Maskrey before rolling over the line.

Within seconds the Rams were back in front when Bentley found the net after Garry had laid on the chance. Three goals in as many minutes had the big crowd buzzing and as Leeds pushed for another equaliser, Maskrey had to be at his best. Then Leeds won the ball back after a Derby free-kick and with

Morris out of position, McLeod was clean through before Nicholas brought him down. McLeod took the penalty himself and the scores were level again, although Maskrey got his fingertips to the ball. Before the interval, Maskrey was again in action, saving brilliantly from Croot.

There were still plenty of incidents to come in the second half. Croot hit a post, then Watson appeared to handle but the referee turned down Derby appeals for a penalty. When Davis was tripped on the edge of the penalty area, however, the Rams were awarded a free-kick and after some scrapping for the ball, Bentley made it 3-2.

At the other end, Morris headed off the line when Maskrey was beaten, but from that moment almost all the play was in the Leeds half and after 60 minutes Bentley completed his hat-trick to make it 4-2 after Nasiby had twice blocked shots.

The Rams' fifth goal came when Ainsworth centred and the ball ran to Bentley and Bevan. At the time the *Derby Daily Telegraph* gave the goal to Bevan, but this was later altered in favour of Bentley. The newspaper commented: 'It is a moot point as to whether or not the goal credited to Bevan was from his foot . . . but he deserves the credit.'

The Rams had to wait a few more seasons before being promoted, by which time Steve Bloomer had returned to the Baseball Ground and Alf Bentley had been transferred to Bolton Wanderers after scoring 112 League and Cup goals in 168 appearances for the Rams. His greatest season came with West Brom, when he helped the Throstles to the League championship in 1919-20. Leeds City, meanwhile, were wound up just after World War One following allegations of illegal payments to players in wartime. They re-emerged as Leeds United.

Leeds City: Naisby; Watson, White, McAllister, Hamilton, Cubberley, Guy, Burnett, McLeod, Roger, Croot.
Derby County: Maskrey; Nicholas, Morris, Atkin, Hall, Richards, Davis, Garry, Bevan, Bentley, Ainsworth.
Referee: A.R.Greaves (Blackpool)
Att: 20,000.

Derby County with Steve Bloomer back in their ranks. Back row (left to right): A.Latham (trainer), Bagshaw, Betts, Scattergood, Sharpe, Garry, Barbour, J.Methven (manager). Front row: Grimes, Bloomer, Richards, Leonard, Bauchop, Barnes, Donald.

Bloomer's Two Goals On A Hero's Return

Saturday, 1 October 1910

Derby County 5   Lincoln City 0

WHEN Steve Bloomer left Derby County for Middlesbrough in March 1906, it brought relegation that much closer.

Bloomer went to Middlesbrough with another Rams player, defender Emor 'Jack' Ratcliffe. 'Boro probably didn't want Ratcliffe, a former Loughborough Corinthians player who was mostly a reserve at Derby, but under the transfer regulations then in force, it meant that Derby could receive a more realistic fee of £750 for Bloomer.

Middlesbrough had been accused of buying their way out of trouble, for after having a bid for Bloomer rejected the previous season, they became the first British club to break the £1,000 barrier when they signed Sunderland's Alf Common.

For Middlesbrough, Steve Bloomer scored 62 goals in 130 League and Cup games — Ratcliffe managed only nine games — and

after a disastrous debut, a 6-1 defeat at Anfield, did much to help 'Boro preserve their survival.

Bloomer, though, never settled in the North-East and when the chance came to return to Derby, he jumped at it. Bloomer had sent manager Jimmy Methven a telegram, recommending a Middlesbrough player called Tommy Wilson. When Bloomer was asked to meet Methven at Middlesbrough railway station in late September 1910, he thought it was to discuss Wilson but instead, Methven asked Bloomer to return to the Baseball Ground.

Methven later recalled: 'I could see by Steve's face that he was under the impression I was pulling his leg. Then it dawned on him that I really meant business, and I never saw such a happy countenance in my life. The transfer fee we paid for Steve was £100, and that sum was nearly the entrance gate at the very first match.'

That game was a Second Division match against Lincoln City at the Baseball Ground on 1 October 1910, when the prospect of again seeing Steve Bloomer in a Derby shirt attracted some 14,000 fans — more than double the attendance for the previous home game, against Blackpool.

The Rams had made a medicore start to the season, losing their opening game 4-1 at

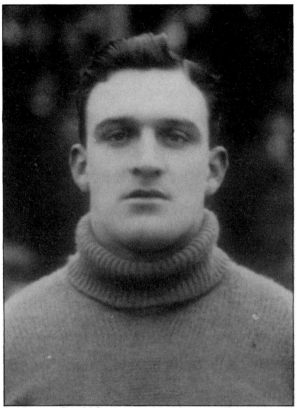

Goalkeeper Ernald Scattergood had just established himself as Bloomer returned and when the Rams won promotion in 1911-12, he was their only ever-present.

home to Chelsea and winning only one of their first six matches. Bloomer was made skipper for his return debut — and what a homecoming it turned out to be.

The *Derby Daily Telegraph* described the scene: 'The great attraction on the Baseball Ground this Saturday afternoon . . . .was the reappearance of Stephen Bloomer for his old club. His sojourn in the North did not by any means lose him all his friends here, and when he made his entry he had a reception which was in the highest degree flattering. The weather was warmer than on many a day last summer, and the spectators enjoyed a great advantage over the players in this respect.'

A brass band was on hand to play *See The Conquering Hero Come* as Bloomer led Derby out into the glorious sunshine. The Rams kicked-off attacking the Osmaston End and for the first 20 minutes play was even. Then Bloomer struck.

Lincoln goalkeeper Fern got in a tussle with Donald and Barnes, the ball ran loose and Bloomer who 'pounced with his old time vigour and scored cleverly'.

That set the scene for the rest of the match, although when the half-time whistle

sounded, the Rams still had only Bloomer's goal to show for their efforts, despite the fact that they had several chances and that City played for most of the time with ten men and no regular goalkeeper after Fern strained his side and was carried off, to be replaced by Wilson, the Lincoln skipper.

Fern returned in goal after the interval but within ten minutes his side were two goals down when Donald swung over a left-wing corner and Horace Barnes headed home past Fern, who struggled to get across to the ball. In the 65th minute it was 3-0 when Bloomer converted a penalty after Lincoln's left-half Miller fisted the ball away and then Lincoln made a half-hearted appeal for a spot-kick when Hunter's shot struck Ben Hall on the forearm.

With 15 minutes remaining, Fern gave up and was assisted off the field, looking back to see Jimmy Beauchop head the Rams' fourth goal from a cross by Barnes. And in the last minute, stand-in goalkeeper Wilson did well to block a shot from Beauchop but the ball went straight to Grimes on the Rams' right wing and he switched it back into the middle for Beauchop to slam home Derby's fifth goal.

The Rams ended the season in sixth place and Bloomer finished as leading scorer with 20 goals in 28 games. Alf Bentley, who missed the Lincoln game through injury, returned to form a good partnership with Bloomer and netted 14 goals.

Derby County: Scattergood; Barbour, Atkin, Garry, Hall, Bagshaw, Grimes, Bloomer, Beauchop, Barnes, Donald.
Lincoln City: Fern; Jackson, Wilson, Fraser, Gardner, Miller, Clarke, Reid, Hunter, Yule, Platts.
Referee: J.H.Smith (Doncaster)   Att: 14,000.

ON the Monday after this match, Rams player Ted Garry was married to local spinster Bertha Robinson at St Joseph's RC Church in Derby. Billy Halligan was best man and other Rams players present were Bloomer, Bauchop, Scattergood, Barbour, Hall and Grimes.

Derby County, 1913. Back row (left to right): Bloomer, Atkin, Scattergood, Barbour, Betts. Middle row: Jimmy Methven (manager), Hardman, Bagshaw, Buckley, Richards, Waugh, Arthur Latham (trainer). Front row: Grimes, Walker, Leonard, Barnes, Neve. John Hardman, who joined the Rams from Oldham, was killed in action in France in 1917.

Second Division Champions At The Last Gasp

Monday, 22 April 1912

Barnsley 0   Derby County 2

WITH the great Steve Bloomer back in their ranks, Derby County made a renewed effort to win back their First Division place and early in the 1911-12 season, the Rams enjoyed a three-month spell in which they went unbeaten.

It began with a 5-0 win over Glossop at the Baseball Ground on 16 September and ended with a 4-0 defeat at Stockport on New Year's Day. In between, Derby won 11 games out of 14, including six victories on the trot.

But then followed something of a hiccup, with only two points from six matches, before the Rams got back to their best form and sailed

to promotion, conceding only one goal in their last 11 games, and that a late equaliser from Wolves' Irish international Billy Halligan, who had left Derby for the Molineux club just over a year earlier.

One of the main factors behind this new-found defensive excellence was the signing of centre-half Frank Buckley, who came from Birmingham in May 1911, and the arrival of full-back Charlie Betts, from Newcastle United, in October.

Up front the Rams also had new faces: Harry Leonard, a centre-forward from Middlesbrough, also joined them in October; and the Rams also had the gifted amateur Ivan Sharpe, who was signed from Glossop, again in October. Sharpe's League debut came in that 5-0 thrashing of his former club, whilst Leonard, who had played alongside Steve Bloomer for Middlesbrough, made his mark with four goals in a 6-1 defeat of Fulham in early November.

When the final League game arrived, a trip to Oakwell to meet FA Cup Finalists Barnsley, the Rams were already assured of promotion. Now they needed victory to take the Second Division championship.

Despite the glorious late April weather and the fact that only 48 hours earlier, Barnsley had drawn the Cup Final against West Brom at the Crystal Palace, there were only about 4,000 at Oakwell. Perhaps the fact that Barnsley could finish only sixth might have been partly to blame; more likely it was because, remarkably, Barnsley had to replay the Cup Final two days later and the Colliers' fans were no doubt saving up for the trip to Bramall Lane (where they saw their side win 1-0 after extra-time).

If the Rams were hoping for an easy task against a weakened Barnsley, they were disappointed. The *Derby Daily Telegraph* applauded Barnsley, saying: "The County certainly had a surprise when they knew that the Barnsley eleven had arrived in the town from the Cup Final barely half an hour previously and that they were turning out at full-strength that evening . . .taking the sporting risk that no player would be injured in any way for Wednesday's replayed Cup Final."

The first half had few thrills to offer, although the Rams might have had a penalty when Bloomer was floored. The *Telegraph* reminded readers that the same official had denied Bloomer a penalty when the teams had met at the Baseball Ground the previous October, a match which ended in a goalless draw.

'Had there been no goals scored in the second half on Monday, then the Derby County Club would have had a bone to pick with this official,' wrote the reporter.

There was no need to hark back to the incident, however. Two minutes into the second half, Grimes sent over a corner and no less than three Derby forwards went for the ball which eventually found its way into the back of the net via Beauchop's head.

Midway through the half, Frank Buckley made it 2-0 with his first goal for the Rams. The ball fell to the centre-half on the edge of the penalty area and he hit a glorious, swerving shot into the top corner, well out of Cooper's reach.

The Rams finished champions, ahead of

Tommy Barbour, the former Kilbirnie defender, receovered from injury to help the Rams into Division One as champions.

runners-up Chelsea on goal average. When the team arrived back at Derby Midland Station that evening, they were met by several thousand supporters who gave them a rapturous welcome.

As the *Derby Daily Telegraph* said: "Now let the supporters rally round the club and help to raise Derby County's name to its former heights."

Barnsley: Cooper; Downs, Taylor, Glendenning, Bratley, Utley, Bartrop, Tufnell, Lilleycrop, Travers, Moore.
Derby County: Scattergood; Atkin, Barbour, Garry, Buckley, Richards, Grimes, Bloomer, Leonard, Beauchop, Barnes.
Referee: H.G.Yates (Bolton)   *Att: 4,000.*

Promotion Again — But Four Years To Wait

Saturday, 24 April 1915

Derby County 2   Preston North End 0

TWO years after Derby County were seeking the Second Division championship on the last day of their season, the Rams found themselves in an identical position after being relegated immediately and then bouncing straight back up.

This time, though, the matter was compounded by the fact that Preston North End, their opponents on the last day of that 1914-15 season, were also assured of promotion and could also take the title. The Rams arrived at the last game with 51 points, Preston had 50, so there was everything to play for.

The other distraction, of course, was that Britain was now at war. The conflict against Germany, to become known as the Great War, finally ignited in August 1914 but football's authorities decided to continue with the season, despite a considerable amount of hostility from people who felt it almost treasonable for healthy young men to be kicking a ball about when others of their generation would soon be dying in France and Belgium.

The truth was, of course, that top-class sport was good for the morale of both troops home on leave and those who worked long hours in munitions factories. Eventually, the League and FA Cup were suspended and the Rams had to wait over four years to resume their place in the First Division.

The Rams did not appear to be letting thoughts of war bother them when the season got under way in September 1914, for they began with a 7-0 hammering of Barnsley at the Baseball Ground, where Norman Fordham, a former Kent League player standing in for the injured Harry Leonard, scored a hat-trick.

Steve Bloomer had made only five League appearances when the Rams went down the previous season and he had now retired and was coaching in Berlin when war was declared. The former Derby star spent the entire war in an internment camp.

One great effect the war was having was on attendances. There were only 2,000 to see the beating of Barnsley and when the Rams visited Glossop in midweek, barely 500 turned up to watch, such was the uncertain nature of these times.

As the season unfolded, attendances improved, particularly for Derby who soon went to the top of the table, helped by a ten-match run which saw them drop only one point. Scoring the goals were Leonard, now recovered, Tom Benfield, a new signing from Leicester Fosse, and Jimmy Moore, who had joined the Rams from Glossop for £1,500 the previous season.

Apart from a shock home Cup defeat by Leeds City, Derby County's last peacetime season was extremely successful one and when the last day arrived, there was only the championship to decide.

Both teams were at full-strength but the attendance was disappointing, probably affected by heavy rain after lunch and into the afternoon. The Rams kicked-off towards the Osmaston End and enjoyed a slight edge upon which they capitalised in the 22nd minute when Grimes put them ahead.

Preston goalkeeper Jones had already dealt with shots from Leonard and Moore, when the ball went out to the Rams left wing, where Baker shaped to cross it back into the middle. Jones anticipated wrongly, the ball going over his head to where Grimes came in from the right flank to score.

Preston had their chances, one coming near the end of the half when Lawrence made a weak clearance and Osborn had a clear shot at goal but put his effort over the bar.

Twelve minutes into the second half, the Rams increased their lead when Leonard scored a fine individual goal, taking a pass from Eadie and forcing his way between two defenders before powering home a shot.

The Rams defence had plenty to do for the remainder of the match but there was never now any doubt about the outcome and for the second time in three seasons, Derby County were crowned champions of the Second Division.

Full-back Jack Atkin joined the Rams from Newhall Swifts, helped them to two promotions and, despite losing three seasons to World War One, clocked up more than 300 senior appearances for the club.

The *Derby Daily Telegraph* reported: 'For some reason or another the opinion had gained ground before the match that the County were going to lose. A reason we heard was given for this was that as the players were not to receive a bonus which the Championship carries with it in normal times, their interest in the result was minimised.'

Apparently, the Rams directors had refused to pay the £25 per head bonus allowed for winning the title, whereas the Preston players had been promised the reward should they top the division. Whatever the outcome of that wrangle, the Rams were, indeed, champions.

Derby County: Lawrence; Atkin, Barbour, Walker, Eadie, Brooks, Grimes, Benfield, Leonard, Moore, Baker.
Preston North End: Jones; Broadhurst, Holbem, Holdsworth, McCall, Broome, Ford, Morley, Osborn, Macaulay, Dawson.
Referee: T.P.Campbell (Blackburn)
Att: 12,000.

The Rams' 1923 FA Cup semi-final team (from left to right): Olney, Chandler, Crilly, McIntyre, Thoms, Plackett, Thornewell, Lyons, Galloway, Moore, Murphy.

So Near To The First Wembley Final

Saturday, 24 March 1923

Derby County 2   West Ham United 5

FOR some time, the Football Association realised that they needed a better home for the FA Cup Final. After several years at the Crystal Palace and a one-season interlude at Old Trafford, the biggest game in the football calendar was switched to Chelsea's Stamford Bridge in the years immediately after World War One.

But that was not particularly satisfactory, especially as Chelsea's pitch was often heavy and difficult at the end of a long League season. So when the Empire Stadium at Wembley was built to house the British Empire Exhibition of 1924, the FA saw it as the natural venue for the Cup Final. And Derby County came within 90 minutes of appearing in that historic game.

The Rams had begun the first post-war season in Division One but in 1920-21 they were relegated and then began a period as a mid-table Second Division club. Their post-war Cup record was nothing special either, until the 1922-23 campaign when they knocked out Blackpool, Bristol City, Sheffield Wednesday and Tottenham Hotspur (their only First Division opponents) to reach the semi-finals, where they met fellow Second Division club West Ham United at Stamford Bridge.

Naturally, the Rams' team had changed beyond recognition from the one that had ended the last pre-war season. In goal was Ben Olney, signed from Stourbridge in April 1912. The full-backs were Albert Chandler, who came to the Rams straight from the Army and having survived a gas attack during the war, and Tom Crilly, who was signed from Hartlepools United in August 1922, brought to Derby by new Rams manager Cecil Potter, who had been in charge at Hartlepools.

The Rams' half-backs were Johnny McIntyre, from Stenhousemuir in June 1921, Harry Thoms, who came with Crilly from Hartlepools, and Syd Plackett, who had been wounded in the Battle of the Somme in 1916 but had recovered to join Derby in January 1921 from Sawley Discharged Soldiers' Federation.

In the forward line were little George Thornewell, a former Rolls-Royce apprentice, Jimmy Lyons, a goalscorer from Hednesford Town who had hit all four in a match against Rotherham County the previous season, centre-forward Randolph Galloway, from local football in Sunderland, Jimmy Moore, the only remaining member of the pre-war team, and Lionel 'Spud' Murphy, signed from Melton Mowbray in February 1922. Moore, who had scored five goals against Crystal Palace on Christmas Day that season, was the Rams' skipper.

It was Derby County's first semi-final for 14 years and it came only a fortnight after the Rams' great quarter-final victory over Spurs, when Galloway scored the only goal of the match.

The teams ran on to a pitch bare of grass for the most part but quite playable after an overnight shower. The weather had cleared up and the sun shone brightly, although the sky was a little hazy. The Rams fielded the

West Ham goalkeeper Ted Hufton punches clear from a Derby attack in the 1923 semi-final at Stamford Bridge. Galloway (nearest the camera) and Lyons are the Rams forwards.

side that had carried them to the penultimate stage, whilst West Ham had skipper George Kay fit after their victory over Southampton in second replay at Villa Park only five days earlier.

Despite the fact that Stamford Bridge was practically a home venue for the Hammers, when the teams came out it was the Derby fans who made the most noise. Alas, they were soon to be silenced as the Rams fell 2-0 behind after only ten minutes.

In the fifth minute, Vic Watson swept the ball out to Jimmy Ruffell, who took it on and then centred for Billy Brown to run through a flat-footed Derby defence to score. Five minutes later, West Ham's Jimmy Moore had the easiest of chances, tapping the ball over the line after Olney had blocked but not gathered a shot from Watson.

The opening ten minutes of the second half where almost a repetition of the start, for within a minute West Ham were 3-0 ahead through Moore. The Rams, though, could feel aggrieved in that they had been awarded a free-kick when Lyons was shaping to shoot. Denied of any advantage, Derby lost the ball and although Chandler regained possession, he then tried to dribble his way out of trouble. Ruffell got the ball off him and set Moore free to score.

After 62 minutes it was 4-0 and the Rams'

Wembley dreams had truly disappeared. With the Derby defence appealing for offside, Watson was allowed to take the ball on. Chandler got in a half-tackle, Olney had left his line in search of the ball, and Brown had plenty of time to put it over the line when it rolled to him.

Eleven minutes later, Derby pulled a goal back when West Ham's Billy Henderson turned Murphy's shot into his own net. Three minutes after that, the Rams scored another when Murphy made the opening and Derby's Jimmy Moore literally walked the ball past Ted Hufton and into the net.

There was to be no sensational fightback, however, and ten minutes from time, Ruffell hit West Ham's fifth from an acute angle following a corner by Kay.

The Hammers lost 2-0 to Bolton in what became known as the 'White Horse Cup Final'. On the same day as that historic game, the Rams lost 1-0 at home to Leeds United, Wembley now a million miles away.

Derby County: Olney; Chandler, Crilly, McIntyre, Thoms, Plackett, Thornewell, Lyons, Galloway, Moore, Murphy.

West Ham United: Hufton; Henderson, Young, Bishop, Kay, Tresadern, Richards, Brown, Watson, Moore, Ruffell.

Referee: H.W.Andrews (Manchester)

Att: 50,795.

Derby County in 1923. Back row (left to right, players only): Ritchie, Olney, Thoms, Cecil Potter (manager), McIntyre. Middle row: Thornewell, Lyons, Galloway, Crilly, Storer, Underwood. Front row: Keetley, Plackett, Moore, Chandler.

Harry Storer's Four-Goal Blast At Bristol

Saturday, 29 September 1923

Bristol City 0   Derby County 8

WHEN Derby County visited Ashton Gate early in the 1923-24 season, they fielded the side that had enjoyed such a good Cup run the previous season, with the exception, that is, of their two inside-forwards, Harry Storer and Jackie Whitehouse.

Whitehouse, who had guested for the Rams during the war, had been signed from

Birmingham in May 1923. Storer, who was also a Derbyshire cricketer and who came from a famous local sporting family, had joined Derby from Grimsby Town in March 1921. Between them they were about to help the Rams become the most prolific scoring team in the Second Division. And Harry Storer was to enjoy a special day out at Bristol.

Storer spent most of his Rams career as a tough-tackling, though, skilful, wing-half, but for this one season he moved to inside-forward with huge success.

The Rams had an indifferent start to the season — three wins and a draw in their opening seven games — and arrived at Ashton Gate after two successive defeats, the most recent a 3-2 defeat by Bristol City at the

Baseball Ground only seven days earlier. No one, then, was prepared for what was about to happen.

The Rams had Johnny McIntyre back at right-half and Bernard McLaverty had to stand down. It was a beautiful afternoon and, according to the *Derby Daily Telegraph*, the pitch was 'as perfect as a billiard table'. City were a little weakened by illness and injury and were forced to make a change to their left-wing partnership where Sutherland and Compton took the places of Drinnan and Pocock. Despite the counter-attraction of a big Rugby game in Bristol, the attendance was a pleasing 20,000.

Bristol were much more enterprising in the opening minutes and, but for Ben Olney, it might have been a different story. In the opening minutes he was called upon to make a string of good saves, one of them from Albert Fairclough, who was to join the Rams the following summer.

After 12 minutes, though, the Rams took the lead and the floodgates opened. Murphy crossed, Storer went down with two City defenders, and the ball ran free to Galloway, who scored from 12 yards out.

Before half-time, the outcome of the game was settled, when Syd Plackett put the Rams 2-0 up after 24 minutes and then Storer scored in the 34th and 41st minutes to give Derby a 4-0 half-time lead.

So often when a team takes a big half-time lead, they do not add further goals in the second period, but in this case Derby went out and doubled the score. Following a corner, McIntyre shot hard and low and Goddard could only parry the ball to Storer, who made it 5-0 only four minutes into the second half.

And as the game began to deteriorate as a spectacle, three goals in as many minutes brought it to life again. First Storer hit home a left-foot volley after 79 minutes; a minute later, Thornewell centred for Galloway to hit the target from 20 yards; and after 81 minutes, the unmarked Thornewell took the ball through himself and ran it into the net, finishing it off with his left foot.

The Rams shooting had been razor-sharp but their great strength had come at half-back. Derby dominated the midfield where McIntyre's skill was outstanding. Thoms was superb at centre-half, despite the fact that he had to leave the field for a short spell, and Syd Plackett was in the sort of form that had seen him retain his place after Storer had recovered from injury and move into the forward line.

At the end of the season the Rams had scored 75 goals and their inside trio of Whitehouse (16), Galloway (17) and Storer (24) had contributed most of them. For Storer there was an additional bonus, for he won the first of his two England caps, against France in Paris.

Yet for all their goals, Derby missed promotion by a whisker. In their last game they needed to beat Leicester City 5-0 at the Baseball Ground to go up on goal-average. By half-time they were 3-0 ahead through Moore, Galloway and Storer, and in the 65th minute went four in front when Moore got his second.

Although Moore and Galloway went agonisingly close, Derby could not find the crucial fifth goal and their valiant effort came to nought. Bury followed champions Leeds United into the First Division, only 0.015 of a goal ahead of the Rams.

Bristol City: Goddard; Hughes, Banfield, Neesam, Hawley, Torrance, Worlock, Paul, Fairclough, Sutherland, Compton.
Derby County: Olney; Chandler, Crilly, McIntyre, Thoms, Plackett, Thornewell, Whitehouse, Galloway, Storer, Murphy.
Referee: H.Mason (Birmingham)
Att: 20,000.

Derby County, 1925-26. Back row (left to right): Plackett, Haley, Collins, Rowe, Carr, Olney, Underwood, Bacon. Second row: Bill Bromage (trainer), McIntyre, Wade, McLaverty, Keetley, Davidson, Barrett, Louis Edwards (trainer). Seated: Moore, Wightman, Crilly, Bedford, Thoms, Storer, Fazackerly, Pumford. On ground: Tootle, Enos Bromage, Whitehouse, Murphy, Thornewell.

Bedford's Hat-Trick Sinks The Swans

Saturday, 3 October 1925

Derby County 5   **Swansea Town 0**

IN August 1925, Derby County made one of the most significant appointments in the club's history when George Jobey became their manager. After a good playing career with Newcastle and Arsenal, Jobey had taken Wolves out of the Third Division North before retiring. The Rams persuaded him out of the hotel business and back into football — and Jobey went on to give his name to one of the most successful eras in Derby County's story.

Jobey was soon into the transfer market and one of his requirements was to strengthen the Rams' strike force. Jobey signed Stan Fazackerley, the former Sheffield United, Everton and Wolves centre-forward who had a proven scoring record (including one for the Blades in the 1915 Cup Final) but after scoring twice in three games for the Rams, Fazackerley was advised to quit for medical reasons.

Having signed Fazackerley, Jobey allowed Randolph Galloway to move to Nottingham Forest for £2,500, so when the new man was sidelined, Jobey had to move again and this time brought Blackpool's centre-forward Harry Bedford to the Baseball Ground for £3,500.

Bedford, who had begun his senior career with Nottingham Forest, made his Rams debut on 26 September 1925 at the City Ground where Thoms and Murphy gave Derby a 2-1 win. The following week, Bedford

Harry Bedford, capped twice for England as a Blackpool player before signing for Derby County.

Harry Storer, opened the scoring for Derby after only three minutes when he headed home Thornewell's cross.

ran out at the Baseball Ground for the first time as a Derby player when Swansea Town, newly-promoted from the Third Division South, were the visitors. It was the first-ever meeting between the clubs.

On a day more suited to championship cricket than football, Harry Thoms won the toss, set Swansea to face the sun, and after only three minutes, Derby were ahead.

Bedford got his first touch and won a corner which Murphy thumped over to the far post. The unmarked Thornewell lobbed the ball back into the middle and Storer jumped to head the Rams in front.

Derby's Johnny McIntyre was knocked out when he took the full force of Harold Wightman's clearance in his face but soon recovered to break up a Swansea attack and then a beautiful move between Thornewell, Murphy, Storer and Bedford finished with the centre-forward getting in a good drive.

After 14 minutes, the Rams went further ahead when Whitehurst finished off a move involving all five Derby forwards.

The home side were now well in command and although Storer missed a good chance, firing wide from 15 yards, the third goal

arrived in the 40th minute. Bellamy was penalised for a push just on the edge of the penalty area and Bedford took the free-kick to hammer a 20-yard shot into the net off the underside of the crossbar. It was a spectacular way to open his account.

In a desperate attempt to head the ball clear, Swansea's centre-half Humphreys fell heavily with Whitehurst and was taken off with a dislocated shoulder.

With the second half only two minutes old, the reorganised Swansea defence conceded a fourth goal. Morley took the ball from Bedford, but Thornewell won it back and hit a low pass across the goal for the Rams centre-forward to back-heel a cheeky effort over the line. How the Baseball Ground crowd were warming to their new star, who had now scored two brilliant goals.

Bedford's third goal was a little messy, a shade controversial, but none the less a result of more brilliant opportunism from Bedford. He looked to be offside but the referee ignored him as Storer shot. The ball bounced off Robson's chest and there was Bedford to complete his hat-trick.

Three weeks later he scored another, in the 7-3 home defeat of Stoke City, and by the end the season had registered a third to finish Derby's leading scorer with 27 League goals. After finishing in third place in the previous two seasons, the Rams were promoted as runners-up to Sheffield Wednesday, and Bedford went on to score over 150 League and Cup goals for Derby before his transfer to Newcastle United in December 1930. Those goals included 13 hat-tricks, including four in a game three times, and he was the Rams' leading scorer for five consecutive seasons. The crowd at the Baseball Ground that sunny October day had enjoyed their initial sight of the first of a long line of great Derby County centre-forwards.

Derby County: Olney; Wightman, Crilly, McIntyre, Thoms, Plackett, Thornewell, Whitehouse, Bedford, Storer, Murphy.
Swansea Town: Robson; Morley, Evans, Collins, Humphreys, Bellamy, Hole, Deacon, Fowler, Thompson, Corkindale.
Referee: T.G.Bryan (Willenhall)

Att: 16,609.

Jack Bowers Begins With A Real Beauty

Saturday, 2 February 1929

Derby County 2   Bolton Wanderers 0

LEGEND has it that when Rams manager George Jobey went to look at a young centre-forward called Jack Bowers playing for Scunthorpe United against Denaby United in a Midland League game towards the end of the 1927-28 season, he was so impressed by the opposing centre-half, Jack Barker, that he signed them both.

Or it might have been the other way around and Barker was the original target but Bowers impressed as well. Whatever the truth of the tale, each went on to play a part in the Rams story between the wars.

Both men made their League debuts the following season, Barker in a 3-1 First Division win over Bury at the Baseball Ground just before Christmas, Bowers when Bolton Wanderers visited Derby some six weeks later. Barker, of course, went on to play in over 350 League and Cup games for the Rams before World War Two ended his career; Bowers was to score 183 goals in 220 senior games before a move to Leicester in 1936, and he also set a Rams goals record and achieved several other notable scoring feats for the club.

On that cold winter's day at the Baseball Ground in 1929, all that was before him, although as the crowd filed out at the end, they had a feeling that they had seen the beginning of something.

After a reasonably good start to the season, the Rams had faltered over Christmas and well into the New Year, enduring a run of six League games from which they gained only two points.

Jobey was forced to bring in three reserves for the visit of Bolton, who were on their way to winning the FA Cup that season. Bowers was given his first taste of League football in place of the injured Tom Ruddy; outside-left Bert Mann, from Nuneaton, was also making his debut, standing in for Jack

Robson (who had himself been deputising for George Mee); and wing-half Tom Robinson, from Burton, was making a rare appearance as the latest stand-in for Johnny McIntyre.

Young Jack Barker was having another outing — it seemed he had displaced former Wolves centre-half Tommy Davison — and on the Rams right wing was Sammy Crooks, the former Durham City player who had just celebrated his 21st birthday.

The opening minutes of the game were fairly even but as the match approached the half-hour mark, an incident occured which swung it Derby's way. Bolton's young full-back Harry Greenhalgh, who had never even seen a Football League game until he made his senior debut for the Trotters in 1925, broke his right leg in a freak accident involving Derby's Jackie Whitehouse.

The two were battling for the ball and Whitehouse won the tussle. But as he was bringing it away, Greenhalgh swung a boot and appeared to catch the Rams player on the heel. Down went Greenhalgh to be stretchered off. He never played League football again.

In those days long before substitutes were allowed, the Rams now had a decided advantage, especially on a pitch which was an even bigger mudbath than it had been the previous Wednesday, when the Rams had lost 3-0 at home to Blackburn in a fourth-round Cup replay.

Just before the interval, Derby took the lead when Harry Bedford, who had switched to inside-left to accommodate Bowers, hammered the ball past reserve 'keeper Gill.

It was Bowers who made it 2-0 in the second half. The *Derby Daily Telegraph* reported: 'Bowers is actually the County's third centre-forward . . . .and the youngster is the eleventh debutant the Rams have introduced to League football this season.

'His goal in the second half was a real beauty, and his general work pleased everyone. There must surely be a great future in store for this smart youngster. He positions himself with the skill of a veteran, and some of his distributive work was a delight to watch.'

Plucky Bolton pulled a goal back through

Jack Bowers, joined the Rams from Midland League Scunthorpe United.

Jack Barker, also a recruit from Midland League soccer with Denaby United.

Wright, who took advantage of a slip by Harry Wilkes, but there was never any doubt that the Rams would take both points.

The *Telegraph* continued: 'Barker, too, was an outstanding performer . . .impressed me more than any of the Derby halves.

'Cooper has never played better than he does nowadays and his selection for the International Trial today, is a well-merited honour.'

Certainly, the Rams had some young lions who would prove the backbone of their team into the 1930s.

Derby County: Wilkes; Cooper, Collin, Robinson, Barker, Storer, Crooks, White-house, Bowers, Bedford, Mann.
Bolton Wanderers: Gill; Haworth, Green-halgh, Kean, Seddon, Thorborough, Butler, McClelland, Wright, Gibson, Cook.
Referee: W.Phipps (West Bromwich)

Att: 9,319.

Derby County's forward line at the start of 1932-33. From left to right are Sammy Crooks, Norman Robson, Jack Bowers, Peter Ramage and Dally Duncan. By the time of the sixth round, Robson had been transferred to Bradford City and amateur international Howard Fabian was the latest to be tried at inside-right.

Ramage's Goal Settles Roker Thriller

Wednesday, 8 March 1933

Sunderland 0   Derby County 1

BY the early 1930s, Derby County were established as one of the better sides in the First Division — they were runners-up in 1929-30 — but their FA Cup pedigree was not so impressive. Indeed, in 1931 the Rams were beaten 3-2 by Third Division South Exeter City; and not since their semi-final appearance in 1923 had they gone far beyond the opening stages.

So their Cup campaign of 1933 was especially welcomed by the fans. The Rams began with a 6-3 win at Molineux, where Jack Bowers hit a hat-trick, and then they won 3-2 at Southend and 2-0 at home to Aldershot before the quarter-final draw paired them with Sunderland, another club who were beginning to emerge as a strength in the First Division.

The tie was certainly a major attraction and at the Baseball Ground on 4 March, the sides fought out a spectacular 4-4 draw before a Rams record home crowd of 34,218, who paid receipts of £2,768 — another record.

Those spectators were treated to six goals in the first 36 minutes: Derby went 2-0 ahead through Dally Duncan and Peter Ramage;

then Sunderland fought back to go 3-2 in front with goals from Connor, Davis and Gurney; and then the Rams levelled the scores when Jack Bowers.

Four minutes after half-time, Gurney restored Sunderland's lead, but one minute from the final whistle, Duncan, a £2,000 signing from Hull City 12 months earlier, hit a sensational equaliser from far out on the left wing.

The scenes at the Roker Park replay were even more remarkable and over 75,000 fans — still a Roker record — packed into the ground for the Wednesday afternoon replay. Two men died in the crush, one in the Shilling Stand after Sunderland had scored an offside goal, the other in the mass outside. Several more were injured, and thousands were locked out and followed the game only through the roars and groans of the massive crowd. Four excursion trains from Derby were turned back on their way to Sunderland when it was realised that their passengers would never gain admittance.

The Rams made one change for the replay, Howard Fabian, the amateur international inside-right, replacing Freddie Jessop, who was still struggling to regain full fitness after breaking his right leg in a Cup tie against Manchester City a year earlier.

The Rams planned a more cautious approach to the replay and centre-half Jack Barker played deeper than usual. Barker was quite brilliant and wing-halves Jack Nicholas and Ike Keen weren't far behind him. Full-backs Tommy Cooper and George Collin defended heroically and goalkeeper Jack Kirby was another rock as Sunderland, inspired by 19-year-old Raich Carter, attacked in numbers.

After 90 minutes there was no score and the game moved into extra-time. In the 11th minute of the extra period, the Rams at last broke the deadlock with a goal of stunning simplicity. Only three Rams players touched the ball from beginning to end of this match-winning goal.

Jack Nicholas won the ball in the centre-circle and swept a brilliant pass between Carter and Edgar, straight to the feet of Crooks. The nippy outside-right took the ball in his stride, swerved past Shaw and sent over a magnificent centre. Up went Jack Bowers, shadowed by a posse of Sunderland defenders, and behind him the unmarked Peter Ramage, formerly of Coventry City, made a terrific leap and powered a header just inside the far post.

The Rams were in sight of a semi-final against Manchester City, but with two minutes remaining, Sunderland's fans were already shouting 'Goal' when Jack Kirby brought off an astonishing save from Davis. And Kirby did not just stop Davis' shot which was going into the top corner, he caught the ball. Said the *Derby Evening Telegraph*: 'Davis got the shock of his life when he saw Kirby make that brilliant save.'

Alas, that was as far as the Rams went, for they lost 3-2 in the semi-final at Huddersfield, but the day at Roker stands out as one of the truly great days in Derby County's history. As Mark Eaton said in the *Telegraph*: 'Peter Ramage's goal . . . .will never be forgotten by the huge crowd which invaded Roker Park . . . .'

Sunderland: Thorpe; Murray, Shaw, Thomson, McDougall, Edgar, Davis, Gallacher, Gurney, Carter, Connor.
Derby County: Kirby; Cooper, Collin, Nicholas, Barker, Keen, Crooks, A.H.Fabian, Bowers, Ramage, Duncan.
Referee: T.G.Gould (London)

Att: 75,118.

Crooks, Bowers and Fabian watch the ball go over the Manchester City bar in the semi-final at Huddersfield.

When Gallacher Went Nap At Ewood Park

Saturday, 15 December 1934

Blackburn Rovers 2   Derby County 5

WHEN centre-forward Jack Bowers badly injured a knee against Spurs at the Baseball Ground in September 1934, Rams manager George Jobey was confronted with a major problem.

Bowers had enjoyed a remarkable record after establishing himself in 1930. In his first full season he had scored a club record 37 League goals, was by now an England international and had been the First Division's leading scorer in consecutive seasons. At the time of his injury, he had scored 146 goals in only 169 League games for the Rams.

Jobey, then, had a major gap to fill and he turned to a wayward talent to fill it. In November 1934, the Rams paid £2,750 for Chelsea's 31-year-old Scottish international centre-forward, Hughie Gallacher.

Despite standing only 5ft 5in tall, Gallacher's scoring record was as remarkable as that of Bowers. Born at Bellshill, a Lanarkshire pit village, Gallacher had joined Queen of the South, then a Scottish non-League club, before moving to Aidrieonians, then Newcastle United (for £6,500) and Chelsea (£10,000). By the time he arrived at the Baseball Ground, he had scored 359 goals in 469 League, Cup and international matches.

He had led Newcastle to the League championship in 1926-27, played in the famous Wembley Wizards team that hammered England at Wembley in 1928, and had achieved five goals in a match on four occasions, one of them for Scotland in Belfast in 1929.

But besides buying a prolific scorer, Jobey also knew that he might be buying trouble. Married at 17 and divorced at 23, known to like more than a few drinks, and with a string of suspensions behind him, Gallacher could have spelled trouble for the Rams.

But Jobey was a disciplinarian whose reputation also preceded him and he felt that Gallacher could be handled. The player moved into a house in Littleover, soon fitted in with his Derby teammates, and when he made his Rams debut, against Birmingham, nearly 20,000 fans braved a rain-soaked day to see him. Within six minutes they were rewarded by a Gallacher goal. His international teammate, Dally Duncan, provided a magnificent crossfield pass and Gallacher rocketed home a stinging left-foot shot past Harry Hibbs.

Gallacher scored in his next game, although the Rams went down 5-1 at Fratton Park, and the move to Derby seemed to have rekindled his appetite for the game. By mid-December he had scored four goals in five games, including two when the Rams hit West Brom for nine at the Baseball Ground. Seven days later they visited Ewood Park and the stage was set for a Gallacher spectacular.

Blackburn had not been a particularly happy hunting ground for the Rams in recent years, but Gallacher was about to put that right. The *Derby Evening Telegraph* reported: 'Hughie Gallacher, the supreme artist in ball control, made goalscoring look the simplest thing in the world . . .

'The spectators enjoyed it too. They had not seen five goals scored by the opposition at Ewood Park this season and this new experience appealed to their sense of humour, for every time a Blackburn player gained possession, the crowd implored him to "give it to Gallacher".

'In scoring all five goals, the Scottish international moved along with the ball at his toe as if he had some magic influence over it. Only two of his goals — the first and the third — came from shots. The other three scoring efforts were typical of the incomparable Gallacher — mere flicks of the ball which left the goalkeeper standing helpless on his line.'

The Rams took the lead in the 22nd minute when Gallacher touched home Stockill's downward header from a Crooks corner. It was his 300th League goal, including his days in Scotland.

Ted Udall conceded a penalty from which Bruton equalised, but just on half-time, Gallacher made it 2-1, tapping the ball home after Crooks had squared a pass to him and

Derby County, 1935. Hughie Gallacher, scorer of five goals at Ewood Park the previous Christmas, is in the centre of the front row. Jack Bowers, the man who Gallacher was signed to replace after he was injured, is third from right of the middle row.

the little Scotsman took it and danced around the goalkeeper in one movement.

Thomson levelled the scores again just after the interval, sweeping past George Collin before beating Vince Blore, the Uttoxeter-born goalkeeper who was standing in for the injured Jack Kirby, but in the 57th minute, Gallacher put the Rams back in front with the best goal of the game.

Duncan ended a brilliant dribble by finding Gallacher, who veered away from goal and, despite the close attentions of Whyte and Pride, screwed home his shot from the tightest of angles.

Three minutes later, Hughie got his fourth after Crooks had again laid on the chance and, after a Crooks' shot hit the goalkeeper full in the face and laid him out, Gallacher made it 5-2 in the 73rd minute.

After the game, a 15-year-old centre-forward who was an amateur on Burnley's books approached Gallacher for advice. "Keep your nose clean and you'll do all right," he was told. The youngster was Tommy Lawton.

Blackburn Rovers: Binns; Gorman, Whyte, Whiteside, Carver, Pride, Bruton, McLean,

New signing Hughie Gallacher meets some of his Rams teammates in September 1934.

Thompson, Brennan, Turner.
Derby County: Blore; Udall, Collin, Nicholas, Barker, Hann, Crooks, Stockill, Gallacher, Ramage, Duncan.
Referee: R.W.Blake (Middlesbrough)
Att: 12,543.

Derby County, 1936-37. Back row (left to right): Hann, Summers, Nicholas, Scattergood, Wileman, Bell, Kirby, Webb, Barker, Roberts. Middle row: Boyd, Hagan, Udall, Bowers, Jessop, Napier, Keen, Gallacher. Front row: Stockill, Ramage, Jones, Crooks, Duncan, Howe.

Bowers Hits Four In Sensational Rams Recovery

Saturday, 5 September 1936

Derby County 5   Manchester United 4

AFTER being injured against Spurs in September 1934, Rams centre-forward Jack Bowers found that recovery was slow and he played only twice more that season and in only 17 games in 1935-36, although the Rams Reserves benefited that season when his 30 goals helped them win the Central League championship for the first time.

By the start of 1936-37, however, the veteran Hughie Gallacher's days at Derby were over — he was transferred to Notts County that September — and Bowers was in the side from the start, as the Rams, First Division runners-up the previous season, looked to go one better

this time and lift the League title for the first time in the club's history.

They began with a 3-1 win at The Hawthorns, where Bowers was on target, but then lost 3-2 in a midweek game at Roker Park before Manchester United, the Second Division champions in 1935-36, visited the Baseball Ground.

United had good reason to remember Jack Bowers because he had scored four times in the Rams 6-1 win over them in April 1931. Now he was about to repeat the feat, although the circumstances would be so much more dramatic.

The Rams took the lead after 13 minutes when Crooks got his head to a Duncan corner and saw the ball trickle slowly between John's legs and over the line after an unaccountable error by the United 'keeper.

Four minutes later, however, United were level when Wassall was perfectly positioned to hit Bryant's pass into the Rams' net off the underside of the crossbar. Welsh international centre-forward Tommy Bamford resisted a challenge from Derby's Ted Udall to put United in front after 24 minutes and then four minutes later, the same player made it 3-1 after Jack Howe had failed to win the ball from outside-right Bryant. The winger put over a perfect centre and Bamford nodded it home with Kirby looking out of position.

Six minutes into the second half, Bamford completed his hat-trick and the Rams looked to be heading for a thrashing. McKay lofted a free-kick into the Derby goalmouth and Bamford beat Ralph Hann in the air to head home the best of his three goals.

The *Derby Evening Telegraph* reported: 'Thus, the stage was set for the Rams' great recovery, which was largely due to Crooks's inspiration, Duncan's judgement and Bowers's opportunism.

'The first of Bowers's four goals, scored in 13 minutes, came in the 64th minute. Duncan sent in a fast centre and Bowers, racing past Vose, dived to meet the ball with his head and send it past John in the twinkling of an eye.

'Derby's third goal was not such a spectacular effort but it spoke well for the centre-forward's quickness that he netted, for when the ball came unexpectedly to him from a mass of players, he had not much time to think before tapping it into the net with his left foot.

'Roaring approval for the Rams' recovery, the spectators went almost delerious when the centre-forward, assisted by brilliant work by Duncan, completed his hat-trick and put the Rams on level terms.

'It really was a splendid effort of Duncan's. Bowers was racing hard up the field as Duncan clashed with Redwood and did not slacken as the winger came through triumphant. Steadying himself, Duncan appeared to gauge Bowers's speed and placed the ball with such remarkable accuracy in front of Jack's down-thrust head that a centre-forward could scarcely have missed it had he tried. Straight and true it went in and gave John no chance.

'Howe, limping after a tackle, went to outside-right with Crooks inside, and the latter gave Bowers the chance of scoring the goal that gave the Rams the victory. Sammy

Sammy Crooks, opened the scoring then saw his side go 4-1 down before Jack Bowers staged a comeback almost single-handedly.

lifted the ball over his head to Bowers who, despite the combined attentions of Vose and McKay, crashed the ball into the net.'

It was, indeed, a remarkable recovery, achieved as much as anything by the courageous opportunism of Jack Bowers. Yet within two months he had been transferred to Leicester City and ended the season with a Second Division championship medal after his 33 goals in 27 games for City helped them to the title.

The Rams, meanwhile, finished in fourth place. In their last game, at Molineux, they needed six goals to score 100 for the season. But they lost 3-1 and so failed to equal their record of 21 away points for a season.

Derby County: Kirby; Udall, Howe, Nicholas, Hann, Keen, Crooks, Stockill, Bowers, Napier, Duncan.
Manchester United: John; Redwood, McLenahan, Brown, Vose, McKay, Bryant, Wassall, Bamford, Ferrier, Manley.
Referee: S.L.Clark (Southgate)   Att: 21,194.

Dally Duncan in action at Highbury as the Rams attack.

Arsenal's Derby Jinx Continues

Wednesday, 14 September 1938

Arsenal 1   Derby County 2

WHEN Derby County travelled to Highbury early in the 1938-39 season, they met one of the truly great club sides in any era of football. Throughout the 1930s, Arsenal had been the major force in the English game. Under the legendary Herbert Chapman they had won the League championship five times since 1930-31 — including a hat-trick of titles — and the FA Cup twice since 1930. The Gunners were the current champions, too, after regaining the title in 1937-38.

But Derby themselves were no slouches in that decade. The Rams had finished runners-up in 1929-30 and 1935-36 and throughout the late '30s they fielded a magnificent side with more than its fair share of international players. Derby had another reason to be optimistic: over the previous ten years they had a good away record against Arsenal.

They began the 1938-39 season — due to the war, the last full League campaign for seven years as it transpired — with a 2-2 home draw against Wolves and then enjoyed 1-0 wins against Huddersfield Town at the Baseball Ground and Aston Villa away before going down 3-0 in the return game at

Huddersfield. On the Saturday before they went to Highbury, the Rams got themselves back on the rails with a 1-0 win over Raich Carter's Sunderland at the Baseball Ground.

On 4 August 1938, the Gunners had paid a British record fee of £14,000 to sign Wolves' Welsh international inside-forward Bryn Jones and expected great things from him.

The same month that Jones joined Arsenal, the Rams had signed goalkeeper Frank Boulton from the Gunners. Boulton had made 42 League and FA Cup appearances for the Highbury club, standing in for George Swindin. Now he returned to face his old teammates.

The Rams fielded another former Arsenal player, inside-forward Reg Stockill, who George Jobey had signed for £2,000 in September 1934, in the face of fierce competition from Liverpool.

It was Stockill, making his first appearance of the season for Derby in place of Harry Travis, who put the Rams ahead midway through the first half. Ronnie Dix and Dally Duncan combined before Stockill shot home past Swindin to silence the Highbury crowd.

It was no more than Derby deserved. Although Arsenal began in storming fashion, after the first ten minutes the Rams took control. England winger Cliff Bastin looked dangerous early on, but Jack Nicholas soon had the measure of him. The young right-wing pair of Nelson and Bremner did well with their quick passing, but near goal they did not have the experience to beat Jack Howe

Derby County, 1938-39. Back row (left to right): Sullivan, Hann, Wilcox, Travis, Smart, Alton, Parr, Nicholas. Second row: Dave Willis (trainer), Bailey, Bell, Bramley, Boulton, Wright, Wood, King, Barker, Howe, Bill Bromage (assistant trainer). Seated: McLachlan, V.Jones, Jeffreies, Hagan, Dix, Astley, Eggleston, Musson, Bradbury, Ward. On ground: Johnson, Brinton, Crooks, Stockill, Lisle, Mee, H.Jones, Duncan, Thompson.

and Tim Ward.

At the other end, Swindin did well to stop a swerving 20-yard shot from Dai Astley and then from a similar distance, Ronnie Dix brought the best out of the Arsenal 'keeper.

The two former Villa players were in rampant mood as the *Derby Evening Telegraph* explained: 'Both Astley and Dix were right on top of their form and a more progessive pair would be difficult to find. They varied their methods wonderfully, linking up with quick short passes, then swinging the ball out to the wings.'

The result of their magnificent contribution was that Sammy Crooks and Dally Duncan enjoyed marvellous service. Time and again Duncan took the ball past England full-back George Male to impress a watching Scottish selector, and whilst Male's England colleague, left-back Eddie Hapgood, was the pick of the Arsenal team that night, Crooks still found a way round him.

After 67 minutes, Arsenal should have drawn level when the ball appeared to hit Howe on the hip but the referee awarded a penalty. Boulton gave Bastin plenty of room to the right with the spot-kick, but the Arsenal man tried to beat the Rams' 'keeper on his left and succeeded only in shooting straight at him.

A few minutes later, however, the Gunners drew level when Ted Drake at last managed to elude Jack Barker and lobbed the ball over Boulton's head. According to the *Evening Telegraph* reporter 'C.B.M.' — who did not come over as entirely unbiased — the Arsenal centre-forward 'appeared to be well offside'.

It hardly mattered, though. Almost immediately the Rams were back in front when Arsenal were caught wide open. Dix got the ball from a clearance, gave it Astley, who transferred it to Crooks for the winger to centre. When the ball came over, there was the unmarked Duncan, running in from the opposite flank to head home the winner.

The Rams had a late escape when Bryn Jones hit the inside of a post but they held on to score yet another win at Arsenal. Indeed, despite the Gunners' pedigree between the wars, Highbury was becoming a happy hunting ground for the Rams, who also won there in 1927-28, 1928-29 and 1934-35 and drew two other games in the '30s. This season Derby went on to finish sixth, one place and one point behind Arsenal, who lost the championship to Everton.

Arsenal: Swindin; Male, Hapgood, L.Jones, Joy, Copping, Nelson, Bremner, Drake, B.Jones, Bastin.
Derby County: Boulton; Nicholas, Howe, Hann, Barker, Ward, Crooks, Astley, Stockill, Dix, Duncan.
Referee: TO COME   *Att: 25,756.*

Derby County on the eve of the 1939-40 season. Back row (left to right): Hann, Bramley, Alton, Redfern, Boulton, Barker, Nicholas, Howe, Peart. Second row: Dave Willis (trainer), Ward, McCulloch, Hinchliffe, V.Jones, Kendrick, Wilson, Wood, Bell, Dixon, Bill Bromage (assistant trainer). Seated: Engstrom, Steel, H.Jones, Walsh, Powell, Brinton, Johnson, Musson, Eggleston. On ground: Stamps, Crooks, Heydon, Wilcox, Duncan.

The Penalty Of War

Saturday, 2 September 1939

Derby County 1   Aston Villa 0

WHEN Derby County and Aston Villa ran out at the Baseball Ground on the first Saturday of September 1939, a hot, humid afternoon, they found the atmosphere unlike anything they had previously experienced.

The attendance was a meagre 8,000 — First Division matches against Villa had hitherto attracted bumper 'gates' in the 1930s — and those fans who had found their way to the ground were hardly in the mood to concentrate on a game of football, for there was a sense of great events impending elsewhere in the world.

War clouds had been gathering over Europe for over a year now and news that Hitler's army had invaded Poland brought the continent to the edge of the precipice. Britain's treaty with the Poles guaranteed that she would come to their aid if they were attacked. Now the attack had come and, as German tanks rolled into action against

Polish horse cavalry and the Luftwaffe appeared in the skies over Warsaw, fevered diplomatic activity sought to avert a world crisis. The man and woman in street, though, knew in their hearts that for the second time in 20 years, their country was about to go to war.

Thus, a football match between the Rams and Villa hardly seemed to matter. Yet there were enough people still interested enough to make their way to the Baseball Ground on this sultry afternoon over half a century ago.

For what it mattered, the Rams had begun the season with a 3-0 defeat at Sunderland, who were skippered by Raich Carter, and then beaten Portsmouth 2-0 at the Baseball Ground with goals from Billy Redfern and Dally Duncan. Nearly 22,000 watched the Roker match but there were just over 10,000 for the midweek game at Derby.

Because of the war, hundreds of players would see their careers cut short, some before they had hardly begun. Redfern was one of those unfortunates. George Jobey had signed him from Luton Town in August 1939, to replace Ronnie Dix who had moved to Spurs, with Reg Stockill moving to Luton as part of the Redfern transfer. Although Redfern played for Wales in a wartime international, by the time the conflict ended, his League career was over.

There was one other 'forgotten man' in Derby's last pre-war line-up, Jim Wilson, who came from Lincoln City and appeared for the Rams once, at inside-right at Roker Park on the opening day of the 1939-40 season. Like Redfern, his name disappeared from the Rams' statistics, for this was their only season and it was about to be obliterated.

Aston Villa came to Derby with one win and one defeat in their previous games — a 2-0 home win over Middlesbrough and a 2-1 home defeat against Everton. The Rams had finished the previous season sixth in Division One, whilst Villa ended in mid-table.

Despite, the unreal atmosphere on the eve of war, the Rams set about their task with such commitment that it looked as though a hatful of goals was on the cards as Dave McCulloch, Jack Stamps and Dally Duncan all went close in the early stages.

The Villa goal appeared to have a charmed life, though, and the West Midlands team were also helped by some outstanding goalkeeping from Joe Rutherford, signed the previous season from Third Division North club Southport.

According to the *Derby Evening Telegraph*: 'Had even half of Derby's scoring efforts suceeded, a 6-0 victory would not have flattered their superiority.'

As it was, the Rams had to make do with a penalty midway through the second half after George Cummings had bowled over McCulloch, a centre-forward who joined Derby from Brentford in March 1938. Skipper Jack Nicholas, who had already brought Rutherford to a brilliant flying save, hammered home the spot-kick.

According to the *Evening Telegraph*,

Cumming had 'knocked McCulloch over by way of showing his disapproval of the quite legitimate tactics used by the Rams' leader in challenging Rutherford while the goalkeeper was trying to get rid of the ball'. These days, of course, it would be the centre-forward who was penalised.

The newspaper also reported: 'The crowd will also remember with pleasure the all-round impressive form shown by Barker, the cool defensive touches that distinguished Howe's play, and the growing confidence of Wilcox, against such a dangerous winger as Broome, and the thrustfulness of Stamps and Redfern.'

In fact, George Wilcox's career at Derby was already on the wane after Nicholas moved to right-back and he joined Rotherham United after the war. Jack Stamps, signed from New Brighton in January 1939, would write his name large in Derby's history with two goals in the 1946 Cup Final. And Frank Broome, so lively on the Villa left wing, would join the Rams for the first post-war League season.

For now, though, the Football League closed down. On the day after this match, Britain delivered her final ultimatum to Hitler, Prime Minister Neville Chamberlain broadcast his famous speech on the wireless that Sunday morning — and as the *Evening Telegraph* commented: 'We will see no more football until the whistle blows on the grim conflict on which Britain is now engaged.'

Derby County: Boulton; Wilcox, Howe, Nicholas, Barker, Ward, Walsh, Redfern, McCulloch, Stamps, Duncan.
Aston Villa: Rutherford; Callaghan, Cummings, Massie, Allen, Iverson, Edwards, Martin, O'Donnell, Starling, Broome.

Att: 8,039.

Home Guard doing PT at the Baseball Ground in the summer of 1940.

The Rams Start Up Again — And A Debut For Tommy Powell

Thursday, 25 December 1941

Derby County 1   Royal Air Force 3

WHEN war was declared in September 1939, the Government ordered the shut-down of football, fearing that large crowds would be in danger from German air-raids. Soon they allowed limited attendances and although the League and FA Cup were suspended, the game's rulers quickly introduced regional competitions with clubs able to use 'guest' players as they had during World War One.

On 30 September 1939, Derby County arranged a friendly game against Leeds United at the Baseball Ground, but only 1,805 people turned up to watch the Rams go down 3-1, so the directors decided to close the club for the duration of the war. However, a Rams side was occasionally fielded, often playing on the Municipal Sports Ground and run by pre-war players Jack Nicholas and Jack Webb. And on Christmas Day 1941, Derby County returned to the Baseball Ground to prepare for re-entry into competitive football the following season.

This time, a crowd of over 10,000 turned up to see the Rams meet an RAF side in game in aid of the Mayor of Derby's War Fund. The RAF team comprised pre-war League professionals and top amateurs. They included Arsenal goalkeeper George Marks, who was serving in Northern Ireland, and they turned out in the Gunners' colours of red shirts with white sleeves and white shorts. Also in their ranks were Jack Barker's brother, Harry, who

was attached to the Rhyl club, Chelsea's Jack Smith, Villa's Frank O'Donnell, Jimmy McCormick of Spurs and Norwich City's Jack Acquroff, who was of Russian extraction.

The Rams, inevitably, had a motley-looking side. In goal was a young goalkeeper from Bedworth called Allsop and the defence included pre-war regulars Ralph Hann and Jack Nicholas as well local youngsters Jack Parr and Walter 'Chick' Musson, and Pallett, a full-back from the Burton area.

The forward line had a much more experienced look with Sammy Crooks, Jack Bowers, Peter Ramage and Dally Duncan. At inside-right, the Rams had selected Jimmy Hagan, another pre-war player, a supremely talented inside-forward who, alas, had not seen eye-to-eye with manager George Jobey and who had been allowed to move to Sheffield United for £2,500 in November 1938.

Apart from Bowers, who was now with Leicester City, Hagan would have been the Rams' only guest player on show, but he was unable to make the journey and into the Derby team stepped a 16-year-old former Bemrose School pupil called Tommy Powell. He was also a Derby lad, living in Sherwood Street, and had first played on the Baseball Ground in a local schools cup final before the war. In the late 1930s, Tommy had been an avid Rams fan . Now his dream had come true, for he was called up to play between Crooks and Bowers, two of the greatest players in English football between the wars.

'Football on the Baseball Ground again!' trumpeted the *Derby Evening Telegraph*. The report continued: 'Even if it was not according to precedent that it should be on Christmas morning, it was just like old times to survey the familar arena from inside, to "pillory" familiar soccer personalities and to see Derby County preserve what is said to be a tradi-

The Rams, like every club, fielded guest players throughout World War Two. This team beat Nottingham Forest 5-0 at the Baseball Ground in September 1944. Back row: Marshall (Burnley), Trim, Bullions, Bilton, Leuty, Musson. Front row: Doherty (Manchester City), Crooks, Tapping (Blackpool), Powell, Duncan. Trim, an RAF officer, was a former Forest player and Doherty, of course, signed officially for the Rams in December 1945.

tional peculiarity, that of losing when they should have won.'

The Rams did indeed mark their return with a defeat, but the RAF team were an experienced outfit. Their goals came from Acquroff (two) and Collins, whilst Jack Bowers scored Derby's goal after earlier missing a penalty when Leek handled his shot on the line.

And what of Tommy Powell? The newspaper said: 'Tom, a big lad with a long stride, need not be downhearted if he felt rather out of it before the course was run. He did at least get one chance to show he had a fine shot in his gun — and he made Marks, a jack-in-the-box Arsenal goalkeeper, do a nose-dive that was nearly a crash-landing near the foot of a post.'

It was, of course, the start of a remarkable career. The following season, when he was still only 17, Tommy Powell scored four goals in a League North game against Birmingham when the *Evening Telegraph* reported: 'He could do no wrong as a marksman once he had tasted blood . . .though he betrayed no disposition to make it a Powell picnic.'

National Service delayed his League debut proper until 1948, but then Powell went on to make 406 first-team appearances for the Rams before retiring in 1962. His son, Steve, made 402 appearances for Derby and now grandson Steve is on the club's books.

Back in 1941-42, however, the Rams continued their programme of friendly games with matches against such varied opposition as the Czechoslovakian and Belgian Armies, Anti-Aircraft Command, the British Army and the Pick of the Derby & District Senior League. The following year they joined the League North and four years on, Wembley beckoned once more.

Derby County: Allsop; Parr, Pallett, Hann, Nicholas, Musson, Crooks, Powell, Bowers, Ramage, Duncan.
RAF: Marks (Arsenal); Shearer (Motherwell), Smith (Chelsea), Barker (Rhyl), Leek (Corinthians), Mulranen (Corinthians), Collins (Wolves), O'Donnell (Aston Villa), Acquroff (Norwich City), McCormick (Tottenham H), Quinn (Everton).

Att: 10,000.

Raich Carter, the great Sunderland and England inside-forward who guested for the Rams before signing officially. He missed the second leg of the Midland Cup Final because he was on England duty.

Rams team which lost at Wolves in a wartime League game in November 1945. Back row (left to right): Musson, Harrison, Hann, Trim, Nicholas, Parr, Boulton. Front row: Doherty, Powell, Duncan, Morrison.

"We Want Peter," Cried The Fans

Saturday, 26 May 1945

Derby County 6   Aston Villa 0

ALTHOUGH wartime football provided welcome relief for men working long hours in munitions factories and for soldiers at home on leave, the nature of the game in those dark years between 1939 and 1945 could certainly be confusing with matches often counting for two and even three different competitions.

When the Rams got under way properly in 1942-43, they competed in the Football League North, which was split into two competitions, one finishing at Christmas, the other going on to the end of the year, and various cup tournaments. In 1944-45, Derby were still competing in the League North,

the War Cup — which developed into a national competition — and the Midland Cup.

By now the Rams had two great players in their ranks. Raich Carter of Sunderland and Peter Doherty of Manchester City were two of the finest inside-forwards the game has ever seen and when both were posted to RAF Loughborough to help rehabilitate injured airmen, they soon found themselves guesting for Derby County. It was the start of a magnificent, if all-too-brief, period in the club's history which culminated in the Rams' only FA Cup Final victory.

This season the Rams headed for a League and Cup double. They had finished runners-up to Huddersfield Town in the 'first championship' and in the second half of the season, beginning in the New Year, their matches in the Midland Cup also counted towards the Football League North 'second championship'.

Derby won the league title on Whit Monday

when they clinched it with a 1-0 victory over Liverpool. Peter Doherty scored the Rams' goal that afternoon and a few days later he would 'go nap' to give Derby the cup trophy as well.

In the Midlands Cup Final, the Rams had disposed of Northampton Town and Leicester City, both on aggregate, before a two-legged Final against Aston Villa. And two days before they confirmed themselves as League champions, Derby opened up a 3-0 lead in the first leg of the Final at Villa Park, where a crowd of 24,000 saw Raich Carter score a brilliant hat-trick.

Peter Doherty with the Midland Cup after his five goals helped hammer Aston Villa in the second leg.

The following Saturday, Carter was missing, playing for England against France in a Victory international, but his inside-forward partner Doherty made sure that he would not be missed.

With a three-goal cushion, the Rams no doubt felt that the destination of the trophy was already assured, but there was sufficient interest for a crowd of 16,000 to turn out — and what a treat they had.

Derby went ahead in the 27th minute when Jack Parr put Doherty clear and the flame-haired Irishman ran from the halfway line, outstripping the Villa defence before cracking the ball past Alan Wakeman to open up an unassailable aggregate lead.

Villa fought back gamely enough but 16 minutes into the second half centre-forward Clarrie Jordan, a Doncaster Rovers player who was guesting for the Rams, put them 2-0 ahead on the day and 5-0 up overall. This time Doherty was the provider, heading down for Jordan to finish the job.

Sammy Crooks and Jack Nicholas both went near before Doherty scored again in the 67th minute. Within four minutes he had scored twice more and eight minutes from time he scored his fifth and Derby's sixth.

Doherty had enjoyed a brilliant afternoon but afterwards he told a reporter: "It could have been anyone. I just happened to be in the right place at the right time."

Arthur Drewery, a member of the League Management Committee presented the Cup to Rams skipper Jack Nicholas and was congratulating the club when the crowd began to chant, "We want Peter, we want Peter."

"I give you Peter Doherty," said Mr Drewery, but although the Irish international was eventually persuaded to approach the microphone, he was too shy to make the speech which everyone wanted.

The *Derby Evening Telegraph* said: 'Whether he will ever again play for the Rams is questionable. But it can be said that no more popular player has ever worn Derby County's colours.'

Of course, Doherty was to stay with the Rams and share in arguably the greatest day in their history.

Derby County: Grant; Nicholas, Parr, Bullions, Leuty, Baxter, Crooks, Powell, Jordan, Doherty, Duncan.
Aston Villa: Wakeman; Potts, Cummings, Massie, Callaghan, Guttridge, Broome, Starling, Parkes, Iverson, Houghton.
Referee: G.S.Blackhall (Wednesbury)
Att: 16,218

Peter Doherty, the great Irish international inside-forward who helped the Rams win the FA Cup in 1946 after he was signed from Manchester City following a spell as a Rams guest. With Raich Carter he formed an inside-forward paiting which became legendary in English football, although they were together for only a brief period.

Birmingham's Mulraney finds the net in the drawn 1946 FA Cup semi-final at Hillsborough. Jack Parr and Vic Woodley are the Derby defenders.

Peter Doherty and Blues defender Arthur Turner go for the same ball – but where is it?

The Rams line-up for the Hillsborough semi-final. Back row (left to right): Harrison, Parr, Woodley, Bullions, Leuty, Stamps. Front row: Musson, Carter, Nicholas, Doherty, Duncan.

80,000 See The Rams Go Through To Wembley

Wednesday, 27 March 1946

Derby County 4   Birmingham City 0

DERBY County's march to the 1946 FA Cup Final was unique in that it was the only time the competition has been contested over two legs in the rounds up to and including the quarter-finals. It was also dramatic in that the Rams enjoyed a thrilling tie against Aston Villa to reach the semi-final and then took two games to beat Birmingham City and go through to Wembley for the first time.

Derby now had the brilliant inside-forward pair of Raich Carter and Peter Doherty officially on their books. Both men had been

signed in December 1945, both for £6,000 and Carter after a midnight taxi dash ensured that he would be available for the FA Cup which had just restarted and where no guest players were allowed, although guests could still play in the regional League games.

For Derby, the road to Wembley began relatively close to the Empire Stadium, at Kenilworth Road, Luton, to be precise, where Jack Stamps scored four goals as the Rams took a 6-0 advantage back to the Baseball Ground, where they completed the job with a 3-0 win. Derby then knocked out West Brom and Brighton (who were beaten 4-1 and 6-0) before meeting Villa in the quarter-final.

By now, the Rams had a new manager. Ted Magner had gone to coach abroad and former Derby player Stuart McMillan took over, combining the job of steering the club to Wembley with that of landlord of the Nag's Head pub at Mickleover.

The first leg of the quarter-final at Villa Park was a remarkable affair as a record crowd of 76,588 saw the Rams equalise three times before Sammy Crooks scored a 90th-minute winner. There were 32,000 at the Baseball Ground to see them go through with a 1-1 draw, although they fell behind at one stage and had Sammy Crooks carried off. For Crooks it was the end of the Cup trail.

Derby had harboured hopes of another League and Cup double, but defeat at Coventry meant that their interest now centered on the FA Cup. There were 65,000 at Hillsborough for the semi-final but they saw a drab 1-1 draw with Carter saving the day for the Rams.

The replay at Maine Road could not have provided a greater contrast. The crowd of 80,407 is still a record for a midweek game between two English clubs and when the teams came out they found spectators wedged up right to the touchlines in scenes reminiscent of the famous 1923 'White Horse' Cup Final.

Jim Bullions recalls: "Before the game we could hear the thunder of people's feet in the stands above our dressing-room. And when we took throw-ins and corners we had to move people out of the way. It was incredible."

After 90 minutes there was no score and the crucial moment came in the fifth minute of extra-time. Dally Duncan won the ball from Birmingham's Ted Duckhouse and took it to the byline before switching it back into the middle, into the path of the onrushing Doherty. Duckhouse had recovered but Doherty reached the ball a split-second before him and slid it into the net.

According to the *Derby Evening Telegraph*: 'A thunderous roar, which seemed to rock the stands, greeted the goal, but silence fell over the ground almost immediately . . .'

There had been a sickening collision and both men lay motionless.

Raich Carter said later: "I heard a crack and thought, 'Oh my God, Peter's broken his leg.' Of course, I didn't want either of them to be hurt but I was so relieved when Peter got to his feet."

It was poor Duckhouse who was stretchered off with a broken left leg and now ten-men

Birmingham were on the rack. After 103 minutes, Duncan slipped the ball through to Stamps and the Rams' centre-forward beat Gil Merrick with an acutely-angled shot.

Nine minutes later, 'a characteristically saucy effort' by Doherty saw the Irishman dribble the ball up to Merrick, feint and then slip his shot through the goalkeeper's legs.

The game was now comfortably won and Carter dawdled on the ball out on the left wing before sending a low pass into the goalmouth for Stamps to stab home for the Rams' fourth goal.

Yet it could have been so different if Birmingham's Harold Bodle had not been denied by former Chelsea goalkeeper Vic Woodley, who had come out of semi-retirement with Bath City after Frank Boulton was injured. Bodle might have given the Blues a 50th-minute lead but Woodley kidded him by leaving him a huge gap — and the Birmingham inside-left shot straight at the 'keeper.

Whether Derby would have equalised is open to question. Certainly, they were the more confident team in the first half and they might well have pulled back had Bodle's shot been true.

The reality was that the Rams were through to their first Wembley Cup Final.

Derby County: Woodley; Nicholas, Parr, Bullions, Howe, Musson, Harrison, Carter, Stamps, Doherty, Duncan.
Birmingham City: Merrick; Duckhouse, Jennings, Harris, Turner, Mitchell, Mulraney, Dougal, Jones, Bodle, Edwards.
Referee: W.H.E.Evans (Liverpool)
Att: 80,407

The Rams have been involved in several other attendance records, setting new marks at Sunderland (75,118 for an FA Cup sixth-round replay in March 1933), Millwall (48,672, FA Cup fifth round, February 1937), Aston Villa (76,588, FA Cup sixth round, March 1946), Portsmouth (51,385, FA Cup sixth round, February 1949) and Lincoln City (23,196, League Cup fourth round, November 1967).

Rams players and officials pictured at their Harpenden hotel before the 1946 Cup Final.

Two Goals For Stamps In Rams' Wembley Glory

Saturday, 27 April 1946

Derby County 4   Charlton Athletic 1

THE 1946 FA Cup Final was what most football fans had been dreaming of for months, if not years. After six war-weary seasons of regionalised soccer with clubs using guest players and untried youngsters, 'real' football was back. Although the Football League would not start up again until August 1946, the Cup began a year earlier and the Rams had fought their way through to meet Charlton Athletic at Wembley.

Yet for some at the Baseball Ground, success was tinged with sadness, particularly for Sammy Crooks, the veteran Rams and England outside-right who was denied this crowning glory to a wonderful career because a knee, injured in the quarter-final, had not recovered sufficiently for manager Stuart McMillan to risk him. His place went to Reg Harrison, the 22-year-old former Derby Corinthians forward who had done so well as Crooks' deputy in the semi-final.

There was also bad news for another former local junior player. Left-back Jack Parr had played right through the 1945-46 FA Cup campaign, including the two semi-final matches. But 24 days from Wembley, Parr broke an arm during a League South game against Luton Town and his place went to Jack Howe, who had deputised at centre-half for the injured Leon Leuty in the semi-final replay.

And goalkeeper Frank Boulton also had to sit out the Cup Final. The Rams' regular pre-war 'keeper, Boulton had been badly injured in a clash with Swansea Town's Trevor Ford during a League South game at the Baseball Ground in February. Boulton had not long returned to the Derby team after four years RAF service in West Africa. Now he too would miss his chance of glory as the Rams had signed former Chelsea and England goalkeeper Vic Woodley for the semi-final.

Angus Morrison could also feel unlucky to miss Wembley. A Scot, signed whilst he was still serving in the RAF, Morrison had played in the first six Cup ties before losing his place when Jack Stamps became regularly available.

Finally, pre-war wing-half Tim Ward had managed only one Cup game — the first, a 6-0 romp at Luton — before Army duties took him back to Germany. Ward returned to England in time to take his place in a Wembley seat, but his number-four shirt was worn by Jim Bullions, a Scots-born miner who had been playing as an amateur for

Vic Woodley loses the ball to Charlton centre-forward Arthur Turner with Leon Leuty covering.

Chesterfield before the Rams snapped him up.

Charlton also had their unfortunates. Full-back Peter Croker had broken a leg shortly before the Final and another defender, Charlie Revell, was also injured and missed the big day. Incidentally, Revell would make 22 appearances for the Rams after joining them in March 1951.

If matters had taken a different course, then the injured players would not have been the only ones missing the 1946 Cup Final. Indeed, there might have been no game at all.

On the Thursday before the game, the Rams players discovered that their wives and girl-friends had been given cheaper seats in an uncovered part of Wembley whilst the directors' wives were to be comfortably seated under cover. Incensed, some of the more experienced players, led by Raich Carter and Peter Doherty, told the board, "No new tickets — no Cup Final!" And Doherty said later: "We meant it. Make no mistake about that."

The club quickly relented and the Final went ahead, begging the question of whether Charlton would have been the first club in the history of the competition to be awarded the trophy by default.

For the first 80 minutes of the 1946 Final, there were no goals, although Carter had netted, only to be ruled offside. Then, with ten minutes remaining, the Rams went ahead. Carter took a throw-in and from it Harrison sent the ball to Stamps, who chipped neatly to Doherty. The Irishman nodded the ball down to Dally Duncan and it was his shot from about ten yards that Charlton defender Bert Turner turned past Sam Bartram for an own-goal, although Duncan said later, "It was definitely my goal. It would have gone in anyway."

Sixty seconds later, however, Charlton were level again and, ironically, it was Turner who was credited with their goal — but Derby claimed an own-goal!

Peter Doherty was convinced that without a wicked deflection off his shins, Woodley would have easily saved Turner's free-kick, and cinema news footage later confirmed that the ball did, indeed, take a big deflection to send the Rams goalkeeper the wrong way.

In the last five minutes of normal time,

This time Leuty heads clear from a Charlton attack during normal time. The Final eventually exploded into life after 80 minutes and in extra-time the Rams took control.

Another Charlton attack is repelled by the Rams as Woodley fists the ball clear.

a Stamps shot looked goalward bound until the ball burst and dropped at Bartram's feet. Said Stamps later, "The bloody thing just went phut!" The ball was to burst in a League South game between the two clubs four days later, and again in the following year's Final between Charlton and Burnley, but it seems that it was more likely the poor quality of the material available in wartime rather than some mystic force.

So the first post-war FA Cup Final went into extra-time and that is when the Rams, and Jack Stamps in particular, took the game over. After only two minutes, Stamps came in from the left and sent in a hard shot-cum-centre which Bartram could only block. The ball ran loose and Doherty almost knocked Duncan over in his eagerness to rifle home a shot which put Derby in front again.

Ten minutes later, Doherty was laying on a goal for Stamps and the big centre-forward went past Oakes and Phipps to put the Rams 3-1 in front. Within seconds of the start of

the second period of extra-time, Doherty laid on another for Stamps, who once again showed confidence in holding on to the ball and beating a man to create an opening for himself, his right-foot shot giving Bartram no chance.

The *Derby Evening Telegraph* told its readers: 'Derby has at last produced a "Crown Derby" football team. In defeating Charlton . . .and so winning the FA Cup for the first time in the club's history, Derby County gave one of the greatest exhibitions of football artistry and team-work ever seen in a Cup Final.

'There is no hard luck story to be told on behalf of the losers; indeed, when one reflects on those pulsating moments of extra-time, it seems difficult to realise that Charlton had survived 90 minutes of Derby County magic.

'With their forward line moving as sweetly as a well-oiled machine; with Leuty and Bullions the outstanding half-backs on the field; and with Nicholas playing a clever

Left: Charlton's Bert Turner turns the ball over his own line. *Right:* Jack Stamps hit one of his extra-time goals.

Peter Doherty brushes Dally Duncan aside to score the Rams' second goal and regain the lead.

waiting game which completely demoralised Duffy, the Rams never looked like losing.'

Reg Harrison was also singled out: 'In the second half he played like a veteran and not only did some of his footwork equal that of Duncan's, but a great left-foot shot of his nearly beat Bartram.'

The paper also gave some interesting statistics: during the game, the Rams forced 12 corners to Charlton's five; the ball went into touch 83 times and each goalkeeper took 15 goal-kicks; the Rams conceded 21 free-kicks to Charlton's 14; the Rams trainer came on to the field six times, Charlton's four; and the receipts of £45,000 were a British record.

On the eve of the Final, Raich Carter's father-in-law, Edgar Marsh of 16 Rupert Road, Chaddesden, had been taken ill and died early on Saturday afternoon. Carter's wife immediately telephoned Wembley and asked that her husband should not be informed until after the game.

Jack Nicholas has just collected the Cup and his winners' medal from King George VI. Beside the King is Queen Elizabeth. FA secretary Stanley Rous looks on and Rams wing-half Chick Musson is next in line.

When they left Wembley, the Rams found that thousands of Rams supporters had stayed behind to cheer them and in every village and built-up area on the way to their hotel at Harpenden, the team bus became snarled up in heavy traffic. Inching slowly along, it was surrounded by all sorts of people who simply wanted to cheer the Cup holders.

On Saturday night there was a musical evening for the players and then on Sunday they either rested or played golf.

Back at Derby's Midland Station, the tired but happy fans began arriving back at about 10 o'clock on Saturday evening and the great trek back from London continued until the early hours of Sunday morning. Many fans arrived back after the last buses had departed and they faced a long walk back to Derby's suburbs.

The Rams party arrived in town on Monday and then on Tuesday evening made their way in triumphant procession, displaying the FA Cup on an Offilers' beer dray from the Blue Peter at Alvaston to the town centre where a civic reception awaited them. All the way they were cheered by thousands of Rams fans — and even by people who had probably never been to a football match in their life. It was, indeed, Derby County's greatest day.

Derby County: Woodley; Nicholas, Howe, Bullions, Leuty, Musson, Harrison, Carter, Stamps, Doherty, Duncan.
Charlton Athletic: Bartram; Phipps, Shreeve, H.Turner, Oakes, Johnson, Fell, Brown, A.Turner, Welsh, Duffy.
Referee: E.D.Smith (Whitehaven)
Att: 98,215.

Back home. Skipper Jack Nicholas holds the FA Cup as the Rams progress on an Offilers beer dray from the Blue Peter to the Council House. This photograph was taken at the corner of Victoria Street and St Peter's Street. Trainer Dave Willis smokes a cigaratte. A police constable from the Derby Borough force stares at the camera.

Broome's Goalkeeping 'Blinder' As Chelsea Are Denied

Wednesday, 29 January 1947

Derby County 1　　　　　　Chelsea 0

AFTER beating Third Division Bourne-mouth with the help of a freak goal by stand-in outside-left Tim Ward in the third round of the FA Cup, holders Derby County faced fellow First Division club Chelsea in the next round and earned a goalless draw at Stamford Bridge.

But when the Pensioners came back to the Baseball Ground for the Wednesday after-noon replay, it looked likely that they would score a shock victory over the holders when the Rams lost goalkeeper Alec Grant only four minutes into the game.

Grant had joined Derby from Leicester City earlier in the season and after taking over from the veteran Vic Woodley, he had kept his place.

The Rams showed other new faces from the side that had lifted the Cup nine months earlier: Bert Mozley, a Derby youngster who was doing his National Service in the RAF, was at right-back in place of Jack Nicholas, who had retired; Tim Ward's talent had seen him take over the right-half berth from Jim Bullions; Angus Morrison was back at centre-forward in place of Jack Stamps, who had switched to inside-left in place of Peter Doherty, transferred to Huddersfield; and on the left wing in place of Dally Duncan, who had moved to Luton Town as player-coach in October, was the former Aston Villa and England star, Frank Broome, who the Rams had signed in September.

Broome was, indeed, a talented footballer who had played in four different forward positions for England before the war. On this day, he was to show even greater versatility after the accident to Grant.

Broome takes up the story: "Alec Grant had this habit of hitch-kicking when he cleared the ball and before we went out to play Chelsea, Stuart McMillan told him to be careful on the bone-hard pitch. As we got into the tunnel, Stuart said it again — 'Remember Alec, no hitch-kicking.'

"Blow me, we'd been going less than five minutes when Alec caught the ball and did his party-piece as he went to kick it upfield. Down he went, dislocated his elbow — and I had to go in goal. I volunteered straight away because I used to keep goal in training and always fancied it."

In training, though, Broome did not have to face centre-forwards of the calibre of Chelsea's Tommy Lawton. But for 116 minutes, Broome and his fellow defenders denied the Pensioners' forward line.

After 25 minutes Grant, his elbow heavily bandaged, returned to the fray on the left wing. The injured goalkeeper was far from a passenger, though, and in the tenth minute of extra-time, with the game still goalless, he swung over a long crossfield pass to Reg Harrison on the opposite wing.

Harrison took the ball past Chelsea defender Willi Steffen, a former Swiss Air Force pilot who was playing as an amateur whilst working in London, and pushed a pass down the centre for Stamps to take on the run. Stamps tricked centre-half Harris, bundled off another challenge and then coolly lobbed the ball over Harry Medhurst's head as the Chelsea goalkeeper came out. It was a superb goal and it won the game for Derby.

The only other real chance of the game had been in normal time when Raich Carter — 'otherwise rather leg weary' according to the *Derby Evening Telegraph* — saw his glorious drive tipped over in equally mag-nificent fashion by Medhurst.

The *Telegraph* commented: 'This Derby Cup victory was no fluke. . . .On a glassy surface that would have been better suited for an ice-hockey match, the Rams won through by determination and team spirit. . . .

'Shining through this Derby County silver lining was their most brilliant star, Leon Leuty, who never once flickered in his tremendous task as Lawton's shadow. The impreturbable centre-half did not put a foot wrong and in his complete supression of the England leader lay the master key to the Rams' ultimate success. . .

Tim Ward, now back in the Rams team. Ward was capped twice by England and later managed Derby County.

Derby County in 1947. Back row (left to right): Bullions, Mozley, Grant, Howe, Musson. Front row: Harrison, Ward, Leuty, Morrison, Stamps, Ken Powell. On ground: Broome, Carter.

Bert Mozley, a Derby-born full-back who gained his place in the side whilst still doing National Service in the RAF. Mozley, too, was capped for England.

'Stamps's goal was fitting reward for his grand, wholehearted display. There was no doubt about it that the Rams inside-forward was the best forward — and that includes Tommy Lawton . . .'

Alas, in the next round, the Rams lost their grip on the Cup when they lost 1-0 before a 44,000 crowd at Anfield, where Jack Balmer scored the Merseysiders' goal.

So the Chelsea replay remained the high spot of Derby's Cup season. Years later, whenever Frank Broome saw Tommy Lawton, he would extend a hand and say, "Tommy, shake hands with the only goal-keeper you never scored against."

Derby County: Grant; Mozley, Howe, Ward, Leuty, Musson, Harrison, Carter, Morrison, Stamps, Broome.
Chelsea: Medhurst; Winter, Steffen, Macaulay, Harris, Machin, Spence, Walker, Lawton, Goulden, Paton.
Referee: T.Smith (Atherstone)   *Att: 19,079.*

The Rams team which reached the FA Cup semi-final in 1948. Back row (left to right): Ward, Mozley, Leuty, Wallace, Howe, Musson. Front row: Harrison, Carter, Stamps, Steel, Morrison.

Stamps, Carter, Steel — And Into Another Semi-Final

Saturday, 6 March 1948

Derby County 5   QPR 0

WHEN Derby County began their 1947-48 FA Cup campaign, goalkeeper Bill Townsend, a pre-war signing from Nuneaton Borough, had made the position his own following the retirement of Vic Woodley, who had kept goal in the 1946 Final. But a freak training injury to Townsend in the Baseball Ground gym on the eve of the fifth-round tie at Middlesbrough in late January 1948 left Derby without an experienced goalkeeper.

Frank Payne, a novice from Ollerton Colliery, made his debut at Ayresome Park and was protected by an experienced Derby defence as the Rams won 2-1. Then manager Stuart McMillan bought Blackpool's veteran Jock Wallace, whose main attraction was that he was out of favour at Bloomfield Road and thus not cup-tied.

Wallace made his Rams debut in happy circumstances — a 5-1 home win over Sunderland when Raich Carter scored four times against the club who, he said, had sold him 'for peanuts' — and was well installed when Derby met Third Division South club Queen's Park Rangers in the FA Cup quarter-final two weeks later.

The game at Loftus Road was a bruising affair and big Jack Stamps was one of the

Brave Jack Stamps, head swathed in bandages, gets above two QPR defenders in the first game at Loftus Road.

Rams players to suffer, finishing the game with his head heavily bandaged following a collision with a Rangers' defender. In the end, Derby were perhaps grateful to escape from London with a 1-1 draw, thanks to a goal from Billy Steel, the brilliant Scottish international inside-left who had joined the Rams from Morton in June 1947, for a British record fee of £15,500. The first game included extra-time, for in those immediate post-war days, the government wanted to avoid midweek afternoon replays which would draw men away from vital factory work as Britain got back on her feet again.

When the sides replayed at the Baseball Ground a week later, they knew that the winners would face Manchester United in the semi-final. And this time the Rams showed that they meant business straight from the kick-off. As the *Derby Evening Telegraph* reported: 'They were complete masters from the first kick and even with 11 sound men, QPR were made to look what they are — just a good Third Division side.'

The '11 sound men' was a reference to the fact that after 38 minutes QPR's goalkeeper Reg Allen, a former prisoner-of-war, had to move on to the right wing with a broken bone in his right hand; and outside-right Bill McEwan twisted his knee and had to watch the second half from the trainer's bench.

By then, however, The Rams were well on the way to an emphatic victory. Steel had put them ahead after only four minutes and Carter and Stamps added further goals before half-time, albeit immediately after Allen had to come out of goal.

Sixteen minutes into the second half, Carter scored his second goal of the afternoon and with a minute remaining, Stamps netted his second to round off an emphatic Derby win.

The *Evening Telegraph* was having none of Rangers' moans: 'Barely had the tumult and shouting died than the first moan was heard from the boys of the Big City: "We wuz robbed." I expected it, but I could not disagree more heartily with it. Derby County beat Queen's Park Rangers by 5-0 in the FA Cup sixth-round replay at the Baseball Ground on Saturday because: (1) they played

the only good football going; (2) they treated QPR to a spoonful of their own football "rough stuff" — and the Londoners found it awful bitter; (3) the Rams cashed in on their luck — something QPR had failed to do the previous week when everything went wrong for Derby.'

The paper's reporter, Frank Nicklin, continued: 'Everybody already knew that the Rams had a great half-back line. Ward, Leuty and Musson were in such fine fettle that there was seldom any danger of QPR's smash-and-grab tactics paying a goal dividend. With Leuty playing the perfect third-back game, supported on either side by cool tackling, safe kicking Mozley and Howe, and Ward and Musson dominating the midfield approaches, the Derby defence looked well nigh impregnable.

'As in the previous encounter, the best forward was, without doubt, Billy Steel, whose ball control and dribbling were uncanny. His distribution of the ball was absolutely first-rate . . .'

Despite what the jeering QPR supporters may have thought of Carter, the Rams captain played a sound tactical game . . .his first-half goal was the finest I have seen this season — a tearing 30-yard snap drive delivered while QPR were still reeling from the blow of losing Allen.

Not surprisingly, there was no mention of Jock Wallace, who had little to do that afternoon. Alas, Wallace would come in for some criticism when the Rams lost 3-1 to Manchester United in the Hillsborough semi-final, where Stan Pearson scored a hat-trick. His first-class career was then almost over and the following August, he was released to Leith Athletic.

Derby County: Wallace; Mozley, Howe, Ward, Leuty, Musson, Harrison, Carter, Stamps, Steel, Morrison.
Queen's Park Rangers: Allen; G.Powell, Jefferson, I.Powell, G.Smith, A.Smith, McEwan, Ramscar, Boxshall, Hatton, Hartburn.
Referee: P.Stevens (Luton)   *Att: 31,588.*

Derby County in 1949-50. Back row (left to right): Ward, Mozley, Webster, Leuty, Musson, Howe. Front row: Harrison, Morris, Stamps, Steel, Broome.

Rams Cup Wobbles Before Record Baseball Ground Crowd

Saturday, 11 February 1950

Derby County 4   Northampton Town 2

ON the second Saturday of February 1950, Derby County's 24-year-old winger Tommy Powell was making his way down Pear Tree Street en route to the Baseball Ground for the Rams' fifth-round FA Cup tie against Northampton Town.

That season the Rams had progressed to the last 16 by way of a 5-3 win over Manchester City — Jack Stamps scoring a hat-trick in front of 53,000 at Maine Road — and a replay

win over Bury when Stamps scored another three. Now they faced the Cobblers, who were chasing Notts County for promotion from the Third Division South.

Interest in the tie was enormous and Northampton brought an estimated 10,000 fans in six special trains and 100 coaches, hoping to see the Cobblers improve on what was promising to be their best-ever Cup run. And in those days when all-ticket matches were a rarity, it meant that thousands of home fans were locked out of the Baseball Ground.

As Tommy Powell pushed his way through the crowds, a disconsolate fan was coming the other way. He didn't recognise Powell and said, "I shouldn't bother, mate. You'll never get in." The Rams' forward smiled: "Well, I'll have a go." And what a contribution he made to the first half as Derby stormed into a 4-1 lead.

Tommy Powell hammers the ball goalwards during the Cup victory over Northampton when a record crowd packed the Baseball Ground. Billy Steel is the other Rams player.

After only 30 seconds, Powell fed Stamps and the burly Rams centre-forward pushed the ball through for Johnny Morris to put his side ahead. Morris was enjoying a brilliant start with Derby, the club he had joined from Manchester United for £24,500 some 11 months earlier when the Rams broke the British transfer record for the second time in less than two years. In his first 13 games for Derby, Morris had scored as many goals.

After his strike gave the Rams a dream start against Northampton, they continued to bombard the Cobblers' goal and six minutes later went 2-0 ahead when Powell beat two defenders before playing a square ball to Hughie McLaren, who hit it into the roof of the net.

After 16 minutes it was 3-0 after Morris robbed Maurice Candlin, the Northampton skipper, pushed the ball to Stamps and watched as the number-nine shimmied past another defender before tapping a through pass to Billy Steel. The little Scotsman fired in the third and the Rams were apparently home and dry, although five minutes later the Cobblers grasped at a lifeline when Arthur Dixon headed home a Albert Mitchell cross.

But three minutes before half-time, McLaren claimed his second goal in controversial fashion. His shot went in off a post with the Northampton defenders claiming that it had not crossed the line.

Ten minutes into the second half, Dixon pulled the score back to 4-2 when Bert Mozley was guilty of some slack marking and the Cobblers' inside-right hammered the ball past Bill Townsend from an acute angle.

Suddenly, the Rams appeared to have a fight on their hands. The *Derby Evening Telegraph* takes up the story: 'Confidence is a great thing . . .but when it comes to cockiness, watch out for trouble. After taking a 4-1 lead by half-time against Northampton Town on Saturday, the Rams were so cocky that they didn't even bother to remember they had a right winger. How wrong they were, for they had to struggle to keep in front.

'For Tommy Powell, the Rams' right winger and most improved forward in the side, the *Harry Lime* zither theme which kept the record Baseball Ground crowd of 38,063 entertained before the match became the 'shiver' theme.

'He was almost completely pass-starved for the whole of the second half when the Cobblers, staging a desperate all-or-nothing rally in which they played some brilliant first-time football, rocking the Rams with a series of defence-splitting raids that might have easily brought them three goals in addition to Dixon's narrow-angle effort.

'Powell had to wander into the middle, out to the left wing, even back to his own penalty area to forage for himself. It was a peculiar state of affairs, for the Rams tried everything . . .They moved Steel to centre-forward and plugged the ball haphazardly down the middle to him; they tried long and short passes out to McLaren — everything except put the ball out to Powell.'

In the end, though, the Rams held on and there was to be no Cup sensation. The attendance, swelled by the huge following from Northampton, easily broke the Baseball Ground attendance record of 37,830, set against Nottingham Forest back in January 1936. Receipts of £4,877 17s 6d from the 38,063 crowd show just how inflation has worked in the ensuing years.

The Rams went out of the FA Cup in the quarter-finals, losing 2-1 at home to Everton with Tommy Powell scoring Derby's goal. Intriguingly, the attendance for that game was only 32,128, the Northampton 'gate' remaining a Baseball Ground record for almost 20 years.

Derby County: Townsend; Mozley, Parr, Ward, Leuty, Musson, Powell, Morris, Stamps, Steel, McLaren.
Northampton Town: Ansell; Smalley, Barron, Candlin, McCoy, Hughes, English, Dixon, McCulloch, Murphy, Mitchell.
Referee: H.Pearce (Luton)   *Att: 38,063.*

The Rams Got Their Skates On In 11-Goal Thriller

Saturday, 16 December 1950

Derby County 6   Sunderland 5

WHEN two middle-of-the-table sides meet in mid-season, there is no reason to suspect that they are going to serve up anything special. But when Derby County and Sunderland — both having average seasons in the First Division — met just before Christmas 1950, they dished up a festive treat for the fans at the Baseball Ground. Eleven goals and plenty of thrills and spills on an icy pitch — the game had it all.

Stars of the show for the Rams were Johnny Morris, their £24,500 record signing from Manchester United, and Jack Lee, a centre-forward who joined Derby from Leicester City in June 1950, for £18,500.

When Rams manager Stuart McMillan signed Lee, he promised him one thing — that if he joined Derby he would win a full England cap. Sure enough, within four months of arriving at the Baseball Ground, Lee had scored on his England debut, in a 4-1 win over Northern Ireland in Belfast.

And when Sunderland arrived at the Baseball Ground two months later, Lee was in brilliant form, scoring four goals in a match the see-sawed in amazing fashion.

The victory, though, had as much to do with the brilliance of Johnny Morris as anything. The *Derby Evening Telegraph* reported: 'The home team won this thrill-a-minute match by 6-5 and they owed much to Johnny Morris, who although finishing without a goal to his name, wriggled and slithered through the Sunderland defence with a speed that would have put Rudolph the Red-Nosed Reindeer to shame!'

At no time were the Rams behind. After 28 minutes they led 2-0 after goals from Lee (nine minutes) and Hugh McLaren. A minute later, Dick Davis pulled a goal back for the Wearsiders but after 36 minutes, Lee restored Derby's two-goal advantage.

Sunderland were then handicapped by an injury to Willie Watson, but two minutes before half-time their fiery Welsh international centre-forward Trevor Ford gave them a 3-2 lead. Four minutes after the interval, Davis pulled Sunderland level.

Lee restored the Rams' lead after 67 minutes and McLaren made it 5-3 in the 70th minute. Two minutes after that, Tommy Wright scored Sunderland's fourth but then Lee his own fourth goal and Derby's fifth. Even then, the excitement was not over and four minutes from the end, Ford picked up a long clearance and found himself with only goalkeeper Harry Brown to beat. The Welshman made no mistake to set up the possibility of an astonishing 6-6 draw, but the Rams' defence held on for both points.

In the *Telegraph* Mark Eaton wrote: 'I award the biggest bouquet to the two Derby men because they realised from the first what was required of them. Their ball control was something to marvel at, and Morris's passes, which he skimmed along just above the snow, repeatedly had the Sunderland defence in difficulties.

'He varied the procedure, too, first swinging the ball out to the opposite wing, and then pushing it firmly but accurately down the middle or through to the lively McLaren, who completed the Rams' scoring. In this way he made at least three of the goals.

'Lee, I should say, gave just about his best display since he was chosen to play for England. He was always master of the ball and his shooting was of a variety that makes one wonder why he does not try more shots.

'As he revealed in this match — and in others — he carries a powerful shot in either foot and I doubt if we shall see any better goals than his first two. In each instance he pivoted on his right foot after beating an opponent, and appeared to hook the ball with his left foot round a "wall" of defenders just inside the far upright.

'. . . .But if there was one incident more than any other that warmed the cockles of my heart on that chilly afternoon, it was when I saw Ken Oliver dispossess Ford, trick another man and then move forward in true Barker fashion before making a delightful pass. Apparently, the days when centre-halves can hold the ball and work it forward are

Johnny Morris (left) was the star of the show, although Jack Lee (right) scored four of the Rams' goals.

not yet past.'

At the end of the season, Derby County finished 11th in the First Division, Sunderland were 12th and both teams had 40 points, the Rams just shading it on goal-average, thanks in part to that remarkable December day at the Baseball Ground.

Derby County: Brown; Mozley, Parr, Ward, Oliver, Musson, Harrison, Stamps, Lee, Morris, McLaren.

Sunderland: Mapson; Hedley, Hudgell, McLain, Walsh, A.Wright, T.Wright, Kirtley, Ford, Davis, Watson.

Referee: A.E.Ellis (Halifax)   Att: 15,952.

Fulham Dazzled By Shooting Star Lee

Saturday, 20 January 1951

Fulham 3   Derby County 5

ONE month after their astonishing 6-5 victory over Sunderland, Derby County continued their high-scoring exploits of the 1950-51 season with a 5-3 win over Fulham at Craven Cottage. The Rams had a long-standing reputation for reserving some of their best displays for London and this was a fine example.

Again, Jack Lee was one of the stars of the show. Said the *Derby Evening Telegraph*: 'The performance of the attack was as bright and colourful as the lights that flashed and twinkled in Piccadilly Circus before the power cut. And the "leading light" was Jack Lee, whose electrifying bursts of speed and shooting earned him his third hat-trick of the season.'

The Rams, who moved Johnny Morris to outside-right in place of the injured Reg Harrison, took the lead in the first minute, although it was Jack Stamps, not Lee, who put them ahead, hammering a lovely corner-kick from Morris low into the corner of Ian Black's goal.

Three minutes later, the Cottagers were level when a free-kick from veteran Archie Macaulay lifted the ball right over the Derby defence and in raced Arthur Stevens to beat the advancing Harry Brown, Derby's former QPR and Notts County goalkeeper.

The game was only six minutes old when the Rams regained the lead. Jack Lee raced away from the centre of the field and held off no less than four defenders before luring Black out of goal and then beating him with a powerful drive from a remarkably narrow angle.

On 13 minutes, Fulham drew level once again. This time Brown was at fault when he punched out, rather than caught, a hopeful lob from Bedford Jezzard. Bobby Brennan was in position to slam the ball back into the empty net.

In the 21st minute, Derby regained their lead again. Bert Mozley's free-kick was met by the leaping Lee, who outjumped Bill Pavitt before steering a backward header past Black.

Four minutes later, the scoreline in this astonishing game became 4-2 to Derby County when Lee's low centre was pushed out by Black, straight into the path of Jack Stamps, who fired it back past the goalkeeper.

With less than half an hour played, the 28,000 crowd had already seen six goals and although the excitement subsided a little, there was still more to come.

Ten minutes into the second half, a fierce shot from Macaulay beat Brown but rebounded back off a post straight to the unmarked Brennan, who simply had to walk the ball into the net.

The fans then had to wait until nine minutes from the end for another goal and to their general dismay it fell to the Rams, who thus opened up a comfortable two-goal margin for the first time in this see-saw game. McLaren broke away down the left and took the ball almost to the edge of the penalty area before slipping it to Lee. The Rams centre-forward pivoted round and hit a first-time shot into the roof of the net. It was, said the *Evening Telegraph*, 'the best goal of the match'.

The newspaper reported: 'This was a game that the fans dream about but seldom see. Midfield play was cut down to a minimum, action being confined almost exclusively to first one penalty area and then the other. The match never lost its pulsating pace, which is a tribute to the fitness and determination of the players.

'Lee was in international form — and that's no exaggeration! He led his forwards with abounding zest and skill. He parted with the ball quickly but intelligently, and was just as swift to run into one of the many gaps that were punched in the home defence, ready to receive the return pass that seldom failed to come.'

At that stage of the season, Lee was the First Division's leading scorer with 22 goals but his eventual total of 29 was one short of Blackpool's Stan Mortensen, although Lee missed the last game of the season.

Bedford Jezzard shoots for goal past Harry Brown as Fulham try to get back into the game, but this effort went wide. The other Rams players are Keith Savin and Ken Oliver.

The Fulham game also proved a whirlwind experience for young left-back Keith Savin, a National Serviceman who was making his League debut after joining the Rams from Oxford City eight months earlier.

Fulham: Black; Bacuzzi, R.Lowe, Quested, Pavitt, Lawler, Stevens, Macaulay, Jezzard, Brennan, Campbell.

Derby County: Brown; Mozley, Savin, Ward, Oliver, Musson, Morris, Stamps, Lee, Powell, McLaren.

Referee: E.S.Vickery (Bristol)   Att: 28,865.

Rams players arrive back at the Baseball Ground after a training run, led by the former Derby Boys player Mike Smith. As Derby dropped from the First Division to the Third North, the playing personnel changed dramatically.

Rams Didn't Go Down Without A Fight

Saturday, 18 April 1953

Derby County 5   Manchester City 0

ALTHOUGH Derby County's outlook was still extremely gloomy as far as avoiding relegation from the First Division was concerned, it brightened slightly following their 5-0 win over fellow strugglers Manchester City at the Baseball Ground towards the end of the 1952-53 season.

The Rams' victory was their biggest since November 1951, when Fulham were defeated by the same margin, and it improved their goal-average to such an extent that it was now no longer the worst of the eight relegation-threatened clubs.

Indeed, on that Saturday, Derby were the only one of the teams in danger to record a win and they were still in with a chance, provided they took full points from their two remaining games, at Stoke and against championship-chasing Preston at the Baseball Ground.

Derby gave a League debut to Rhodesian outside-left Cecil Law, and he saw plenty of the ball as the Rams hammered a Manchester City side that would finish 20th that season, only one point from a relegation place.

Jack Lee headed Derby into the lead in the ninth minute, following a McLaren corner. Seven minutes later, the same player made it 2-0 with a low shot which beat City's former prisoner-of-war, the German Bert Trautmann, as the visitors appealed for offside.

A minute before the interval, when City centre-half Dave Ewing was off the field following a collision with Law, Jack Stamps added Derby's third, and in the 55th and 60th minutes the two-goal hero of the 1946 FA Cup Final laid on chances from which McLaren, who had moved into the middle following an injury to Lee, headed Derby's

Derby County, 1952-53. Back row (left to right): Jack Bowers (assistant trainer), Mozley, Mays, Parr, Middleton, Oliver, Nielson, Musson, Jack Poole (trainer). Front row: Harrison, Morris, Lee, Stuart McMillan (manager), Stamps, Powell, McLaren, Law.

fourth and fifth goals.

McLaren's first goal was a remarkable affair, for he was lying on the ground when the ball rolled to him and he managed to steer it with his head into the empty net.

In the *Derby Evening Telegraph*, Milburn Shanks reported: 'So it seems that the Rams are not going down without a fight.

'Although they were opposed on Saturday by a team possessing a defence as shaky as I have seen this season, this should not be allowed to detract from the merit of their performance.

'I have seen the Rams meet some poor teams before and completely fail to clinch their superiority with goals. This time, however, the forwards played their part well — although Lee was a limping passenger on the right wing for all the second half after injuring his left leg in a duel with Ewing.

'My only criticism is that they "allowed" the scoring to come to an end after the 60th minute. For a team in the Rams' position,

to whom goal-average might assume such vital importance, it was certainly a case of "the more goals the better" on Saturday.

'....In the Rams' attack, principal honours were taken by the lively Powell, working hard and using the ball supremely well under the hard ground conditions which suited him best; McLaren, a little lost at outside-right but as persevering and tenacious as ever as a deputy inside-forward; and Stamps, who, in the first half, saw to it that Law, making his First Division debut, got the ball often.'

Concerning City, Shanks wrote: 'As I saw it, Revie — a great worker who found time to inspire several promising attacks — was the one Manchester man to enhance his reputation. Even Trautmann, lacking any form of co-ordinated cover, was below his best.'

The Rams went to win 2-1 at Stoke, with goals from Lee and Stamps, but lost 1-0 to Preston in what was the last First Division match to be played at the Baseball Ground for 16 years. Preston's goal came from a Tom Finney penalty in front of 31,496 fans but it was not enough to give them the title, Arsenal taking it by one-tenth of a goal. A victory would not have kept the Rams up, incidentally, because Chelsea — who Derby could have overhauled — beat Manchester City 3-1 at Stamford Bridge, Derby thus joining Stoke in the drop.

Two years later, the Rams were down again, into the Third Division for the first time. Certainly, their five-goal hammering of Manchester City was one of the few great days of an otherwise depressing era.

Derby County: Middleton; Mozley, Savin, Mays, Oliver, Musson, McLaren, Powell, Lee, Stamps, Law.
Manchester City: Trautmann; Branagan, Hannaway, Revie, Ewing, Paul, Anders, Spurdle, Whitfield, Hart, Cunliffe.
Referee: A.Murdoch (Sheffield)   Att: 15,618.

In March 1954, the Rams lost 2-0 to Leeds United in the middle of a run of 13 matches without a win. That season they finished 18th in Division Two, prior to the drop to the Northern Section. Here, Tommy Powell is beaten in the air. The other Rams attackers are Ken Hawden (right) and Jimmy Dunn.

Derby County in 1955-56, their first season in the Third Division North. Back row (left to right): Barrowcliffe, Mays, Ryan, Webster, McDonnell, Savin. Front row: Ken Harrison, Parry, Ackerman, Pye, Powell.

Alf Ackerman's Four-Goal Comeback

Saturday, 7 April 1956

Derby County 6   Accrington Stanley 2

THE 1955-56 season saw Derby County appear in the Third Division for the first time, the Rams taking their place in the Northern Section after tumbling from Division One in the space of three seasons. Not surprisingly, manager Jack Barker had not survived relegation and Derby had appointed another former Rams player, Harry Storer, as their new boss.

Storer soon set about strengthening the side. Reg Ryan, West Brom's Irish international inside-left, was signed in July, along with Martin McDonnell, a rugged defender who had now joined Storer at three different clubs. In January, outside-left Dennis Woodhead moved from Sheffield Wednesday. And two months later the Rams signed Birmingham City full-back Roy Martin.

With this blend of experience, skill and steel, Derby might have made it back to Division Two at the first time of asking. But that was reckoning without the resurgence taking place at Blundell Park, where former Manchester United centre-half Allenby Chilton was turning Grimsby Town from re-election no-hopers into promotion material.

The Rams lost 2-1 at Grimsby in late October and then in March went down by 3-1 before a Baseball Ground crowd of 33,000. The most significant factor that day, however, was the loss of leading scorer Jack Parry, who had netted 24 goals that season. Parry injured his back in a clash with Mariners' full-back Ray de Gruchy and missed the rest of the campaign.

On the first Saturday in April, the Rams were still top of the table — Grimsby had games in hand — and entertained the only other serious promotion candidates, Accrington Stanley. Back into the Derby side that day came South African forward Alf Ackerman, although he was on the transfer list at his own request.

Jack Barker had paid Hull City £6,600 for Ackerman and his Hull teammate, Ken Harrison, in a desperate bid to stave off relegation. Now he returned to the Derby side for his first game since the end of February, replacing the injured Jesse Pye. Unhappy at being left out, Ackerman had asked for a move — now he was determined to grab this latest chance to prove Storer wrong.

Ackerman soon made his point. After 12 minutes, he put Derby ahead, controlling a Mays through-ball at the second attempt before slotting it past Willie McInnes. It meant that the Rams were the first team to score 100 League goals that season.

Sixteen minutes later, Accrington were level when Wattie Dick beat Terry Webster with a shot which was not all that well hit and appeared to go under the goalkeeper's body as he dived to his left. And three minutes after that, Stanley grabbed the lead after Joe

McInnes had sliced his shot across goal and Joe Devlin popped the ball home.

Three minutes before half-time, Derby were level when Ray Straw had two stabs at a Tommy Powell cross-shot, and 14 minutes into the second half it was Straw, again, who restored Derby's lead with a powerful header from Powell's centre.

The Rams were back in control and the scene was now set for Ackerman to stage a one-man show. After 72 minutes, he jumped high to send a spectacular header past Willie McInnes for the 100th League goal of his career; after 84 minutes he made it 5-2 after a pin-point pass from Woodhead; and in the final minute, Ryan split the Accrington defence and Ackerman was on target again.

But if Ackerman had done supremely well, it was the Rams' right-wing triangle of Mays, Ryan and Powell who had, between them, created five of Derby's six goals.

The South African, meanwhile, came in for some criticism from the *Derby Evening Telegraph's* Wilf Shaw, who wrote: 'His goal hungry attitude was a joy to see, but I wish he would realise all the time that football is a team game. It was not until late in the game that he began to move the ball to better-placed colleagues.'

Ackerman retained his place for the rest of the season, scoring twice in the last four games to finish second-highest scorer with 16 goals, but early the following season he was transferred to Carlisle United.

Derby, meanwhile, ended the season runners-up, five points adrift of Grimsby. Only the champions of the Northern and Southern Sections were promoted and the Rams had to wait another 12 months. Accrington Stanley, who had fielded an all-Scottish team at the Baseball Ground, dropped out of the Football League midway through 1961-62.

Derby County: Webster; McDonnell, Barrowcliffe, Mays, Oliver, Upton, Powell, Ryan, Straw, Ackerman, Woodhead.
Accrington Stanley: W.McInnes; Ashe, McCreadie, Hunter, Harrower, Sneddon, Devlin, Wright, Stewart, Dick, J.McInnes
Referee: J.Powell (Rotherham)

Att: 22,993.

In October 1955, the Rams beat Chesterfield 3-0 at the Baseball Ground. Terry Webster collects a high ball with defenders Frank Upton, Reg Ryan (6) and Albert Mays (4) in attendance. The crowd numbered 22,616.

Chesterfield Hit For Seven — And The Rams Are Almost Up

Saturday, 22 April 1957

Derby County 7   Chesterfield 1

WHEN Easter Monday 1957 dawned, Derby County sat on top of the Third Division North, despite a Good Friday hiccup with a 2-2 draw at mid-table Chesterfield and a 3-2 defeat at lowly Southport on Easter Saturday. If they were to begin the climb back to respectability, the Rams, with three games remaining, now desperately needed victory in the return game over their Derbyshire neighbours.

For once, Derby did not keep their supporters in suspense and the Rams were the only team in it, rattling up a 7-1 win, the club's biggest League victory since they beat Manchester City 7-0 at the Baseball Ground

in December 1949, in what was Bert Trautmann's third appearance for City.

Chesterfield did not have much of a reputation for battling it out away from home, but it is doubtful whether any team in the Northern Section could have lived with the Rams on this form. Derby moved the ball about quickly until they got in front of goal, where their finishing was clinically efficient. They cut out the temptation to try a pass too many and really had a go. The result was spectacular.

Derby took the lead in the 23rd minute when Ray Straw's shot flew off Tommy Flockett's foot and past Ron Powell into the Chesterfield net. Three minutes later, Powell failed to hold a Woodhead cross and Straw was on hand to make it 2-0.

The Chesterfield defence simply collapsed. Flockett had a nightmare game against outside-left Dennis Woodhead and on the other flank, Gerry Sears had almost as many problems coping with Tommy Powell. Down the middle, centre-half Dave Blakey tried hard to stop Straw and his cause was hardly helped by Barry Hutchinson's desire to get forward

Eighteen months later, Ray Straw hits one of his hat-trick of goals as Chesterfield are hammered before a near-30,000 crowd.

Derby County, Third Division North champions 1956-57. Back row (left to right): McDonnell, Mays, Oliver, Webster, Martin, Davies, Young. Front row: Parry, Powell, Brown, Straw, Ryan, Woodhead, Crowshaw.

at every opportunity. Hutchinson's forays, although largely in vain, left too many gaps at the back.

Indeed, it was Hutchinson, later to join Derby along with his Chesterfield teammate Keith Havenhand, who put the Rams 3-0 ahead in the 41st minute. For once he did not neglect his defensive duties, but succeeded only in deflecting Tommy Powell's cross inside an upright with goalkeeper Ron Powell going the wrong way.

Hutchinson did pull a goal back after 44 minutes — it came from the penalty spot after Webster had fouled Havenhand — but any thoughts that Chesterfield might have

harboured about staging a remarkable recovery were put into place four minutes into the second half, when Woodhead beat Flockett twice and then Whitehurst before cracking the ball into the net.

In the 63rd minute, Reg Ryan got in on the act, throwing himself forward for a perfectly-timed header after good work by Mays, Tommy Powell and Woodhead. Derby 5 Chesterfield 1.

Seven minutes from the end, Tommy Powell and Straw combined to give Powell his first League goal of the season and with five minutes remaining, Straw completed his hat-trick after Ryan had set him up.

It was Straw's 35th League goal of the season and with two games to go, he needed three more goals to beat Jack Bowers' record set in the 1930-31 season, although that came in the First Division and from a 42-match programme compared with this 46-game Third Division season.

The victory was even more remarkable for the fact that the unlucky Jack Parry had wrenched an ankle after ten minutes and spent most of the game as little more than a passenger, whilst Rams skipper Reg Ryan started the game with a leg injury. For this reason, Ryan played deeper than usual, allowing Albert Mays a more attacking role in which the Rams right-half revelled.

In the *Derby Evening Telegraph*, Wilf Shaw commented: 'The more Mays saw of the ball, the better he played it. Davies, if not quite as noticeable as an attacker, backed up cleverly without straying too far behind to be on hand to prevent Havenhand from breaking through.

'Young had a fine return, playing Lewis cool and competently; McDonnell and Barrowcliffe were never in the slightest trouble.

'Webster, however, was the odd man out. Never quite so composed as the rest of the side, he lost his head to give away the penalty.

'But altogether it was a magnificent Rams show.'

Second-placed Accrington Stanley met Hull City that evening but went down 3-0 at Peel Park, leaving Hartlepools United as the Rams' only challengers. The following Saturday, however, Derby beat Southport 2-0 at the Baseball Ground to clinch the championship and the only promotion spot.

Ray Straw scored both their goals and two days later, when the Rams went to York for their final game of the season, Straw needed one goal to pass the great Jack Bowers' record.

In a dreary game, Derby drew 1-1 with a goal from Woodhead. Straw missed two early chances and then shaped up to take a penalty before the referee, having first pointed to the spot, changed his mind. Late in the game, York equalised and the curtain came down on an entertaining season. Derby's journey back had begun.

Derby County: Webster; McDonnell, Barrowcliffe, Mays, Young, Davies, T.Powell, Parry, Straw, Ryan, Woodhead.
Chesterfield: R.Powell; Flockett, Sears, Whitehurst, Blakey, Hutchinson, Walker, Havenhand, Lewis, Smith, Cunliffe.
Referee: F.Cowen (Manchester)
Att: 29,886.

David Coleman, ancient BBC microphone in hand, talks to Jack Parry, Tommy Powell and Ken Oliver.

Derby County, 1958-59. Back row (left to right): Harry Storer (manager), Smith, Mays, Upton, Oxford, Adlington, Powell, Martin, Brown, Ralph Hann (trainer). Middle row: Barrowcliffe, Hannigan, Ryan, Hunt, Parry, Clark, Womack, Young. Front row: Daykin, Woodhead, Bowers, Davies, Darwin.

Lucky Preston, Despite Those Rams Errors

Saturday, 10 January 1959

Derby County 2　　Preston North End 2

DECEMBER 1958 saw a 'White Christmas' in Derby. It also brought that Monday lunchtime ritual — the third-round FA Cup draw when those workers or schoolboys near a 'steam radio' — no transistors in those days — tuned in to find out who the Second Division Rams would be playing. They were hoping for a home game against First Division giants like Billy Wright's Wolves, the current champions, or perhaps Manchester United, albeit a club still struggling to come to terms with the awful Munich air tragedy.

The Rams had their home draw and if it was not against one of the true glamour clubs, it was still an attractive prospect — Preston North End, the previous season's League championship runners-up.

By the time the game came around in mid-January, the winter weather was still with Derbeians and the Baseball Ground pitch presented a pretty picture, with the snow-covered surface rolled flat, the lines painted in blue, and the Rams in red shirts and white shorts and Preston in blue and white, for both teams had to change in a Cup tie where their normal colours clashed.

Cup fever had been evident in town all week and most of the 29,237 crowd were in place well before the kick-off of a game which was not all-ticket. And what a treat the fans had, especially in a remarkable opening 19 minutes.

The game was only two minutes old when Jack Parry put the Rams ahead. It was a dream start for Derby and for Parry in particular. Because of injury, the Derby-born inside-forward had missed big chunks of the Rams' highly-entertaining Third Division North

Jack Parry puts the Rams ahead against Preston with Fred Else well beaten.

seasons before re-establishing himself in the Second, and he would end 1958-59 as the club's top scorer.

Three minutes after Parry's sensational opener against Preston, the First Division side were level when Mayers and Farrall took advantage of a misunderstanding between Geoff Barrowcliffe and Les Moore. Derby hearts sank further when Glyn Davies tripped Lambert, but Rams' goalkeeper Ken Oxford, signed from Norwich City the previous season, brilliantly saved Hatsell's penalty.

After 19 minutes, Derby were back in front, thanks to a fine piece of opportunism from George Darwin, the little inside-left from Mansfield Town who had enjoyed such a brilliant start to his brief career at the Baseball Ground.

Former Sunderland winger Johnny Hannigan was enjoying a superb game and Wilf Shaw reported in the *Derby Evening Telegraph*: 'Hannigan, who provided the final passes which brought the Rams goals,

continued to look a vastly improved player at centre-forward. He was masterful in the air and an enthusiastic leader who did not have the best of luck with his shooting.'

It was a no-holds barred, often exciting, always entertaining Cup tie and one which the Rams should have won, but for an unfortunate error by wing-half Albert Mays. There were only 12 minutes remaining on referee Frank Coultas' watch when Mays, with plenty of time to clear the ball upfield, turned from well outside the Rams' penalty area and sent an ill-advised back-pass towards Oxford.

It would have been a risky thing to do on a perfect pitch at the start of the season. On the snow-covered surface it proved suicidal. The ball slowed up on the snow and turned into the perfect through-pass for Derek Hatsell to put Preston level. For years afterwards, the image would be etched on the minds of those Rams fans present.

It was all so sad. Wilf Shaw wrote: 'A stranger to both teams would surely have

George Darwin lashes in Derby's second goal against First Division Preston.

Albert Mays, whose back-pass led to Preston's equaliser.

The following Monday, the Rams learned that they would be at home to Third Division Bradford City if they won the Deepdale replay, and whilst that did not set the pulse racing, it did give them a real chance of progressing to the fifth round for the first time in nine years . . . .IF!

The original replay date found Deepdale shrouded in fog and when the second game finally got under way on 19 January, the Rams went down 4-2, both their goals coming from Dave Cargill (one of them a penalty). It would be several more years before Derby County enjoyed anything approaching a Cup run.

picked wrongly if asked to identify which was challenging for the First Division title. Many times the Preston defenders cleared their lines with the big-kicking methods I was associating with the Gatesheads and Crewes of a couple of years ago.'

Derby County: Oxford; Barrowcliffe, Martin, Mays, Moore, Davies, Powell, Parry, Hannigan, Darwin, Cargill.
Preston North End: Else; Cunningham, Walton, O'Farrell, Dunn, Smith, Campbell, Farrall, Hatsell, Lambert, Mayers.
Referee: F.B.Coultas (Hull)   Att: 29,237.

The Rams in 1960. Back row (left to right): Young, Thomson, Parry, Arthur Hobson (masseur), Newbery, Buxton, Waller. Second row: Jack Bowers (assistant trainer), Powell, Barrowcliffe, Upton, Oxford, Smith, Hutchinson, Daykin, Ralph Hann (trainer). Seated: Swallow, Fagan, Hannigan, Davies, Conwell, Scarborough, Cargill. On ground: O'Shea, Richardson, Webster, Darwin, Hopkinson.

Porter's Blunders In Rams' First League Cup Tie

Tuesday, 11 October 1960

Watford 2   **Derby County 5**

THE 1960-61 season saw the introduction of a new competition, the Football League Cup. For nigh on a century there had been only one knockout competition that mattered — the FA Cup. Now League clubs had their own, although in the early days it was not supported by the leading First Division clubs and, indeed, until it was given the glamour of a Wembley Final and the winners gained qualification for the UEFA Cup, the League Cup did not catch the imagination.

Never the less, there were nearly 11,000 fans

Frank Upton, one of a match-winning quartet.

present at Watford's Vicarage Road ground on a Tuesday evening in October to see the Third Division promotion hopefuls entertain Derby County, then mid-table in the Second.

The Rams' team for this historic match included goalkeeper Terry Adlington, who was enjoying a rare extended run following an injury to Ken Oxford, who had fractured a cheekbone at Ipswich in only the third League game of the season. Jack Parry had put the Rams ahead at Portman Road before going in goal after Oxford's injury. Then Adlington, who joined Derby from Blackwell Colliery MW in 1956 but had been in the shadows ever since, got his chance.

The Rams' forward line also included three Derbyshire cricketers, Ian Hall, Ian Buxton and Ray Swallow, the last of their breed because soccer and cricket were soon to become too demanding with generous overlaps of the seasons making it impossible for a man to play both professionally.

An example of how seriously the League Cup was regarded in that inaugural season was the fact that Third Division Watford fielded no less than six reserve-teamers against Derby.

Yet they went ahead in the third minute when Heard got past Geoff Barrowcliffe and then put in a cross which Benning touched on for Fairbrother to side-foot past Adlington.

Watford's real dangerman, though, was the former Arsenal forward Cliff Holton and he put in one fierce shot which fizzed over the Rams' crossbar with Adlington beaten.

After 26 minutes, Derby drew level and the honour of scoring their first-ever League Cup goal fell to Ian Buxton. One minute later, the Rams were ahead through Ian Hall. Wilf Shaw described the goals in the *Derby Evening Telegraph*: 'Swallow tricked Lawson and flighted a centre which Buxton headed in and then a corner by Swallow saw Hall pirouette like a ballet dancer to beat Linton with a chip shot which could not have been bettered, even though it was blessed by a little bit of luck.'

Watford fought back and it was 2-2 in the 44th minute when Holton rattled a low drive into the back of the net, but then Watford left-half Andy Porter dashed his side's hopes with two awful mistakes.

With 52 minutes played, Porter headed a cross from Frank Upton into his own net to restore Derby's lead. Thirteen minutes later he steered a back-pass intended for Linton straight to the feet of Barry Hutchinson, who lost no time in hammering home his first senior goal for the Rams since signing from Chesterfield in July that year.

Watford were now utterly demoralised and Hutchinson saw his shot rattle the crossbar before Dave Cargill made amends for an otherwise moderate display by scoring the goal of the match with a cracking left-foot volley after 84 minutes.

Wrote Wilf Shaw: 'It was no easy match to win. Any side possessing as much endeavour as Watford did takes a bit of beating.

'Special bouquets, therefore, to Adlington, Parry, Upton and Hall — match-winning quartet.

'Adlington once again looked a most capable 'keeper and four of his saves — from Gregory, Fairbrother (twice) and Catleugh couldn't have been bettered.

'The task of Parry and Upton was made to look an arduous one because neither Hall nor Hutchinson did much to prevent the Watford wing-halves from taking the ball through.

'But both the Rams wing-halves spared nothing. They worked and harried in non-stop fashion throughout.

'Hall goes into the honours list despite his lack of urgency in defence. He was the Rams' most dangerous attacker. In possession, he invariably got a defender out of the way with his body swerve before using the ball intelligently. Furthermore, he always looked a potential scorer.'

In the next round the Rams beat Barnsley 3-0 at the Baseball Ground before going down 4-1 at home to Norwich City before a remarkable attendance of 21,864.

Watford: Linton; Bell, Lawson, Catleugh, McNiece, Porter, Benning, Gregory, Fairbrother, Holton, Heard.
Derby County: Adlington; Barrowcliffe, Conwell, Parry, Young, Upton, Swallow, Hall, Buxton, Hutchinson, Cargill.
Referee: J.E.Cooke (Waterbeach)

Att: 10,936.

Imps Find Curry Too Hot To Handle

Saturday, 22 October 1960

Lincoln City 3   **Derby County 4**

WHEN Rams manager Harry Storer signed centre-forward Bill Curry from Brighton in October 1960, for £12,000, he not only paid out Derby's biggest fee for some time but also brought to the Baseball Ground one of the most colourful players to appear for the club for some years.

Curry, who had won an England Under-23 cap as a Newcastle player soon endeared himself to Rams supporters, not least because he was the club's leading scorer in each of his first three seasons as a Derby player.

Curry did not score on his debut, which resulted in a 2-1 defeat at Swansea, but when Derby fans had their first sight of him a week later, he netted twice in a 4-1 win over Luton Town at the Baseball Ground.

A week after that, the Rams travelled to Sincil Bank to meet Lincoln City, a team already struggling to avoid relegation from the Second Division. The stage was set for Bill Curry to score his first hat-trick for Derby County — and it was as well he did, for the Rams' defence suffered something of an off day.

It took Curry only 12 minutes to put Derby ahead, when he ran on to a neat pass from Barry Hutchinson, and in the 27th minute the Rams' new star made it 2-0 after good work from Tommy Powell and Ian Hall.

It appeared that Derby were going to win in a canter, but 11 minutes into the second half, Barrowcliffe handled and Linnecor scored from the penalty spot.

Fourteen minutes from time, however, Curry extended the Rams' lead back to two goals as he completed the first hat-trick by a Derby County player since Jack Parry's three goals against Grimsby Town in February 1959. Curry cracked home a great shot after Powell had fed him with a pin-point pass.

On 80 minutes, the game seemed quite definitely beyond Lincoln's reach when Hall scored with a brilliant piece of opportunism after Hutchinson had badly mishit his own shot.

Still the Imps weren't quite finished, though and a minute later Linnecor made it 4-2 after a quickly-taken free kick. Three minutes from time, a long-range free-kick from Middleton beat Adlington to set up the prospect of a remarkable comeback, but the Rams' defence held out to take both points. At the end of the season, Lincoln were relegated after finishing bottom of the table.

In the *Derby Evening Telegraph*: Wilf Shaw commented: 'I can't pay too high a tribute to Curry. Undoubtedly, he is the man behind the Rams' revival. He was the major reason for the Imps' defence often being at twelves and thirteens rather than sixes and sevens.

'What a difference it has made to the Rams' attack to have a centre-forward who can get goals. In this game, Curry was as powerful as ever in the air, even though all his goals came from shots.

'He led the line with a lot of intelligence, lacked nothing for pace and emphasised that he must be one of the gamest players in modern football.

'Lesser mortals might have cried-off last Friday. His shoulder wasn't 100 per cent after his battering in last Wednesday's League Cup-tie, nor was his ankle.

'But Curry apparently shrugs off knocks as part and parcel of the game — and he certainly got his reward.'

Altogether, Bill Curry scored 76 goals, including two more hat-tricks, in 164 League and Cup games before being transferred to Mansfield Town in February 1965. Strangely, despite Wilf Shaw's glowing praise, there were some of his playing colleagues who questioned Curry's commitment in away games when the going got tough.

What is without question is that he was a player who brightened an otherwise often dreary era and he is certainly held in affection by those Rams fans who saw him play. After Mansfield he appeared for Chesterfield and did the rounds of East Midlands non-League football. He certainly appeared a battling centre-forward but he lost his last fight, against cancer, at Mansfield in August 1990.

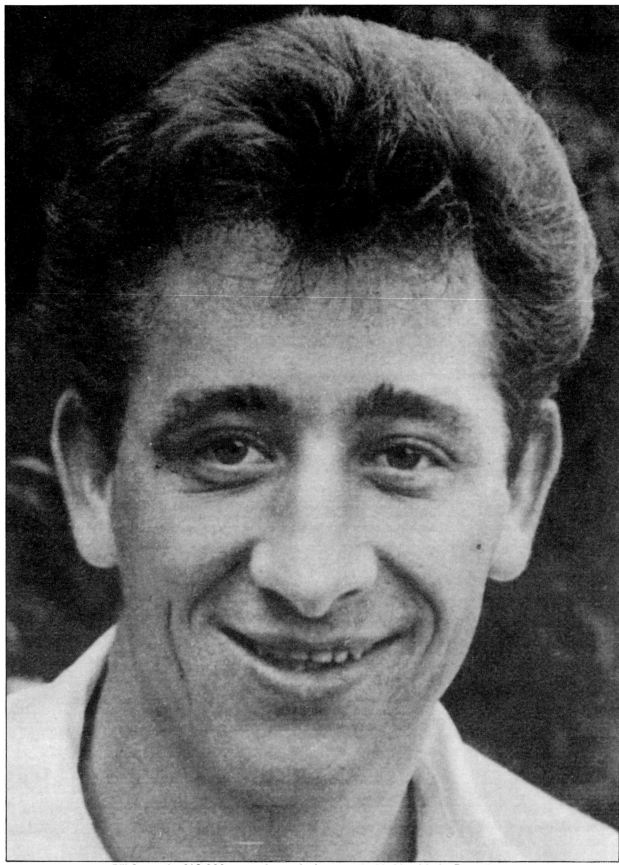

Bill Curry, the £12,000 centre-forward who proved a big hit with the Rams fans.

Lincoln City: Heath; Allen, Smith, Middleton, Gratton, Buick, McClelland, Linnecor, Commons, Hawksworth, Dunwell.
Derby County: Adlington; Barrowcliffe, Conwell, Parry, Young, Upton, Swallow, Hall, Curry, Hutchinson, Powell.
Referee: Mr A.Murdoch (Sheffield)
Att: 9,325.

Derby County, 1961. Back row (left to right): Young, Davies, Daykin, Oxford, Adlington, Parry, Hutchinson, Swallow. Middle row: Jack Bowers (trainer), Thompson, Barrowcliffe, Webster, Hopkinson, Curry, Conwell, Ralph Hann (trainer). Front row: Roby, Stephenson, Palmer, Campion, Richardson, Waller.

Hoppy's Great Goal Sinks Liverpool

Saturday, 21 October 1961

Derby County 2   Liverpool 0

'CAST emotions to one side, banish any tendency towards local loyalties, and it still sticks out a mile — Derby County, and not Liverpool, were the side which looked an elegant, promotion-bound outfit at the Baseball Ground on Saturday.'

That was how the *Derby Evening Telegraph's* Wilf Shaw began his Monday evening report after the Rams had beaten Second Division promotion favourites Liverpool in a tension-filled match. Alas, the paper's news pages were also full of the Merseysiders' visit, but for a different reason as Liverpool supporters appeared before Derby magistrates after the town's first real experience of football hooliganism, some of which had been triggered by a sensational off-the-ball incident during the game.

For six years, Liverpool, now managed by Bill Shankly, had come near to regaining the First Division place they lost in 1954. Shankly was building a new side, eventually to become the springboard for all the glories that the club would achieve over the next 30 years. They came to the Baseball Ground in October 1960, expecting to take both points from a Rams side that was destined to finish in the bottom third of the table that season.

In some ways the game was viewed as might a cup-tie might be seen between teams from different divisions, but the Rams competed on equal terms, battling hard, snapping in at the tackle and displaying just as much good football as their opponents.

In the 43rd minute, all this fine work had its reward when Mick Hopkinson, the Rams' 19-year-old Ambergate-born wing-half, put Derby ahead with one of the most memorable goals ever scored at the Baseball Ground. Hopkinson, growing in confidence all match, took the ball forward, waved Palmer and Hutchinson aside and then struck a perfect cannonball shot past Slater.

Hopkinson did his share of defending, too, and prevented Roger Hunt from adding to

The Rams had a good home record against Liverpool in the mid-1950s. In October 1957 they beat the Reds 2-1 at the Baseball Ground. Here, Terry Webster is beaten as defenders Upton, McDonnell, Mays and Barrowcliffe look on.

his tally of 16 League goals already that season.

Ten minutes from time, the Rams made the game safe with another goal. Bill Curry, who had harried and hassled the Liverpool defence all afternoon, flicked the ball over his shoulder and over the giant Liverpool centre-half Ron Yeats, and then twisted around in the same movement, collected Hutchinson's return pass and raced fully 40 yards before planting the ball past the onrushing Slater. The roar from the 27,000 crowd could be heard for miles around.

Until then it had been a brilliant, pulsating afternoon with both sides playing good football and giving and taking no quarter. But an incident involving Yeats and Curry led to the Rams centre-forward being carried off, a small pitch invasion by some Popside fans, and disgraceful after-match scenes at Derby's Midland Railway Station.

Wilf Shaw told the story: 'For 80 minutes, Liverpool centre-half Ron Yeats, had been a bastion of a tired and overworked defence. But after Curry had made him look like a village novice when scoring the Rams' second goal, Yeats lost his self-control.

'He appeared to kick Curry on his way up for a Liverpool corner when the ball was 70 yards away. The fans wouldn't have been British if they hadn't resented that.

'He felled Curry with a rash, unfair and unnecessary tackle (the ball already appeared to be out of play) which resulted in the Rams player being carried off on a stretcher and might have maimed him for life.'

Shaw added: 'True Britishers readily become incensed at that type of conduct.'

As it transpired, Curry was fit to resume his place in the Rams' side the following week, but the incident provoked a fierce response and chants of "Off, Off," reverberated around the Baseball Ground.

It was sad that such a splendid game should end in that fashion, for the Rams had given a tremendous display, none more so than skipper Glyn Davies. The Welsh wing-half will never be remembered as a skilful player, but his commitment was never in question and on this day he not only tackled with fire but also found from somewhere the ability to collect and use the ball well as the Rams turned defence into attack.

At the end of the season, Liverpool were promoted as champions, eight points ahead of runners-up Leyton Orient. The Rams finished 16th, but their defeat of the Merseysiders entered Derby County folklore.

Derby County: Oxford; Conwell, Davies, Parry, Young, Hopkinson, Roby, Havenhand, Curry, Hutchinson, Palmer.

Liverpool: Slater; White, Byrne, Milne, Yeats, Lewis, Leishman, Hunt, St John, Melia, A'Court.

Referee: H.G.Wilson (Stockton-on-Tees)

Att: 27,355.

Derby County in 1965-66. Back row (left to right): Daniel, Waller, Upton, Matthews, Boulton, Saxton, Thomas, Buxton. Front row: Parry, Hughes, Durban, Hodgson, Richardson, Webster. On ground: Draper, Hopkinson.

Durban's Hat-trick As Rams And Blues Share Ten Goals

Saturday, 9 April 1966

Birmingham City 5   Derby County 5

WHEN the Rams met Birmingham City in the 1965-66 season there were goals galore between the two Second Division clubs — 18 in all — yet no side had hammered the other by any stretch of the imagination.

When the Blues visited the Baseball Ground on 30 October that season, the Rams won an eight-goal thriller 5-3 with Eddie Thomas and Frank Upton each scoring twice and Alan Durban providing the other goal for the Rams.

In the return game at St Andrew's in April, Durban was on the mark again, this time as

a hat-trick hero in a game that swung either way before both sides had to settle for a point each.

The game was remarkable from start to finish, but 16 minutes of the first half were truly amazing with five goals.

Birmingham took the lead after 14 minutes when Alec Jackson rounded Hopkinson and Daniel before centring to the onrushing Trevor Hockey who whipped the ball home.

Four minutes later the Rams were level when Durban dashed in to slam the ball into the roof of Jim Herriot's net. At the time, many people thought that Mick Hopkinson was the scorer and that was how it appeared in the Saturday evening sports editions.

In the 20th minute, Hopkinson played Durban through and the Welshman placed the ball wide of the advancing Herriot and then watched as it trickled over the line.

Two minutes later Jackson, cutting in from the right, was tripped by Bobby Saxton and Beard beat Reg Matthews from the penalty spot to drew Birmingham level again.

Alan Durban scored a hat-trick against Birmingham. Durban's early days at the Baseball Ground saw him as a high-scoring inside-forward.

On the half-hour, Jackson fired a low centre across the face of the Rams' goal and Saxton, dashing back to cover, could only divert the ball into his own net for the Blues to regain the lead.

Two minutes into the second half the scoring started all over again. Gordon Hughes beat Birmingham's offside trap with a well-timed pass to Ian Buxton, who cut in from the right and hammered a fierce shot just inside the post with Foster challenging.

In the 50th minute, Beard met a Jackson corner first time and saw his shot go in off the post to make it 4-3 to Birmingham.

The crowd had to wait another 20 minutes for the next goal, when Geoff Vowden rose high to head Hockey's centre just inside the post as the Rams defenders appealed for offside against Hockey.

It seemed that Birmingham had neatly reversed the Baseball Ground score of six

months earlier, but ten minutes from time Hopkinson crashed a loose ball into the goalmouth and Thomson could only turn it into the net.

Then, with only two minutes remaining, Frank Upton found Buxton with a good pass and the centre-forward went to the by-line before pulling the ball back for Durban to complete his hat-trick and earn the Rams a point from an astonishing match.

The *Derby Evening Telegraph's* George Edwards reported: ' It was just one of those extraordinary games in which both teams forgot about involved defensive systems and got on with the job of trying to score goals.

'This, plus the fact that the muddy surface made it difficult for defenders to turn, meant that the odds were on the forwards throughout.

' . . . .Ian Buxton, in addition to scoring a brilliant goal and creating the last-minute equaliser, played extremely well and Alan Durban took advantage of the fact that Ron Wylie's defensive qualities are almost non-existent to play his best game for some time.

'Durban grabbed a splendid hat-trick and could have had two more goals as he forged through the gap left by Wylie.

' . . . .But the most exhilarating part of the game was the approach of both teams. There was no negative football and no eight and nine-men barriers.

'If only there were more matches like this one, perhaps the grounds would start to fill up again. Unfortunately, one sees very few.'

The Rams ended the season in eighth place in a Second Division table won by Manchester City from Southampton. Birmingham ended up two places below Derby.

Alan Durban's goals helped him on the way to ending the season as the Rams' leading scorer with 17 goals, ahead of Hughes (13) and Thomas (12).

Birmingham City: Herriot; Fraser, Martin, Wylie, Foster, Beard, Jackson, Vincent, Fenton(Thomson), Vowden, Hockey.
Derby County: Matthews; Richardson, Daniel, Webster, Saxton, Upton, Hughes, Thomas, Buxton, Durban, Hopkinson.
Referee: L.W.Faulkner (Liverpool)
Att: 13,078.

Kevin Hector signs for Derby County watched by chairman Sam Longson and other directors.

They Cheered Him Off The Pitch

Saturday, 24 September 1966

Derby County 4   Huddersfield Town 3

WHEN Derby County paid £40,000 for

Bradford striker Kevin Hector in September 1966, it was a signing which surprised, if not shocked, Rams fans everywhere. For years the club had adopted a make-do-and-mend approach to team building.

Of course, there had been some extremely good players coming into the Baseball Ground — Alan Durban and Eddie Thomas to name two who were excellent buys and went on to give the club remarkably good value for money — but the last really interesting signing, one which created a buzz when the player made his bow before the home fans, was that of Bill Curry back in 1960.

And popular and colourful though he was, even Curry was not the sort of player who fans genuinely believed could go much further in the game. Indeed, his career had wavered after early promise with his first club, Newcastle United.

Kevin Hector, however, was an utterly different proposition. From the moment Baseball Ground fans saw him they knew that Tim Ward had signed a player of high quality — and all credit to Ward for persuading a parsimonious Rams board to part with the club's record fee.

Hector made his first appearance in a Derby shirt on 17 September 1966, in a poor game at Selhurst Park where the Rams lost 1-0 to Crystal Palace and Hector had little support from his off-colour colleagues.

The following week was a different matter. The team played well, Hector played brilliantly and, as George Edwards reported in the *Derby Evening Telegraph*: 'They cheered him off the pitch, then they waited half-an-hour and cheered him out of the ground, jostling to pat him on the back. And no wonder, for nobody could have asked more of a player on his debut than £40,000 Kevin Hector provided at the Baseball Ground on Saturday.

'Alan Durban worked tirelessly and scored a hat-trick of fine goals . . . .yet he had the thunder stolen from him by dashing, darting Hector in the Rams' 4-1 win over Huddersfield Town.

' . . . .I am prepared to stick my neck out and say that Derby County at last have a true star. This is the sort of player who will make sports fans leave comfortable chairs and warm firesides in the winter to stand in the cold on the terraces.'

The Rams had fallen behind to a fifth-minute goal from John Quigley after Saxton was caught on the wrong foot, but 20 minutes later, 21-year-old Hector made his mark with the first of many goals for Derby County.

Ian Buxton headed the ball on and, for the first time, Rams fans saw the full power of Hector's finishing when he fought off the attentions of John Coddington before cracking home a brilliant equaliser.

Ten minutes later, Derby went behind again when Saxton felled Tony Leighton and Colin Dobson scored from the penalty spot. But in 38th minute, Durban made it 2-2 with a superbly-flighted free-kick after Hector had been brought down.

Three minutes before half-time the Rams were back in front and again Durban was the scorer, shooting home from Hector's pass.

There were 13 minutes remaining when Durban headed his hat-trick goal from close range after good work from Hodgson and Hughes, and in the very last minute Leighton made it 4-3 from Mike Hellawell's cross.

Edwards continued to drool over Hector: 'Not one of the Rams fans could have been dissatisfied with his performance on Saturday. There was a buzz of excitement every time he accelerated on to a pass . . . .a gasp every time he burst away from astonished defenders . . . .a roar every time he fired in a shot.

' . . . .Any player who can impudently show the ball to a seasoned international like Meagan, then waltz around him, drift past two more defenders and miss by a foot with a wickedly powerful angle is worth going a long way to see.'

At the end of the season Hector was the Rams' leading scorer, with 16 goals from only 30 games, and he maintained that position for the next two seasons and was top scorer twice more in the early 1970s. He shared in all the glories under Clough and Taylor, and under Dave Mackay, and eventually finished his Rams career with 201 goals in all senior matches, second only to the great Steve Bloomer. His 589 senior appearances (eight as a substitute) put him way out in front as the Rams' record appearance holder.

Derby County: Matthews; Richardson, Daniel, Webster, Saxton, Waller, Hughes, Hector, Buxton, Durban, Hodgson.
Huddersfield Town: Oldfield; Atkins, Cattlin, Meagan, Coddington, Ellam, Hellawell, Dunsdale, Leighton, Quigley, Dobson.
Referee: K.E.Walker (Blackpool) Att: 15,029.

Derby County in 1967. Back row (left to right): Daniel, Webster, Thomas, Boulton, Matthews, Rhodes, Saxton, Waller, Hopkinson. Front row: Hughes, Cleevely, Hector, Durban, Hodgson, Draper, Richardson.

Clough's First Game In Charge — And O'Hare Makes His Debut

Saturday, 19 August 1967

Derby County 3　　　**Charlton Athletic 2**

SOME 19,000 spectators — only the sixth highest in the Second Division that day — saw Derby County make a satisfactory start to the 1967-68 season when they overcame a workmanlike Charlton Athletic side.

The Rams' performance was far from a great one, but it was certainly promising, especially in the second half. After Charlton had looked to be settling and threatened danger, Derby had worn them down.

The real significance of the game, though, was that it was Derby's first League game under Brian Clough. And making his debut for the Rams that day was John O'Hare, a young centre-forward from one of Clough's old clubs, Sunderland. Over the next few years, both men would share some remarkable successes in football.

Clough had succeeded Tim Ward as manager the previous May. Under Ward, the Rams had been a fairly moderate side,

although with the exception of the £40,000 he had to buy Kevin Hector, Ward was given precious little money to strengthen the team.

Now the attitude of the board was changing and Clough, a prolific goalscorer with Middlesbrough and Sunderland before injury ended his career, had moved up the managerial ladder after setting Fourth Division Hartlepool United on the road to better things. He had brought with him, Peter Taylor, a former Middlesbrough goalkeeper who had been managing Southern League Burton Albion before Clough tempted him to Hartlepool.

Both men must have been pleased with this, the first Rams game under their control, and they were given the best possible start when Charlton centre-half Ian King put the Rams ahead with a spectacular seventh-minute own-goal after good work by Hector and Alan Durban.

Eight minutes later, however, Bob Curtis put Charlton level after Len Glover swept in a cross and there was now the feeling that if the visitors had scored again soon after, the Rams might have found things awkward.

It was Hector, though, who scored next. In the 23rd minute he weaved his way through the Charlton defence before being brought down. Durban took the free-kick and fired it towards the far post where Hector stormed in to restore Derby's lead.

The Rams celebrate another goal against Charlton, this time in November 1968. O'Hare is the scorer.

Two minutes after half-time, O'Hare capped his debut with a goal. Ron Webster paved the way before O'Hare rifled a right-foot shot past Wright to make it 3-1.

Hector was in fine form and twice in the later stages he went close with quite brilliant left-foot shots and also laid on a chance from which Durban might have given the scoreline a more emphatic look.

Instead, four minutes from time Alan Campbell closed the gap to one goal but there was no shock equaliser and the Rams ended the day with the best possible start to their season.

In the *Derby Evening Telegraph*, George Edwards commented: 'Nobody can fairly complain, although one would not have fancied the chances of the defence against a side with more power in front of goal.

'At times they were in utter confusion with Saxton far from happy and both full-backs vulnerable on the outside, but none the less there was much to encourage Rams fans.'

Edwards continued: 'What was most encouraging, perhaps, was that the Rams got to grips with the game after letting it slip very much Charlton's way. At one point the hard-working Campbell was doing what he liked in midfield, but the Rams, by sheer endeavour, regained the initiative.

'Clearly, they were nervous at the start, particularly new centre-forward O'Hare, who also looked a little short of fitness and therefore mobility.

'In his case, one must reserve judgement and give him time to settle in, and it is worth remembering that he rattled in the only chance that came his way without wasting much time.

'The hero of the day, so far as the crowd were concerned, was Hector, although Durban deserves all credit for forcing his way into the game after an uncertain start.

'The poise, calm and complete self-confidence that marks so much of Hector's work was what delighted the fans and it was almost certainly his display as much as anything that sent them home happy.'

When he arrived at the Baseball Ground, Brian Clough had declared that, whatever else happened, he would get Derby into a higher position in the Second Division in his first season. In fact they finished 18th — one place lower than in 1966-67 — but the fans did not seem to mind. They felt that something positive was happening to their club. Events proved them right.

Derby County: Matthews; Daniel, Hopkinson, Webster, Saxton, Waller, Hughes, Durban, O'Hare, Hector, Hodgson.
Charlton Athletic: Wright; Curtis, Kinsey, Reeves, King, Halom, Peacock, Campbell, Went, Moore, Glover.
Referee: Mr V.James (York)   *Att: 19,412.*

Hector's Hat-Trick — The First of Many

Saturday, 23 September 1967

Cardiff City 1   Derby County 5

WHEN Derby County visited Cardiff City for a Second Division match early in 1967-68, history decreed that the Rams could expect little from the trip, for they had never before won at Ninian Park. Moreover, Cardiff could look back to the previous Boxing Day for their most recent home defeat. Brian Clough's Derby side had only the comfort that they had won their last two games, one of them a difficult match at Loftus Road where Kevin Hector's goal was sufficient to inflict defeat on the team that would finish Second Division runners-up that season.

The game began quietly enough with plenty of uneventful sparring before Hector put the Rams ahead with a fine individual goal after 22 minutes. Thirteen minutes later it was 2-0 to the Rams when John O'Hare netted an equally good goal with the Cardiff defence flat-footed and appealing for offside. Suddenly it appeared that Derby were going to break their Ninian jinx after all.

On the hour mark, Hector scored his second and the game was indeed now beyond the Welshmen's grasp and even though Bird made it 3-1 from the penalty spot after he had been brought down by Peter Daniel, the result was now not in doubt. Sure enough, in the 81st minute Hector completed his first-ever hat-trick for Derby County and six minutes from the end, O'Hare made it 5-1.

It had been an excellent performance from the Rams, although it has to be recorded that this Cardiff side looked ripe for defeat. Their defence, which included former Derby County left-back Bobby Ferguson, was remarkably disorganised for most of the game, showing a particular naivity when it came to covering from set-pieces, whilst the Bluebirds' attack gave a lacklustre performance, displaying precious little method or initiative.

Indeed, the *Derby Evening Telegraph's* Brian McDermott commented: '. . . Cardiff's defence looked so thoroughly pedantic that it would have difficulty stemming the advance of three backward toddlers. Their chances against Hector, O'Hare and Hughes in fine form were therefore non-existent.

Although Hector was the obvious Rams star with his hat-trick sealing their superiority, perhaps Alan Durban had an even better game without getting on the scoresheet. The former Cardiff inside-forward skippered the Rams on his return to Ninian Park, standing in for centre-half Bobby Saxton who was suffering from lumbago. Wearing the number-eight shirt, Durban played just behind Hector and O'Hare and kept both men well supplied, having a hand in at least three of the goals.

McDermott ended his report: 'This was undoubtedly a Rams performance of outstanding merit, but now the biggest battle must be against complacency.

'It is still not a world-beating side, not necessarily a Second Division beating side. Having said, after successive away victories, that the true test is yet to come may seem miserly. However, it still holds good — but if the standard of opposition remains the same it could be said with more significant meaning at the end of the season.'

The Rams won their next game 4-1 at home to Rotherham, when Hector weighed in with another two, and a Second Division promotion challenge looked a real possibility at that stage. Alas, Derby won only one more game out of their next 11 - a run which included four consecutive defeats — and finished the season in 18th place, although there were great days just around the corner.

For Kevin Hector, of course, there were many more goals to come, including another six hat-tricks or better.

Cardiff City: Wilson; Coldrick, Ferguson, Williams, Murray, Harris, Jones, Allen, Toshack, King, Bird.
Derby County: Matthews; Daniel, Richardson, Webster, McFarland, Waller, Hughes, Durban, O'Hare, Hector, Hodgson.
Referee: H.New (Portsmouth)   *Att: 15,375.*

Out But Not Down After League Cup Semi-Final

Wednesday, 7 February 1968

Leeds United 3   **Derby County 2**

ALTHOUGH Brian Clough's first season at the Baseball Ground brought about no improvement in Derby County's Second Division fortunes, for the first time since the Football League Cup was founded, the Rams enjoyed quite a run in the competition. Indeed, it was this as much as anything in Clough's first season that persuaded fans that there were greater times ahead, although ironically, neither Roy McFarland nor Alan Hinton, two of the main players in future promotion and championship successes, could take part because they were cup-tied.

Coincidentally, the Rams' League Cup trail began with a 4-0 win over Fourth Division Hartlepools United, Clough's former club. John O'Hare scored a hat-trick and he was on target again in the next round, when Birmingham City, like the Rams a Second Division side, were beaten 3-1 at the Baseball Ground, the other goals coming from Hector and Billy Hodgson.

Fourth Division Lincoln City then held the Rams 1-1 at Derby before O'Hare (2) and Hector put them through on a rain-soaked night at Sincil Bank before Lincoln's record attendance of 23,196.

Derby were in the quarter-finals for the first time and when the draw gave them a home game against Darlington, a team from the bottom half of the Fourth Division, it seemed that the Rams had an easy passage into the semi-finals. Darlington, though, fought hard and the Rams eventually went through by the odd goal in nine.

Their opponents in the semi-finals were Don Revie's Leeds United, one of the First Division giants. The game was to be played over two legs in mid-January and early February and, in the way of these things, fate conspired to give Derby a visit to Elland Road in the third round of the FA Cup, in between the League Cup legs.

The first leg of the League Cup tie was staged at the Baseball Ground on the Wednesday evening of 17 January and the Rams battled hard before going down 1-0 to a Johnny Giles penalty after Bobby Saxton inexplicably handled the ball in the area.

The Rams lost 2-0 in the FA Cup at Leeds, hardly the best preparation for their return there 11 days later.

The tragedy was, of course, that Derby did not enter the game on level terms, but they soon were equal on aggregate when Hector scored a fine early goal.

O'Hare held the ball brilliantly out on the right before releasing it at just the right moment for Hector to time his move to perfection, rattling a header past Gary Sprake.

Alas, Leeds were soon level through Rod Belfitt. The Rams had given away several free-kicks on the edge of their penalty area and from one of them there followed an almighty scramble before Belfitt lashed the ball home.

O'Hare almost restored the Rams' lead on the night, his shot dipping just over the crossbar, before Eddie Gray shugged off two challenges and then toe-ended the ball over the line one minute before the interval.

In the second half, Belfitt made it 3-1 on the night from another free-kick and then Giles hit the post with a penalty before Arthur Stewart, a signing from Irish League football, scored what was effectively a consolation goal for Derby near the end.

So Leeds went through 4-2 on aggregate to meet Arsenal in the Wembley Final, which Revie's team won 1-0. The Rams were disappointed, of course, but it had been a great run and simply whetted the appetite for what was surely to come.

Leeds United: Sprake; Reaney, Cooper(Bates), Bremner, Madeley, Hunter, Greenhoff, Lorimer, Belfitt, Giles, Gray.
Derby County: Matthews; Daniel, Richardson, Webster, Waller, Stewart, Hughes, Barker, O'Hare, Hector, Durban.
Referee: K.Howley (Middlesbrough)
Att: 29,367.

Derby County, 1967-68. Back row (left to right): Webster, Daniel, Saxton, Matthews, Boulton, McFarland, Waller, Hopkinson. Front row: Richardson, Hughes, Hector, O'Hare, Barker, Durban, Hinton. On ground: Wright, Butlin.

The Shape Of Things To Come As Rangers Are Hammered

Saturday, 17 February 1968

Derby County 4   Queen's Park Rangers 0

WHEN Queen's Park Rangers arrived at the Baseball Ground in mid-February 1968, they sat on top of the Second Division and were definitely the team of the moment. Promoted only a few months earlier, and still basking in the glory of a sensational League Cup Final win over First Division West Brom at Wembley, Rangers were now setting the pace again.

But the Rams had already taken both points from Loftus Road earlier in the season and now they set about the Londoners again to record the only League double over them that season.

Derby went ahead after ten minutes when Hinton took a pass from Stewart, cut past Clement and then crossed low. O'Hare cleverly stepped over the ball, allowing Hector to race in for his 20th goal of the season.

After 14 minutes, Springett failed to hold a corner and the ball bounced loose for Hinton to move in quickly and hit a fierce volley just under the bar.

Writing in the *Derby Evening Telegraph*, George Edwards commented: "The Rams slipped in to their stride and Hector, especially, simply bubbled over with confidence. He slid away from tackles with such ease and moved so quickly while keeping possession that Rangers were completely demoralised.

'Hinton, too, snapped straight into his stride and, for the first time, showed the Rams crowd how he won three England caps. He

Kevin Hector, scored the first goal against QPR and simply bubbled over with confidence as the Rams beat the Second Division leaders.

beat Clement for speed on the outside and his goal was a terrific effort which Springett never looked like stopping.''

It was 17 minutes into the second half before the Rams extended their lead when Arthur Stewart brought the ball down on the edge of the penalty area and with the Rangers players expecting him to pass, the Rams skipper instead tried a snap shot which went in just under the bar.

Eight minutes from time, Hinton did well to beat Clement and then pulled the ball back for Roy McFarland to score his first goal for Derby County.

Rangers had one real chance when Webster was adjudged to have tripped Rodney Marsh. It looked a harsh decision and when Reg Matthews brilliantly saved Keen's penalty, perhaps justice was done.

It had indeed been a magnificent performance from the Rams, for whom McFarland and Webster had been outstanding in defence. Webster had shadowed the brilliant, unpredictable Rodney Marsh all afternoon and had never been tempted into a hasty tackle. The result was that Rangers' main dangerman had been effectively shackled and the visitors had no one else of sufficient individual skill to turn the game their way.

On the other side of the coin, Derby had not one but three such players in their attack — Hector, Hinton and O'Hare. Danger came from all angles and, as a result, Hector revelled in the unaccustomed space he enjoyed. Normally, it was becoming a case of 'stop Hector and you stop Derby' but on this showing the Rams were a considerable threat in almost every department.

Indeed, Brian Clough was getting it right up front with a vengeance. In the 1967-68 season, the Rams scored 71 League goals, six more than they were to achieve the following season when they stormed away with the title. In all competitions they played 50 games in 1967-68, scoring 89 times; in 1968-69 they scored 77 goals in 51 League and Cup games.

Interest, too, was booming and at the end of this season the Rams could look back on average attendances of 20,194, compared with 15,908 in 1966-67. Considering that they finished one place lower, it was quite remarkable.

Derby County: Matthews; Richardson (Waller), Hopkinson, Webster, McFarland, Stewart, Durban, Barker, O'Hare, Hector, Hinton.
Queen's Park Rangers: Springett; Clement, Harris, Keen, Keetch, Hazell, I.Morgan, Sanderson, Leach, Marsh, R.Morgan.
Referee: J.Finney (Hereford)   Att: 22,854.

Chelsea Floored In Baseball Ground Night Of Passion

Wednesday, 2 October 1968

Derby County 3   Chelsea 1

THERE can surely have been few greater Baseball Ground occasions than this League Cup third-round replay. In Brian Clough's second season as Rams manager, Derby County were bound for a long-awaited return to Division One. But before that there was some cup fun including a night which would go down in Rams folklore, a night vividly remembered by every Derby fan lucky enough to be wedged into this famous old ground which has seen so many epic moments.

In the early rounds of the League Cup, a competition the Rams had made a mark in only the previous season when they reached the semi-finals before being knocked out by First Division high-flyers Leeds United, Derby beat Fourth Division Chesterfield and Third Division Stockport County, both at home. Against Stockport, former England winger Alan Hinton, a £30,000 signing from Nottingham Forest a year earlier, scored four times in the 5-1 win.

This Rams team was significantly changed from the one which had battled through to the semi-finals in 1967-68. Then, the reserve team had contributed several key figures when players like Roy McFarland and Hinton were cup-tied. Now they were available and joined by important signings in Willie Carlin and, staggeringly, the former Spurs legend Dave Mackay. Carlin's appearance in the side, after his £60,000 move from Sheffield United in August, had heralded a 13-match unbeaten run. Mackay's move from Tottenham had been a masterstroke by Clough, for he would be the inspirational figure in promotion.

On this October night, however, all

Dave Mackay heads clear from a Chelsea attack with Roy McFarland backing up.

Roy McFarland tests Peter Bonetti with a shot, watched by Ron Harris and Kevin Hector.

thoughts of First Division football were temporarily laid aside. The third-round draw had sent the Rams to Stamford Bridge and they came away with an excellent goalless draw against a side riding in the top third of the Division One.

Suddenly, cup fever hit Derby and there were overnight queues for the replay tickets. When York referee Vic James got the game under way on a balmy autumn evening, there were over 34,000 inside the Baseball Ground, the electric atmosphere hadn't been such since the heady days of the immediate post-war years, and the stage was set for a magnificent occasion. The Rams were already on a high, unbeaten for nine games and with their promotion drive beginning to gather pace.

From the start they hammered away at the Chelsea defence but as the first half wore on, it seemed that the Londoners would weather the storm. And there was always the danger that they would break away.

That was exactly what happened in the 26th minute when Peter Houseman, later to lose his life so tragically in a car crash, laid on a goal for Alan Birchenall. The Chelsea inside-forward hammered in a brilliant shot from fully 30 yards, beating Les Green in the top corner and sending Derby hearts sinking.

There were only 13 minutes remaining when the Rams' relentless pressure finally paid off. It was a peach of a goal. Carlin impishly backheeled the ball into the path of Dave Mackay and he levelled the scores with a dipping 30-yarder.

The Rams were now not going to be beaten and in the 83rd minute, Jim Walker robbed Derby-born Ian Hutchinson, not once but twice, and then burst down the left before crossing perfectly for Alan Durban to head past Peter Bonetti.

The Baseball Ground shook to the roar which greeted Durban's goal and four minutes later it erupted again. Young full-

Chelsea's Eddiee McCreadie tries to block another Rams effort as Derby stream forward, roared on by a packed Baseball Ground.

back John Robson sent over a great centre, O'Hare almost turned it in and then the ball broke between Hector and Bonetti. The Derby star got there first and a famous victory was at hand.

In the *Derby Evening Telegraph*, George Edwards summed up: 'Chelsea went under as wave after wave of white shirts hit them time and again. They were not just outfought — THEY WERE OUTSKILLED.'

It was more than even that, however. It was the night that the new Derby County came of age.

Derby County: Green; Webster, Robson, Durban, McFarland, Mackay, Walker, Carlin, O'Hare, Hector, A.Hinton.
Chelsea: Bonetti; M.Hinton, McCreadie, Hollins, Webb, Harris, Osgood, Tambling, Hutchinson, Birchenall, Houseman.
Referee: V.James (York)   Att: 34,346.

Gordon West punches away as Kevin Hector closes in with John Hurst behind him.

Everton The Victims In Another Cup Glory Night

Wednesday, 23 October 1968

Derby County 1   Everton 0

AFTER their great victory over Chelsea, Derby County met another leading First Division side in the next round of the Football League Cup. This time the draw paired the Rams with Everton, FA Cup Finalists the previous year and boasting the considerable midfield skills of Howard Kendall, Colin Harvey and Alan Ball.

Again, the Rams managed a goalless draw on their First Division opponents' ground, and again the Baseball Ground was packed to the rafters for the replay seven days later.

From the start, Everton looked anxious to show that the draw at Goodison Park had been simply an oversight on their part and twice they burst through dangerously in the opening minutes and also let the Derby attackers know they were there. Little Willie Carlin came in for some particulary robust tackling and had to have lengthy treatment after one heavy challenge from Ball. Then Hector was sent flying by Harvey. For all their skill, the Merseysiders' midfield had plenty of steel to offer.

Gradually, though, the Rams got on top and in the 30th minute they went ahead through a brilliantly-taken goal. Walker, under tremendous pressure, somehow pulled a cross back and Kevin Hector, with his back to goal, did the rest.

The Rams star pulled the ball down, turned quickly and hammered in a great shot which flew past Gordon West and into the back of the Everton net off Brian Labone.

Still Everton put themselves about and Ball

Dave Mackay, in another faultless display, heads clear from an Everton raid.

reacted to Hector's goal with a series of petulant tackles which earned him a hail of boos and other abuse from the crowd. But the match was still full of good football and before half-time, Hector shot over after good work by O'Hare and then Kendall saw a rocket of a shot fly just over Les Green's crossbar.

The Blues began the second half looking for the goal that would prevent yet another cup upset, but the Rams simply stepped up a gear, too, and Carlin robbed Johnny Morrissey with one quite brilliant tackle after the winger had turned Ron Webster. West held a cracking shot from Alan Durban and then it was Webster's turn to come to the rescue, turning the ball away for a corner after McFarland had slipped on the greasy turf.

Joe Royle handled, but still did not manage to get the ball into the net, and then came the first really dangerous move for the Rams when Royle headed back across goal from a centre and Ball only just missed the ball with the Derby defence looking very vulnerable.

As Everton continued their revival, Hurst flipped another shot over the bar from close range and then Carlin got himself out of a terrible position. Facing his own goal, only three yards out, the midfield star simply sold two defenders a perfect dummy and then dribbled his way out of trouble before releasing a perfect pass to O'Hare.

Ball then brought Walker down as the Rams staged another attack, although it was becoming evident that increasing Everton pressure was leaving Derby vulnerable.

Gordon West is helpless as Kevin Hector turns to crack home the only goal of the game.

But another famous victory was imminent and just before the end, Mackay pulled the ball down on the Rams penalty spot, then rolled it to Robson. The Rams left-back saw two men bearing down on him and clipped a pass to Walker who rounded Kendall. Suddenly the ball was deep in Everton's half again and it became so apparent that this Derby County side was competing with the best on football skills, not simply on blind endeavour. Indeed, the fans were complaining that it should have been more than 1-0 when the whistle sounded to end the match.

Alas, the cup run ended in anticlimax with a 1-0 replay defeat at Swindon Town, who were on their way to promotion from the Third Division. But it had been a memorable campaign — and there was still the First Division ahead.

Derby County: Green; Webster, Robson, Durban, McFarland, Mackay, Walker, Carlin, O'Hare, Hector, Hinton.
Everton: West; Wright, Brown, Kendall, Labone, Harvey, Humphreys(Wilson), Ball, Royle, Hurst, Morrissey.
Referee: E.T.Jenning (Stourbridge)
Att: 34,370.

Rams Hit Five — And The Long Wait Is Over

Saturday, 5 April 1969

Derby County 5   Bolton Wanderers 1

ON the first Saturday of April 1969, Derby County stood poised to re-enter the First Division they had left behind in 1953. The last time the Rams had played in Division One, Queen Elizabeth II's Coronation was six weeks away, Winston Churchill was Prime Minister and Mount Everest was still unconquered. Now the Rams had climbed their own mountain, and although they still had to be crowned champions, Brian Clough was most definitely the number-one man so far as Derby fans were concerned.

After a faltering start — only two points from their first four games — the Rams had signed Willie Carlin and embarked on a run of 22 League games which saw them lose only once. Their run-in to the season's end was equally impressive with nine straight wins. Crystal Palace, who went up with the Rams in second place, were the last side to beat them, 1-0 at the Baseball Ground on 5 March, and

Goalmouth action as promotion nears in the second half of the game against Bolton Wanderers. Frank Wignall heads goalwards. John O'Hare is the Derby number nine.

Kevin Hector hooks the ball over the head of former England goalkeeper Eddie Hopkinson, set against the nostalgic backdrop of the old Popular Side.

when Bolton Wanderers came to Derby, the Rams needed only two points to clinch promotion, even though there were still four games to play after the Trotters' visit.

A crowd of over 30,000 was present to see what they hoped would be an historic day. The form book would certainly have led them to be confident, for earlier in the season Derby had won 2-1 at Burnden Park and Bolton were now languishing in the bottom half of the table.

But perhaps even the most ardent Rams fan could not have foreseen just how emphatically the side would collect the points to enter the top flight, although a bone-hard pitch and a gusting wind made the job more

difficult than the final score suggests.

The Rams attacked from the start and forced a number of corners, taken from either side by Alan Hinton and continually troubling former England goalkeeper Eddie Hopkinson.

When the first goal came, however, it was a combination of a long punt downfield by Derby 'keeper Les Green and a piece of individual brilliance from Kevin Hector. Green's clearance bounced once just outside the Bolton penalty area, and as it bounced for a second time, Hector swooped in from the left to glance the ball wide of Hopkinson after 21 minutes.

Seconds before half-time, the Rams went

John O'Hare beats Hopkinson to put the Rams 3-1 ahead.

2-0 in front when Mackay chipped a free-kick forward, McFarland raced square with the goal to chest the ball into the path of Frank Wignall and the former Forest, Wolves and England forward struck it home.

Roy Greaves pulled a goal back for Bolton after 12 minutes of the second half and that was the signal for the Rams to go into top gear. In the 61st minute, Wignall sent Hector away and he lifted the ball over Hopkinson for John O'Hare to apply the finishing touch. Four minutes later, Derby County's place in Division One was assured when Hector and O'Hare combined beautifully before setting up a chance which Carlin took to make the score 4-1.

The Rams' fifth goal, four minutes from time, was scored by Roy McFarland, who was celebrating his 21st birthday. The ball bobbled about in the penalty area before McFarland, who had enjoyed a magnificent game at the heart of the Rams defence, stepped up to hammer it just inside the post with his right foot.

George Edwards wrote in the *Derby Evening Telegraph*: 'The dark days of the Third Division seemed far, far away as the cheers rang round the Baseball Ground at twenty minutes to five on Saturday. Sixteen years in the wilderness were forgotten and the only thing that mattered was that Derby County had secured a place in the First Division next season.'

Peter Taylor, the Rams assistant manager, had missed the celebrations — he was watching a player elsewhere — but Brian Clough spoke for them both: "Well, that's phase one completed." Clough continued: "We won't set 'em alight up there, but we'll surprise a few people."

Derby County: Green; Webster, Robson, Durban, McFarland, Mackay, Wignall, Carlin, O'Hare, Hector, Hinton.
Bolton Wanderers: Hopkinson; Cooper, Farrimond, Williams, Marsh, Rimmer, Phillips, Hill, Byrom, Greaves, Taylor.
Referee: B.H.Daniel (Rainham)   Att: 30,684.

Derby County in 1969 with the Second Division championship trophy. Back row (left to right): Wignall, Durban, Green, Webster, Robson, McFarland, Walker. Front row: McGovern, Carlin, Mackay, Hector, O'Hare, Hinton.

Durban's Hat-trick As The Rams Sign Off With Five

Saturday, 19 April 1969

Derby County 5   Bristol City 0

THERE was never any doubt that this match was going to be a formality from the moment that Bristol City, from the lower reaches of Division Two, strolled awkwardly on to the Baseball Ground pitch while champions Derby County were in the middle of their lap of honour.

After confirming promotion against Bolton in early April, the Rams had continued their great run-in with victories over Sheffield United, Millwall and Norwich City. Now well over 31,000 supporters came to salute Brian Clough's men as they brought down the curtain on a marvellous season.

During the first half, Derby put on a great display of soccer skills which surpassed anything they had produced in the League

that season — and it had been quite a season. The goals were all special, with Alan Durban in devastating form.

The first came after 16 minutes and followed a glorious build-up on the left involving Hinton and Durban. Parr could only head Hinton's eventual centre high into the air and as the ball fell invitingly, Durban was nicely in position to head wide of Watling and into the net.

Kevin Hector was the architect of the Rams' second goal after 34 minutes. He headed on a pass from McFarland and again it was Durban who applied the finishing touch, moving powerfully through to beat Watling as the goalkeeper came off his line. A minute before half-time Durban completed a genuine hat-trick — three on the trot — courtesy of Willie Carlin who outfoxed the Bristol defence by shaping to shoot and then stepping over the ball to allow Durban the easiest of chances to prod it over line with the City defence flat-footed.

It was all so easy but the fans had to wait until nine minutes into the second half for the best goal of the match. Mackay, who was

Rams hat-trick hero Alan Durban accepts congratulations from Ron Webster and Alan Hinton.

strolling through the game like a collossus, clipped the ball forward for Carlin to give chase. Carlin moved into position at just the right time and then cheekily back-heeled the ball into the path of Hinton, who, without having to check his stride, lashed a left-foot drive into the top corner of the net.

'The ball never rose more than six inches off the floor and was the nearest thing to an unstoppable shot one is ever likely to see,' wrote George Edwards in the *Derby Evening Telegraph*.

For some 20 minutes of the second half, the Rams went off the boil and there was even the sight of Ron Webster having to kick a Garland header off the line with Green well beaten. Derby soon replied, however, and two minutes later, Hector steered a powerful header past Watling, following a Hinton corner.

That made it 5-0, yet the Rams should already have had five in the bag because a few minutes earlier, Hinton had missed a penalty. O'Hare was bundled off the ball by Briggs but Hinton's powerfully-struck spot-kick cannoned back to safety off a post.

There were many chances that went astray

and Roy McFarland was perhaps unlucky not to have matched Durban's first-half hat-trick. First he grazed the crossbar with a magnificent header, then he saw a left-foot volley hit the bar and finally had a fierce right-foot shot deflected from its goalbound path.

The Rams' promotion season saw them break several records: Their win over Bristol City gave them club records of nine successive victories and 26 wins in a 42-match League season. Their 32 goals against was also a club record and the best Second Division figure since Birmingham City's all-time record of 24 in 1948-49. And their 63 points equalled the number gained by Leeds United in the 1962-63 season and was one better than Liverpool's promotion total of two seasons earlier.

Derby County: Green; Webster, Robson, Durban, McFarland, Mackay, McGovern, Carlin, O'Hare, Hector, Hinton.
Bristol City: Watling; Jacobs, Briggs, Wimshurst, Connor, Parr, Skirton, Kellard, Bartley, Garland, Sharpe.
Referee: F.Cowen (Oldham)   *Att: 31,644.*

We're back – and as champions. The Rams players parade the championship trophy to the Popular Side after ending their season with a resounding win over Bristol City.

Just part of the record attendance who saw the Rams thrash Spurs.

Spurs Massacred Before Record Baseball Ground Crowd

Saturday, 20 September 1969

Derby County 5   Tottenham Hotspur 0

'IT wasn't a match, it was a massacre. Sustained brilliance with a dash of sheer cruelty enabled Derby County to reduce Spurs to an inept shambles of a team at the Baseball Ground on Saturday. At times it was simply not a fair contest. Jimmy Greaves and Co were just not capable of giving the Rams a decent game.'

That was how the *Derby Evening Telegraph* positively gloated after the Rams, in only their 11th game back in the First Division, hit the might of Tottenham Hotspur for five before a crowd of 41,826, the highest Baseball Ground attendance and

now, of course, a figure which will never be surpassed.

The Rams had certainly made a memorable start to their first season in Division One for 16 years. A goalless draw at home to Burnley on the opening day of the campaign was followed by a 1-0 win at Ipswich and by the time Spurs arrived at the Baseball Ground towards the end of September, Derby County had still to taste defeat and were looking to extend their current winning run to five matches. They managed it with something to spare.

This was a Tottenham side containing so many famous names — Greaves, Jennings, Mullery, England, Gilzean and the rest — but any kind of pedigree counted for nothing against the onslaught which Brian Clough's Derby County side unleashed that day.

The goal timetable went like this . . .15 minutes: Mike England, already in something of a turmoil after the Rams front three ran him ragged, tried to turn the ball back to Jennings — or he might have been trying

Pat Jennings is helpless as the Rams score again.

to reach Mullery — but Durban nipped in to snap it up before steering a brilliant shot past the Spurs 'keeper.

19 minutes: O'Hare took the ball from a throw-in, left England standing and then pushed a pass through to Hector, who warded off a challenge from Collins and hammered home a glorious shot.

23 minutes: After Knowles had headed out for a corner, Hinton sent over a perfect flag-kick and little Willie Carlin, timing his leap to perfection, beat Mike England and Peter Collins — both six-footers — to head Derby into a 3-0 lead.

62 minutes: Carlin took the ball around three men and then pushed it forward to Durban. The Welsh international eliminated another defender and then pulled back a pass for O'Hare to crack home.

70 minutes: Hector burst through on the right, kept the ball in play when it looked to be going out for a throw-in, and then pulled back a great cross for O'Hare to head home for the Rams' fifth.

Admittedly, Spurs were down to ten men

for the last 20 minutes when Pratt limped off and they had already used their only substitute, Want, to replace Morgan at half-time, but by then it was all over. A minute after Pratt went off, incidentally, the Rams lost Durban with a groin strain.

The victory was all the more remarkable for the fact that Tottenham had arrived at the Baseball Ground with the best away record in the First Division and had won their previous four away games.

The Rams had dominated from start to finish but the killer period had been those three goals — and brilliant goals at that — in seven and half first-half minutes. After that they hardly seemed to get a kick and were truly down and out. When Spurs manager Bill Nicholson asked, "Was Dave Mackay playing today?" he was simply underlining the fact that the Rams had no need of the former Tottenham star's abilities as a sweeper.

The Rams midfield of McGovern, Carlin and Durban did almost as they liked, but it still did not daunt young John McGovern from dashing over to seek out Jimmy Greaves

Kevin Hector, John O'Hare and Willie Carlin celebrate the latter's goal.

Carlin (8) celebrates another Rams goal with John O'Hare as McGovern and Hector run to join in the fun.

as soon as the final whistle sounded. Afterwards, McGovern said, "I just wanted to shake his hand, he's such a great player."

Derby County: Green; Webster, Robson, Durban(Wignall), McFarland, Mackay, McGovern, Carlin, O'Hare, Hector, Hinton.
Tottenham Hotspur: Jennings; Beal, Knowles, Mullery, England, Collins, Pearce, Greaves, Gilzean, Pratt, Morgan(Want).
Referee: L.Callaghan (Merthyr Tydfil)
Att: 41,826.

Bill Shankly: "It's No Disgrace To Lose To Derby."

Saturday, 1 November 1969

Derby County 4   Liverpool 0

DERBY County's return to the First Division in 1969-70 proved more successful that even Rams fans dared hope. From the moment they made their bow in the top-flight, Brian Clough's team never looked out of place and there were some memorable victories including, of course, the five-goal thrashing of Tottenham Hotspur before a record Baseball Ground crowd.

Equally impressive was the Rams' display against Bill Shankly's Liverpool seven weeks later. Liverpool had finished runners-up to Leeds United the previous season and were on the brink of their greatest era. But when they arrived at Derby on the first day of November, they were made to look an ordinary side.

The game attracted yet another bumper Baseball Ground attendance of over 40,000 and, altogether, the Rams would play before seven 40,000 plus home 'gates' between September 1969 and January 1971 — five League games (against Spurs, Manchester United, Manchester City, Liverpool and Leeds) and two in the FA Cup (against

Rare action in the Rams half as Les Green attempts to punch clear a Liverpool attack. The other players are (from left) Roy McFarland, Alan Hinton, Ian St John, Peter Thompson, Dave Mackay, Chris Lawler, Peter Daniel and Bobby Graham.

Kevin Hector's diving header from Hinton's cross which gave the Rams a 3-0 lead and Hector his second goal of the afternoon.

Sheffield United and Wolves, both fourth-round games).

This Liverpool display was by no means a poor one, but for all their pressure they never looked on par with the Rams, who took the lead in the 15th minute through a brilliantly-taken effort by John McGovern. Hinton crossed the ball and then a succession of shots reigned in until the ball rebounded clear for a throw-in.

From the throw, the ball ran to McGovern on the right-hand edge of the penalty area and the midfielder hit a curving shot with the outside of his right foot, through a mass of players and into Tommy Lawrence's net.

Less than a minute later, the Rams went 2-0 ahead when Strong was caught out when trying to control a bouncing ball some 40 yards out on the right. Hector robbed him, burst into the penalty area, and as Lawrence came out, the Rams striker lifted the ball perfectly between the goalkeeper and the far post.

If these were great goals, the one which took the Rams 3-0 in front was even better. McGovern switched the ball inside to Durban, whose magnificent pass inside Lawler sent Hinton clear. The winger chipped the ball to the far post and there was Hector, racing in to fling himself at the ball and send a flashing header into the net after 53 minutes.

Liverpool could not cope and in the 68th minute, Hector left Strong behind and took the ball to the edge of the penalty area before sending a pass on to the overlapping Durban. He played the ball into the goalmouth, where O'Hare almost nonchelantly back-heeled it into the net. Alas, up went the linesman's flag for offside, presumably against Durban, although Tommy Smith was standing on the goal-line.

It hardly mattered, though. Less than a minute later, Hector beat the offside trap with O'Hare sensibly running just behind him. Hector could not have been blamed for going for his hat-trick goal, but instead he unsel-

Hector is floored with Strong and Lawrence as O'Hare salutes Hector's goal.

fishly rolled the ball to O'Hare and the centre-forward had an easy task in placing it into an empty net.

The *Derby Evening Telegraph's* George Edwards commented: 'It had to come. Somebody had to suffer for the frustration Derby County have endured since their last League win on 4 October and, unhappily for half of Merseyside, it was Liverpool.

'They played some clever football at the Baseball Ground on Saturday — but all of it across the pitch. The Rams, in sharp contrast, went forward quickly and incisively and scored five brilliant goals, one ruled marginally offside, without reply.

'Liverpool for all their pressure — and there were times when they held the ball for longish periods — managed only one on-target effort throughout the 90 minutes . . . .a header from Ron Yeats which Green, who played impeccably, saved with a flying dive to his left.

' . . . .They were outplayed in midfield where John McGovern, in the first half, put on a display of high skills. Emlyn Hughes seemed ponderous, clumsy and predictable, while St John was never in it.'

The Rams went on to finish fourth — a great achievement on their return to Division One — but were denied a place in European competition after it was discovered that there had been adminstrative problems, resulting in some irregularities, at the Baseball Ground.

But as Bill Shankly said after his team had been slaughtered: "It's no disgrace to lose to Derby."

Derby County: Green; Webster, Daniel, Durban, McFarland, Mackay, McGovern, Carlin, O'Hare, Hector, Hinton.
Liverpool: Lawrence; Lawler, Strong, Smith, Yeats, Hughes, Callaghan, Hunt, Graham, St John, Thompson.
Referee: P.Baldwin (Middlesbrough)
Att: 40,993.

United On The Rack In Boxing Day Thriller

Saturday, 26 December 1970

Derby County 4   Manchester United 4

MANCHESTER United's visit to the Baseball Ground on Boxing Day 1970 brought back recent memories of their appearance there in the Watney Cup Final the previous August, when the Rams hammered them 4-1. Today, the Watney Cup would not set the pulse racing, but 13 years ago there was tremendous interest, even though it was played out of season and with an experimental offside rule. Indeed, a crowd of over 32,000 saw Derby beat United in the Final.

When the players celebrated with champagne, Brian Clough scoffed. "We haven't played a real match yet," he said. And by mid-November it appeared that he was right to be cautious. Now, hopes of another successful season following the Watney victory were dashed as Derby slumped to 19th place by mid-November.

Wins at home to Blackpool and at Forest eased matters but then followed a 4-2 home defeat at the hands of West Ham. So when United came for this Christmas fixture, Derby County were on something of a knife edge.

After 22 minutes, however, the Rams were 2-0 ahead. It had taken only three minutes for them to get in front, when Ian Ure pushed Frank Wignall and Dave Mackay thundered in a superb left-foot free-kick. Then Wignall hammered the ball home from close-range after Law failed to clear a McFarland effort from a Mackay free-kick.

The game was full of incident, despite the atrocious playing surface after recent rain and snow, and the Rams might have extended their lead before Denis Law pulled a goal back for United, when he took a return pass from Willie Morgan to head over Les Green's head and into the net. It was a goal that Green could have stopped, had he been in position.

Nine minutes into the second half, Green did well to tip a fierce shot from Kidd over the crossbar, but a minute later United were level when Charlton took a corner on the right, Sadler back-headed the ball on, Green dropped it and George Best nipped in to score.

In the 59th minute it was United who were in front. Green was again in the thick of the action, this time making a fine save from Kidd. But Roy McFarland failed to clear and Law, astonishingly all alone, was allowed a free header, which he stooped low to steer home.

The Rams' heads did not drop, however, and Hector and Gemmill went close before

Bobby Charlton in action during the eight-goal Boxing Day thriller.

Derby scored a magnificent equaliser in the 65th minute. Gemmill beat three men in a great run down the right and then held the ball until Hector was moving forward. The little Scot then chipped a perfect pass and Hector scored with a right-foot shot from ten yards.

Five minutes later, the Rams were back in front. Hennessey fed Hector, who returned an earlier compliment by pushing the ball through for Gemmill to make it 4-3 with a right-foot shot which Ure touched, the ball going in off a post.

There were 16 minutes remaining when Charlton swung over another corner, Green was again out of position and Kidd got up highest to level the scores once more.

Gerald Mortimer, writing in the *Derby Evening Telegraph*, said: 'Derby County, two goals up at half-time, allowed a match which should have been dead and buried to slip from their grasp . . . .Manchester United, for lone periods a pathetic husk of a great side, came back to lead and finally take a point from a 4-4 draw. Tremendous entertainment for the spectators, certainly, but the Rams had thrown another point down the drain.

' . . . .Largely as a result of Green's goalkeeper errors, Manchester United, without playing particularly well, suddenly found themselves 3-2 ahead after scoring three times in five minutes . . . .'

Green's errors were uncharactaristic, but like his United counterpart, Jimmy Rimmer, he was dropped for the next game and, indeed, never played for the Rams' first team again.

Derby County were on the road to recovery, though. Two fine spells — a run of five successive wins and then only one defeat in their last eight games — saw them finish ninth. The springboard for the ultimate success was in position.

Derby County: Green; Webster, Daniel, Hennessey, McFarland, Mackay, Durban, Wignall, O'Hare, Hector, Gemmill.
Manchester United: Rimmer; Fitzpatrick, Dunne, Crerand, Ure, Sadler, Morgan, Best, Charlton, Kidd, Law.
Referee: H.Williams (Sheffield)   Att: 34,068.

Archie Gemmill (partly hidden) sees his shot enter the net off Ian Ure to make it 4-3 to Derby.

Leeds Slammed — And the Championship Is In Sight

Saturday, 1 April 1972

Derby County 2   **Leeds United 0**

IN MARCH 1972, five days after losing a marathon FA Cup fifth-round tie to Arsenal — they eventually went down 1-0 at neutral Leicester in a second replay — Derby County beat Leicester City 3-0 at the Baseball Ground to move into second place in the First Division.

When Leeds United, also challenging for the title, arrived at the Baseball Ground on Easter Saturday, the Rams were still in second place and had dropped only one point from their previous seven matches. The League championship still seemed a long way away

John O'Hare gets in a left-foot shot during the vital win over challengers Leeds.

— Liverpool and Manchester City were also up there and running hard — but victory over Leeds would keep Derby in there too.

It appeared a daunting task, for Don Revie's Leeds side were one of the most clinically professional in the game. Unloved by most people outside the Yorkshire City, of course they had great skill, too, but it was their method which irritated at best and made them reviled at worst. On this day, though, Derby County took them apart.

Revie had announced that his Irish international midfielder Johnny Giles would be ruled out because of a muscle strain, but then produced him at the last possible moment. It mattered not to Derby. John McGovern had his name taken in only the fifth minute after clattering Giles, but after the Irishman had supplied the pass for Eddie Gray to slip the ball into the Rams' net, only to be pulled up for offside, Giles was snuffed out of the game by McGovern, who also found time to

supply plenty of passes through to the Rams' strikers.

Derby soon had the Leeds defence in a tizzy and Hector, in particular, proved a big handful. Gemmill might have scored early on, when his rocket of a shot was bravely headed off the line by Paul Reaney, but it took Derby only 16 minutes to go in front when John O'Hare, on his 200th League appearance for the Rams, headed Durban's left-footed centre into the corner of the net. It was a beautiful goal, both in creation and execution.

From the restart, the Rams simply surged back and Hector, McFarland, Gemmill and O'Hare all went close before the tangled Leeds defence conceded an own-goal.

Hector split them wide open with a superb diagonal pass which fell right into the path of O'Hare. The centre-forward's shot bounced off Sprake, who was well off his line, and Norman Hunter was helpless as the ball hit

Derby celebrate their second goal but Leeds 'keeper Gary Sprake can only ponder on the error which led to the Rams going 2-0 in front.

Jim Walker hits a shot but Paul Reaney cleared the ball off the line. Left to right are McGovern, Walker, Giles, McFarland, Madeley, Charlton and Robson.

him and looped back over the line.

There were no more goals but the result hardly emphasised just how much the Rams had been on top. In the *Derby Evening Telegraph*, Gerald Mortimer said: 'It may come as a surprise to those who follow football only through the medium of television and newspapers, but Leeds United are fallible. Derby County, brilliant, indefatigable, utterly ruthless, did not so much beat Leeds at the Baseball Ground on Saturday as massacre them. The score was 2-0 and, but for some heroic last-ditch defending, it could have been five or more to Derby.

'This was a complete team performance by Derby County, produced when it was most needed, at a time of maximum pressure.

'The belief persisted until late in the game that Leeds could pull something out to shake Derby. It was a view based on past evidence and not upon what was happening on the pitch.

' . . . .The Rams so pulled the Leeds defence out of shape that it resembled a buckled iron bar, its strength no longer adequate. In midfield, Derby ruled and the Leeds strikers could make no impact.'

After such an epic performance, it was perhaps no surprise that on the Easter Monday, Derby lost 1-0 at home to Newcastle United, thus bringing to an end a magnificent run of 26 home games without defeat, stretching back to March 1971. Newcastle, incidentally, were the only visiting side to win at the Baseball Ground in 1971-72, but the Rams still had all to play for.

Derby County: Boulton; Webster, Robson, Durban, McFarland, Todd, McGovern, Gemmill, O'Hare, Hector, Walker.

Leeds United: Sprake; Reaney, Cooper, Bremner, Charlton, Hunter, Lorimer, Clarke, Madeley, Giles, Gray.

Referee: D.W.Smith (Stonehouse)

Att: 39,450.

Aerial combat in the Derby penalty area. Combatants are (left to right): McFarland, Lawler, Powell, Lloyd, Todd and Robson.

Liverpool Beaten — And Then The Long Wait

Monday, 1 May 1972

Derby County 1　　　　**Liverpool 0**

THE Easter Monday defeat by Newcastle United, when the Rams lost Roy McFarland for a short spell while he had five stitches inserted in a head wound and Colin Boulton was nursing a fractured finger, was soon put behind Derby County and they reached their last game of the 1971-72 season still in the hunt for the League championship.

Of course, if Rams fans were at all realistic they did not expect the title to come their way. Both Leeds and Liverpool had a game in hand over Derby and even if the Rams succeeded in their last game, against the Anfield club, it would still take an unlikely set of results to hand Derby the trophy.

Nevertheless, on that warm early May evening, over 39,000 fans packed the Baseball Ground for a match vital to both sides, with some 3,000 ticketless Liverpool fans locked out.

When it was announced that Brian Clough had decided to play 16-year-old Steve Powell at right-back in place of the injured Ron Webster, there were gasps of astonishment from the crowd. Normally, the last game of a season might be considered a good time to blood a youngster, and of course, Powell had already tasted senior football that season and thoroughly impressed. But in the pressure-cooker atmosphere of this match? And against a team such as Liverpool with Keegan, Toshack and company? It was asking a lot.

Powell, though, did more than just not let Derby down. He provided a cool head, mature beyond his boyish years, and abundant skill, too. Gerald Mortimer wrote: 'Powell was brilliant. Not brilliant for a 16-year-old: just brilliant.'

Welsh referee Clive Thomas perhaps erred on the side of caution in keeping a tight hold on a potentially explosive game. Many promising moves were strangled at birth and it was pretty obvious that one goal would probably settle the match.

That goal came in the 62nd minute with the Rams attacking the Normanton End. Kevin Hector took a throw-in on the right and Gemmill collected the ball and then took it across the face of the Liverpool goal, looking for an opening. He turned back, found Durban and the Welsh international dummied over the ball, allowing it to go to John McGovern, who beat Ray Clemence.

It was a fine goal but there was still almost half an hour to play and Liverpool were hardly going to give up. Substitute McLaughlin had Colin Boulton at full stretch with a testing shot, but that was as near as the Merseysiders came to snatching a point.

It had been a magnificent Derby County performance. In defence, Todd and McFarland were magnificent in front of Boulton, who had this season proved himself to be a First Division goalkeeper of the highest class.

In midfield, Alan Durban had a superb game, perhaps his best-ever in a Derby shirt.

John McGovern falls as he strikes the only goal of the game and, as it turned out, the one that sealed the title for Derby.

Young fans of both sides congratulate their heroes. Left to right are Colin Todd, Tommy Smith, Brian Hall and Roy McFarland. Derby had won but Liverpool, or Leeds, could still overtake them.

Trainer Jimmy Gordon holds up the Football League championship trophy. Alongside him are Ron Webster, Alan Hinton and Kevin Hector.

Never the quickest man on the field, Durban had always possessed an astonishing ability to read a game and against Liverpool, always managing to find space, he was a key factor in the Rams' success.

He had helped lay on the goal with a piece of unselfish quick thinking and in the first half, his flick on from a McFarland header had almost provided a goal for Hector. And in the closing moments he was there to hammer the ball to safety after Boulton had stopped McLaughlin's effort.

Up front, Hector and O'Hare had caused the Liverpool defence plenty of headaches.

Despite this great victory, however, on the same night Leeds beat Chelsea and it still seemed that either they or Liverpool would lift the title. The Rams, now top of the table, were on holiday in Majorca — minus Clough who was with his family in the Scilly Isles — when seven days later, both Leeds and Liverpool failed and Derby County were confirmed as Football League champions for the first time in the club's history.

Derby County: Boulton; Powell, Robson, Durban, McFarland, Todd, McGovern, Gemmill, O'Hare, Hector, Hinton.
Liverpool: Clemence; Lawler, Lindsay, Smith, Lloyd, Hughes, Keegan, Hall, Heighway(McLaughlin), Toshack, Callaghan.
Referee: C.Thomas (Treorchy)   Att: 39,159.

Benfica Parlaysed By Magnificent Rams

Wednesday, 25 October 1972

Derby County 3   **Benfica 0**

ACCORDING to the critics the European Cup tie between the Rams and Portuguese champions Benfica would be rather one-sided — and they were right, but for the wrong reason. Before another packed Baseball Ground house, it was Derby County, not the so-called Eagles of Lisbon, who dominated from first to last whistle with a breathtaking display of powerful attacking football.

The Rams first-ever European campaign had begun with a tie against the Yugoslavian champions, FK Zeljeznicar, and ended in a 4-1 aggregate victory for the English cham-

pions. That brought Benfica, one of the greatest names in club football, to the Baseball Ground for a game which would not have seemed possible only five years earlier.

The Portuguese, who were managed by pre-war Rams player Jimmy Hagan, included some world-class players, none greater than Eusebio, the man from Mozambique who the Press had dubbed 'the Black Pearl'. But on this glorious Baseball Ground night, Eusebio and his illustrious teammates were outplayed by Brian Clough's Derby County.

The first 45 minutes were quite fabulous. The Rams took the lead while some latecomers in the 38,000 crowd were still fighting their way to their positions.

Derby went straight on to the attack and forced a corner. Alan Hinton swung over one of his specials and Roy McFarland, running across goal from right to left, headed the cross down firmly, out of the reach of the Benfica goalkeeper.

A near miss in the Benfica penalty area. Terry Hennessey is left open-mouthed.

When Derby took a 2-0 lead it was again from a corner. This time McFarland strained to reach Hinton's kick and the ball glanced off his head, falling to Kevin Hector whose left-foot shot dipped into the top corner.

It was a remarkable start and there was more to come. Hector won the ball in the air and then John McGovern controlled it nicely before hitting a great shot into the far corner. Thus, well before half-time, the Rams had opened up a 3-0 lead and there was really no way back for the Portuguese champions, although such was their reputation that despite the big lead, Derby could afford no slackening of intent in the second half.

There were no further goals, although Hector twice might have made it 4-0, once from what looked like an easy header and once when he beat two men but then tried a shot from a narrow angle when colleagues looked better placed.

In the *Derby Evening Telegraph*, George Edwards reported: There were those who said that Benfica were a disappointment. To say that is an insult to Derby County and, in particular, to two great defenders, Roy McFarland and Colin Todd.

'Have they ever played better? Surely not, for to say they were world-class would be to devalue their performances.

'This was exceptional. Derby County have their critics and they have struggled in the League, but last night they went to town. They took on opposition whose reputation borders on the legendary and beat them out of sight before the tea had been made for half-time.'

Even a 20-second floodlight failure in the second leg at the Eastadio da Luz — the Stadium of Light — with Eusebio bearing down on Colin Boulton, could not help Benfica and the Rams went through after a

Roy McFarland surges in to head home a Hinton corner as the Rams overrun the Portuguese champions.

John McGovern hits a fine shot into the far corner of the Benfica net to leave the Portuguese floundering at 3-0 down.

goalless draw in the Portuguese capital. Then a quarter-final victory over Spartak Trnava of Czechoslovakia set up another mouth-watering tie against the Italian giants, Juventus.

Derby County: Boulton; Robson, Daniel, Hennessey, McFarland, Todd, McGovern, Gemmill, O'Hare, Hector, Hinton.
Benfica: José Henriques; da Silva, Humberto, Messias, Adolfo, Jaime Graca, Nene, Toni, Batista(Jhordao), Eusebio, Simoes.
Referee: B.Loow (Sweden) *Att: 38,100*

Don't Blame Bob Wilson — Praise The Rams

Saturday, 25 November 1972

Derby County 5   **Arsenal 0**

FOLLOWING their League championship success, Derby County made a disappointing start in their bid to retain the title in 1972-73. The Rams went four matches before their first victory and in their first 17 matches gained only 15 points. Then Kevin Hector's goals gave them a 2-1 win at Upton Park and the Rams began something of a revival. The following week Arsenal, League and Cup double winners two years earlier and now challenging for the title again, visited the Baseball Ground and were put to the sword by a rampant Derby team in which Alan Hinton was the star amongst stars.

The Gunners were second in the table when they arrived at the Baseball Ground and had goalkeeper Bob Wilson back in action after a seven-month lay-off following a cartilage injury. By the end of the afternoon, Derbyshire-born Wilson was surely wishing that he had delayed his comeback by at least this match.

In front of him the Arsenal defence was overwhelmed by a Derby side that dominated the midfield and thus gave them their forwards a tremendous amount of service.

Kevin Hector revelled in it, of course, and Roger Davies, a £12,000 signing from Southern League Worcester City in September 1971, began to confirm himself as a player of First Division quality.

Arsenal had looked the more dangerous in the opening stages but after 21 minutes John McGovern gave the Rams the lead after Wilson had failed to hold a centre from Gemmill and Hector had worked the ball on to McGovern who turned to hit the ball cleanly into the net.

That was the signal for the Rams to power back on to the attack. First Hennessey might have had a penalty when Peter Simpson appeared to push him, then McFarland had a goal disallowed when the referee was not ready for Hinton's free-kick.

Before the interval, however, Derby put the game beyond Arsenal's reach with three goals inside five minutes. First Hinton cut inside Pat Rice and netted with a fierce shot after Simpson had failed to dispossess Hector.

Then a short corner between Hinton and Webster saw the Arsenal defence trail Davies, leaving McFarland to nod the Rams into a 3-0 lead in the 40th minute. And two minutes later, Hinton curled in a perfect free-kick for Hector to head in.

The second half was less than two minutes old when Storey fouled Hector and when Hinton curled in another superb free-kick from the right, Davies rose to head home a fine goal. It was a fitting climax to Davies' home League debut, for he had displayed

Roy McFarland (5) leads the celebrations as the Rams increase their lead over Arsenal.

Roger Davies, on his home League debut, shows typical skill in shielding the ball from Peter Simpson.

immaculate close control and caused the Gunners' defence, particularly McLintock and Simpson, plenty of problems. Five-nil to the Rams was a scoreline which must have raised eyebrows elsewhere, but it was a result which did not flatter Derby County and one man, in particular, has to be singled out for special mention.

Said Gerald Mortimer in the *Derby Evening Telegraph*: 'The pure skill of Alan Hinton reduced Arsenal's defence to a rabble . . .He scored a goal of savage beauty and laid on the next three as the Rams raced to a crushing 5-0 victory, their best in the League since they put five past Spurs in the first season back in Division One.

' . . .It was a day on which Roger Davies confirmed his enormous potential, on which Colin Todd again embarrassed the FA who have banned him from international football, on which David Nish showed true pedigree and Kevin Hector played like a great striker.

'. . .There were only just over 31,000 spectators present. The others should get to the Baseball Ground now, for on Saturday they missed some of the most devastating football I have ever seen.'

Derby County: Boulton; Webster, Nish, Hennessey, McFarland, Todd, McGovern, Gemmill, Davies, Hector, Hinton.
Arsenal: Wilson; Rice, McNab, Storey, McLintock, Simpson, Marinello(Armstrong), Ball, Radford, George, Kelly.
Referee: A.W.S.Jones (Ormskirk) Att: 31,034.

Davies Hat-Trick Makes It A Glory Night For Derby

Wednesday, 7 February 1973

Tottenham Hotspur 3   Derby County 5

ALTHOUGH Roger Davies had earned Derby County a draw in the fourth round of the FA Cup against Tottenham Hotspur at the Baseball Ground the previous Saturday, the task of visiting White Hart Lane for the replay against the UEFA Cup holders and League Cup Finalists looked difficult. And when, after 78 minutes, Spurs led 3-1, it looked impossible.

But then Davies got to work again. The big centre-forward who joined the Rams from Worcester City of the Southern League in September 1971, was still a relative novice. Although Brian Clough had seen enough potential to invest £12,000 in the non-League player, Davies had to serve his apprenticeship in the Rams Reserves — helping them win the Central league title for only the second time in the club's history — and had his first taste of League action whilst on loan to Preston. In 1972-73, though, he forced his way in, and on this night at White Hart Lane he staked a place in Derby County's history.

In truth, the Rams should never have been two goals down in the first place. They had outplayed Spurs from start to finish and restricted the Londoners to only four on-target efforts all night. Unfortunately for Derby, three of them went in. Tottenham took the lead in the 20th minute — after Pat Jennings had made two brilliant saves as his

Roger Davies (9) and Kevin Hector cause the Tottenham defence plenty of problems as Mike England attempts a clearance.

side looked like being overrun — when Cyril Knowles broke down the right and his low diagonal cross was met by Martin Chivers.

Still the Rams swept forward, Hector hitting the bar and Gemmill having a shot blocked on the line, but before half-time Tottenham were 2-0 ahead after Alan Gilzean's first header had rebounded off the crossbar for him to head home at the second attempt.

The second half was 23 minutes old when Hector pulled a goal back for Derby, hooking his shot just under Jennings' bar. But with 12 minutes to play, Ralph Coates pushed Webster and as the Rams defender fell on the ball, the referee awarded a free-kick against Derby for hands. From it, O'Hare was also adjudged to have handled and Mike England hit the penalty past Colin Boulton.

The Rams had replaced Terry Hennessey with Alan Durban, a move which had given Derby an even better shape, and two minutes after England's penalty, Durban was involved a move which finished with Davies shooting home through a crowded goalmouth to make it 3-2. Six minutes later, Davies scored a truly magnificent goal. O'Hare controlled the ball magnificently on the by-line and then pulled it back for Davies to volley home, even though he was well short of the near post. The score was 3-3 and Davies disappeared under a mass of delighted teammates.

The Rams might have won it in normal time, for Hector hit Jennings with a shot and then appeared to be brought down as the rebound came back to him, but there were no further goals and extra-time was needed.

Although the first 15 minutes of the extra period brought the Rams no reward, there was surely no doubting the result now, for Tottenham looked out on their feet as brilliant Derby swarmed forward. It was no surprise, then, when Davies completed his hat-trick in the second minute of the second half of extra-time, heading home Hector's corner after Jennings had hesitated.

Six minutes later they scored again, when a long clearance caught the Tottenham defence square and Hector raced clear of Beal to shoot past the oncoming goalkeeper. It capped one of the truly great Cup come-backs. Three times in the last five minutes Derby

Roger Davies, the so-called Rams 'super sub' who played the full 120 minutes again Tottenham and helped the Rams stage an epic Cup fightback.

could have scored again and, as George Edwards said in the *Derby Evening Telegraph*, Spurs 'were comprehensively outclassed.'

Tottenham Hotspur: Jennings; Evans, Knowles, Pratt, England, Beal, Gilzean, Perryman, Chivers, Peters, Coates(Pearce).
Derby County: Boulton; Webster, Nish, Hennessey(Durban), McFarland, Todd, McGovern, Gemmill, Davies, Hector, O'Hare.
Referee: D.Biddle (Bristol) *Att: 52,736.*

Kevin Hector, scorer of the first ever English goal in a European tie in Italy, in action in Turin. The Juventus players are Roberto Bettega (left) and Sandro Salvadore.

Hector's Historic Goal Gives Rams Hope In Turin

Wednesday, 11 April 1973

Juventus 3   Derby County 1

DERBY County in the European Cup semi-finals — it was something that no Rams supporter would have dared dream of five years earlier as he set off for Carlisle or Northampton. Now, though, the Rams had eliminated three of Europe's champion clubs, including mighty Benfica, to reach the penultimate stage of one of football's greatest competitions.

The barrier which now stood in their way was Juventus, like Benfica a legendary name.

The first leg was to be played in the Italians' daunting Stadio Communale, an awesome task for any club. Indeed, no English side had ever scored a goal in a European Cup match in Italy — that was how difficult a task Derby faced.

After 28 minutes Juventus went ahead when Anastasi went past Webster and Todd before laying on a goal for 34-year-old José Altafini.

Two minutes later, though, Derby County were level with an historic goal. John O'Hare, playing at centre-forward in place of the injured Roger Davies, had a magnificent match and he gave the pass for Hector to score a simple but clinically taken goal. The first time an English club player had scored in such circumstances, it gave the Rams great hope for the return leg, even though they could not remain on level terms.

Causio might have put the Italians back in front before half-time, but the Rams negotiated the period to the interval quite satisfactorally, with McFarland and Todd outstanding in defence and the midfield of McGovern, Powell and Durban matching the Italians for skill. There was still no obvious need for concern in the opening moments of the second half, but then Cuccureddu was taken off after colliding with Todd and the West German star Helmut Haller came on.

Whilst Haller did nothing remarkable, his presence seemed to lift the Italian side and they regained the lead in the 66th minute. It was a bad goal to concede because the ball went across the face of the Derby goal and back again before Causio, with plenty of room, turned and hit it into the corner of the net.

Now the Rams were coming under pressure. Boulton had to react quickly to stop a McFarland attempt at volleying away Causio's centre, and then Causio saw his shot hit a post. At the other end, Durban went close, but seven minutes from time, Altafini made it 3-1 with a brilliant effort to give Juventus a two-goal lead to take to the Baseball Ground.

The Rams had plenty of cause to grumble, though. Both McFarland and Gemmill would miss the second leg after being booked — McFarland for an accidental collision of heads with Antonello Cuccureddu and Gemmill for eventually reacting to continual rough

Juventus goalkeeper Dino Zoff comes under pressure in the second leg at the Baseball Ground.

After his dismissal in the second leg, Roger Davies is led off by Jimmy Gordon.

treatment from Giuseppe Furino. Furino would also miss the second game, but as Gerald Mortimer said in the *Derby Evening Telegraph*: 'Furino . . .went around the field systematically and cold bloodedly tripping, holding and obstructing . . .His treatment of Gemmill was deplorable and it was hard to see how he was allowed to remain on the field.'

The game in Turin had been controversial, to say the least. There was a sensational incident at half-time when Peter Taylor was all but arrested after complaining that substitute Haller and referee Schulenberg — both West Germans — had 'had their heads

together.' And the second leg at Derby, which ended in a goalless draw after Hinton missed a penalty and Davies was sent off, was clouded by a story that someone had tried to bribe the Portuguese referee, Lobo, into seeing that Juventus did not lose. Nonetheless, the Rams had done English football proud in Turin.

Juventus: Zoff; Spinosi, Marchetti, Furino, Morini, Salvadore, Causio, Cuccureddu (Haller), Anastasi, Capello, Altafini.
Derby County: Boulton; Webster, Nish, Durban, McFarland, Todd, McGovern, Hector, O'Hare, Gemmill, Powell.
Referee: G.Schulenberg (West German)
Att: 72,000.

Derby County at the start of the 1973-74 season. Back row (left to right): Jimmy Gordon (trainer), Peter Taylor (assistant manager), Hennessey, Nish, Sims, Moseley, Boulton, Webster, Daniel, Todd, Brian Clough (manager). Front row: Powell, Davies, McGovern, Gemmill, McFarland, O'Hare, Hinton, Durban, Hector.

Hector Scores, The Rams Go Third — But The End Of An Era

Saturday, 13 October 1973

Manchester United 0   Derby County 1

ON the Saturday evening of 13 October 1973, Derby County manager Brian Clough pictured Leeds United boss Don Revie studying the top of the First Division to see who posed his team the greatest threat. Said Clough: "He'll be thinking about Liverpool or Newcastle. But one club will hit him in the eye. Us. And I reckon we'll be ready when they come to Derby at the end of November."

Certainly, the Rams were nicely placed — third — after that afternoon's fine victory at Old Trafford where Kevin Hector's fourth-minute goal had been enough to earn Derby their first away win of the season. But the game was to go down in Derby County's history as more than just an excellent win. It would also prove to be the last match under Clough, and when Leeds did arrive at the Baseball Ground the following month — when, incidentally, they drew 0-0 — the Rams had a new boss in Dave Mackay.

There had been rumblings for weeks. Clough's colourful and often abrasive style, especially on television, had seen his once close relationship with club chairman Sam Longson — "Like father and son," Longson said more than once — deteriorate dramatically as the game's establishment apparently told Longson to 'control your manager.' But after the Rams' win over United, what was to follow was nothing short of sensational.

The win at Old Trafford was well-deserved if not achieved with any great flourish.

Happier times. Brian Clough and Peter Taylor with Sam Longson on the day the pair joined Derby County.

Hector's early goal was the result of a combination of a dreadful error by Alex Forsyth, playing his first League game of the season, and a splendid piece of opportunism by Hector.

The United defender tried to work the ball back to goalkeeper Alec Stepney, but the pass was poor and whilst Stepney still had a chance to redeem the situation, he was left standing by Hector, who nipped in to tuck his shot into the far corner of the net.

The Rams might have extended their lead as the game wore on — Hector was presented with another chance by James and then Stepney was grateful to grab at the ball and catch it after a Davies effort had struck him on the arm. And if United came more into the game in the second half, Derby must have known it was their day when in the 79th minute, successive shots from Brian Kidd and Tony Young came back off the Rams' crossbar with Boulton well beaten.

'Derby, although making their fair share of mistakes, were still comfortably better than the worst Manchester United side I have ever seen,' wrote Gerald Mortimer in the *Derby Evening Telegraph*.

But the writing was on the wall for the mangerial pair. Mrs Clough and Mrs Taylor had to watch the match from the United directors' box because Derby County had not provided them with any guest tickets. And when Clough and Taylor returned to the Baseball Ground that evening, to toast a good win, they found that the bar in the manager's office had been cleared.

Two days later, what amounted to an ultmatum from the chairman said that, in future, all articles attributed to Clough must first be submitted to the board for approval. That was the enough. Clough and Taylor resigned in one of the most sensational and well publicised episodes in the game's history. Protest marches and meetings, a threatened players' strike — the saga had it all — but at the end of the day, Brian Clough and Derby County parted company. It was certainly not a great day for Derby County — indeed, it was probably one of the worst in the club's history — but this game at Old Trafford stands to be remembered as the end of the greatest era in the Rams' story.

Manchester United: Stepney; M.Buchan, Forsyth, Greenhoff, Holton, Jones, Morgan, Young, Kidd, Anderson, Graham.
Derby County: Boulton; Webster, Nish, Newton, McFarland, Todd, McGovern, Gemmill, Davies, Hector, Hinton.
Referee: E.D.Wallace (Crewe)   Att: 43,724.

Derby County at the start of 1974-75. Back row (left to right): Des Anderson (assistant manager), Hector, McGovern, O'Hare, Webster, Boulton, Moseley, Daniel, Powell, Todd, Jimmy Gordon (trainer). Front row: Hinton, Bourne, Nish, Gemmill, Dave Mackay (manager), McFarland, Davies, Rioch, Thomas, Newton.

Rams Go Marching On After European Epic

Wednesday, 6 November 1974

Atletico Madrid 2   Derby County 2
(aggregate 4-4; Rams won 7-6 on penalties)

DESPITE the turmoil which followed Brian Clough's departure from the Baseball Ground in October 1973, Derby County under Dave Mackay recovered sufficiently to finish third in Division One and so qualify for a place in the following season's UEFA Cup.

By the time the Rams took their place in that competition, however, there had been two significant changes in playing personnel. First, in May 1974, centre-half and skipper Roy McFarland, was seriously injured whilst playing for England in the Home International Championships. A severed Achilles tendon meant that McFarland would not play First Division football again for 11 months and his place was taken by Peter Daniel, an unsung hero who had been on the Rams' staff

since the days of Tim Ward's managership.

The second major change to the Rams team came when Mackay signed the former England striker Francis Lee from Manchester City for £100,000. It was an inspired move and Lee was to make a major contribution as Derby lifted the League championship again. Mackay's other major signing was Bruce Rioch, the Aston Villa midfielder who cost £200,000 in February 1974.

The Rams UEFA Cup campaign had begun quietly enough with a game against the Swiss side servette, with less than 18,000 turning up at the Baseball Ground to see the first leg. A 6-2 aggregate win over the Swiss earned Derby a second-round tie against Atletico Madrid, the previous season's European Cup runners-up who had been involved in a brutal game with Celtic on their way to the Final. Their manager, Juan Carlos Lorenzo, had been in charge of the 1966 Argentinian side dubbed 'animals' by Alf Ramsay.

The first leg at the Baseball Ground ended in a 2-2 draw. David Nish had equalised Ayala's long-range effort when the referee awarded two controversial penalties. First

Boulton was dubiously penalised and then Lee fell in the box and Rioch levelled the scores again.

At the Vincente Calderon Stadium in Madrid, the Rams knew that they must avoid conceding an early goal, but the game was only four minutes old when Adelardo chipped in a free-kick and the unmarked Luis headed past Boulton. It was a dreadful piece of defending by the Derby rearguard. It was disappointing, but before half-time both Gemmill, playing his 200th game for Derby, and Rioch might have drawn the Rams level again.

Nine minutes into the second half, however, the Rams scored through Rioch, who came through to fire home after Davies had headed down a centre by Hector. Inside ten minutes the Rams were ahead for the first time in the tie when Lee, although challenged by Diaz, rolled the ball back to Gemmill and this centre was breasted down by Hector before the Rams striker finished the job with a shot into Reina's net.

That was the signal for the Spanish crowd to call for the head of Juan Carlos Lorenzo and for a time it looked as though the Atletico players were a beaten side. But when Henry Newton was rather harshly penalised for hands, the veteran Luis beat Boulton with a magnificent curling free-kick.

Extra-time failed to produce another goal and the tie went to penalties. Rioch and Hector scored for Derby, Luis and Ayala for Atletico. Then Reina saved from Davies and the Spaniards went 3-2 up when Salcedo scored. Nish kept Derby in it, then Capon shot over and after Lee and Irureta both netted, it was on to sudden death.

Gemmill, Newton and Powell scored for Derby, Benegas and Garate for Atletico. Then came the deciding kick. Eusebio shot to Boulton's right, the Rams' goalkeeper guessed correctly, dived to push the ball on to the post, and it did not matter that Eusebio banged the rebound into the net. The Rams were through.

Gerald Mortimer, in the *Derby Evening Telegraph*, picked out Steve Powell as the star — 'His composure was uncanny, his authority total' — but said: 'They all deserve a medal, just read through the names of the team and savour them, for this performance matches anything Derby County have ever achieved.'

Atletico Madrid: Reina; Capon, Diaz, Adelardo(Marcelino), Benegas, Eusebio, Alberto (Salcedo), Luis, Garate, Irureta, Ayala.
Derby County: Boulton; Webster, Nish, Rioch, Daniel, Powell, Newton, Gemmill, Davies, Hector, Lee.
Referee: F.Biwersi (West Germany)
Att: 35,000.

Steve Powell cannot stop this shot from an Atletico player but Powell was one of the penalty scorers who took the Rams through to the next round of the UEFA Cup.

Glory For Lee — But Great Defending Earned The Points

Saturday, 28 December 1974

Manchester City 1   Derby County 2

THIS was always going to be Francis Lee's day. On his return to Maine Road, the ground which he had so often graced as a Manchester City player, Lee received the warmest of welcomes and then, just as City looked as though they would assume complete command of a game vital to Derby County's championship aspirations, he scored a brilliant goal and gave the initiative back to his new club.

The Rams went to Manchester just after Christmas 1975, looking back over recent League results which had gone a little astray following their controversial elimination from the UEFA Cup at the hands of Velez Mostar. Bob Latchford's header had settled the game against Everton at the Baseball Ground and a week later, Derby had lost at bottom-of-the-table Luton Town to slip to tenth, albeit only five points behind the current leaders, Ipswich, in the constantly changing First Division.

Hitherto, Luton had won only one of their 21 League games that season but after beating the Rams, they won at Ipswich, while Derby beat Birmingham 2-1 at the Baseball Ground to get themselves back into the hunt and also mark Ron Webster's 500th game for the club.

The visit to Maine Road thus assumed great importance and when Henry Newton put the Rams in front after 21 minutes, all looked well. Newton won a centre from Rioch and when the ball fell to Lee, the former City star played it sideways back to Newton for him to score his first goal of the season with a fine shot just inside the top corner of Joe Corrigan's goal.

It was perhaps fitting that this first strike of the season for Newton should come on an afternoon when he was quite magnificent, tackling and covering brilliantly as the Rams sought to counter City's threat. In disconcert-

ing conditions — the wind swirled around Maine Road all afternoon — Boulton had to make a brilliant save from a Doyle header, Newton robbed Tueart with a superb tackle as the City man was about to shoot, and Marsh and Tueart again also went close, while there was a nasty moment when Bruce Rioch, attempting a clearance, managed only to loft the ball straight up into the air before it dropped uncomfortably near the Derby goal.

After 63 minutes, City finally equalised and the goal was a classic. Asa Hartford found Rodney Marsh with an exquisite pass and Marsh rolled the ball sideways into the path of Colin Bell, who beat Boulton with a first-time shot. At that point it seemed that the Rams would be pleased to take a point, but two minutes later they were back in front.

This time Lee turned and shock off Alan Oakes and the attentions of two other defenders before taking the ball across the face of the penalty area, then hammering a fierce shot into the far corner of the goal it was a brilliantly executed goal and one which seemed scripted for a boys' adventure comic — the local hero returns to sink his former club.

Said Gerald Mortimer in the *Derby Evening Telegraph*: 'Lee is the man for the big occasion and he changed the course of the match in one memorable moment.'

But perhaps the real heroes had been the Rams' defence, heartening for they had given away some silly goals that season. And City, who included centre-forward Joe Royle, signed on Christmas Eve but hardly match fit for the First Division after languishing in Everton Reserves, might have felt they were worth a point because Corrigan was under-employed in the second half.

The points meant that Derby ended the year only three points behind the top teams Ipswich and Middlesbrough. The championship was still wide open.

Manchester City: Corrigan; Hammond, Donachie, Bell, Doyle, Oakes, Horswill, Royle, Marsh, Hartford, Tueart.
Derby County: Boulton; Webster, Nish, Rioch, Daniel, Todd, Newton, Gemill, Davies, Bourne, Lee.
Referee: J.Gow (Swansea)   *Att: 40,188.*

Colin Todd, the magnificent Rams defender who held firm as Derby took both points from Maine Road.

Roger Davies leaps to head the first of his five goals against Luton Town. Paul Futcher (left) later joined the Rams.

Davies dives to head home again but this effort was disallowed for offside. The Luton player is Steve Buckley, who later proved such a magnificent servant to the Rams.

Five-Goal Davies Kept Rams On Title Course

Saturday, 29 March 1975

Derby County 5   Luton Town 0

DEFEAT at home to Stoke City on 15 March 1975 put Derby County out of the running for the League championship as far as the national newspapers were concerned. But when the Rams hit back with a 2-0 win at Newcastle a week later, they were back on course. Then came three vital games over the Easter holidays. Derby needed the points and they began by hammering struggling Luton Town. It was a crucial victory — and for one man in particular, a day never to be forgotten.

Roger Davies had not been the most prolific of scorers this season — six goals in 31 League games, four of which had come in the first seven matches — but against the Hatters, Davies gave a performance which elevated him to a very select group of players in Derby County's history. He took only just over half

an hour to complete his hat-trick, netted twice more in the second-half — and had other efforts disallowed.

Although Luton were still next-to-bottom of the table, they came to Derby on something of a roll, having won their previous three games. The Hatters also included two future Rams players, Steve Buckley and Paul Futcher.

Davies opened his account in the ninth minute. Hinton had a right-foot shot turned around by Barber for a corner and the winger floated in the flag-kick for Davies to rise high above the defence and head home via a post.

Four minutes later it was 2-0 and again Davies was the scorer. This time Hinton sent Todd away down the right. He got the ball back to Rod Thomas and although the Welsh international full-back mishit his cross, Davies managed to get his head to it and Barber was again left groping. After 33 minutes, Davies completed his hat-trick, chasing a long pass from Thomas and then flashing the ball past Barber who had decided to stay on his line.

Within a couple of minutes, Davies had the ball in the net again but was ruled offside.

Luton goalkeeper Keith Barber is helpless as another Davies effort sails towards his net.

Barber is again in trouble as Davies, who seemed to pop up every time there was a chance in the Luton penalty area, chips goalwards.

The big centre-forward was causing the Luton defence all manner of problems and before half-time he thought he had scored a fourth, but this time the linesman flagged to indicate that he had used an arm when chesting down a curling pass from Hinton.

Early in the second half, Davies drove a pass from Hector narrowly over the bar and later mishit his final shot after flicking Hinton's centre over Faulkner's head. Then Futcher was booked after aiming a kick of frustration at Davies' ankles. Still the Rams' centre-forward was looking for goals and brought a good save from Barber after Gemmill laid on the chance.

Eventually, in the 78th minute, Davies did get his fourth. John Ryan headed back a long pass and Davies, ever the opportunist, got there first and hit the ball into the net with the Luton defence in tatters. He thus became the first Derby County player to score four goals in a League game since Alf Ackerman, who achieved the feat against Accrington Stanley in the Third Division North in April 1956.

There were four minutes left when Davies added his fifth goal of the afternoon. Faulkner misjudged Hinton's long ball forward and Davies ran in to slip his shot under Barber. The points had been in the bag for some time, of course, but the goals were still vital, building up the Rams' goal-average.

This time one had to look back to December 1934 and a nap hand by the great Hughie Gallacher for the last time a Derby player had scored five goals in a game.

It was a great start to Easter and the Rams went on to beat Burnley and Manchester City to make it six points out of six over the holidays. They were well and truly back in the hunt.

Derby County: Boulton; Thomas, Nish, Rioch, Daniel, Todd, Powell, Gemmill, Davies, Hector, Hinton.
Luton Town: Barber; John Ryan, Buckley, Anderson, Faulkner, P.Futcher, Jim Ryan, Husband(Seasman), R.Futcher, West, Aston.
Referee: R.Tinkler (Boston)   Att: 24,619.

For old time's sake. Former Rams stars join hands to sing *Auld Lang Syne* before the start of the Carlisle game which marked another championship success and the end of the infamous Baseball Ground pitch.

Another Title — And Farewell To That Pitch

Saturday, 26 April 1975

Derby County 0   **Carlisle United 0**

FOR the second time in four seasons, Derby County learned that they were Football League champions whilst sitting in a nightspot. In May 1972, they were in Majorca when news came through that both Liverpool and Leeds had failed to overtake the Rams. In late April 1975, the players were attending the club's annual awards night in Derby when they learned that Ipswich Town had dropped a point at Maine Road and therefore could not catch the Rams.

Derby could have wrapped it up the previous Saturday, but a goalless draw at Leicester left them hanging on the Ipswich result. Now, three days after being confirmed as champions, the Rams played their last home game of the season, against relegated Carlisle United, when they said hello to a parade of former stars and goodbye to the Baseball Ground's infamous pitch.

For decades, the surface was a footballer's midwinter nightmare of cloying, often waterlogged mud. Players squelched around on it, sometimes ankle-deep in the quagmire — more than one boot was wrenched off by the suction — and by April, the only grass was to be found in the four corners. In a dry springtime, the majority of the playing area resembled a giant brown, dusty diamond. Now the club had decided to dig up the pitch, sell pieces of it, hermetically sealed, to supporters for souvenirs, and lay a new carpet. Alas, the problems were far from over in this regard and even in 1993, players were still complaining, only now it appeared that the pitch drained too quickly.

Before the game, the Rams lined up a parade of former stars. It was a Derby County supporter's dream as some of the greatest names in the club's history came on to the pitch. There were at least 11 players — George Thornewell, Freddie Knowles, Harry Bedford, Dai Astley, Sammy Crooks, Jack Stamps, Tim Ward, Jack Webb, Jack Howe, Freddie Jessop and Billy Townsend, who had started

Roger Davies head over the Carlisle crossbar with the goal at his mercy.

The Rams parade the Football League championship trophy. Back row (left to right): Dave Mackay (manager), Davies, Newton, Boulton, McFarland, Hinton, Lee, Nish, Daniel, Todd and Powell. Front row: Thomas, Rioch, Gemmill and Hector.

with the Rams before World War Two.

Others like Peter Doherty, Tommy Powell, Jack Parr and Jim Bullions had joined Derby during the war, whilst Johnny Morris was a British record signing in the early post-war era, Reg Ryan, Ray Young and Reg Matthews played later and Willie Carlin and Terry Hennessey had starred in the rise under Brian Clough. Ron Webster, Steve Powell and Player of the Year Peter Daniel, all out with injuries, represented the current side in the parade of stars.

Football League vice president Sam Bolton presented Rams skipper Archie Gemmill with the championship trophy and the players then went on a lap of honour, to huge acclaim from the near-37,000 crowd.

Alas, the game itself was an anticlimax. In the *Derby Evening Telegraph* Gerald Mortimer summed up: 'The celebrations before the match were splendidly emotional, the enthusiasm afterwards exhilarating. Unfortunately, the game itself was a complete bore. Derby County, released from the tension of the last two months, were totally unable to concentrate. Carlisle United, neat but entirely without venom, were simply not good enough to take advantage. If the Rams had not already been hailed as League champions, the crowd would have had plenty to say.'

Said manager Dave Mackay: 'We simply did not play at all, but had we needed a point to make sure, the game would have been completely different.

There were chances for the Rams, the best falling to Gemmill, without a League goal that season, but he chipped the ball wide of the advancing Alan Ross. The crowd didn't really mind, though. On a hot afternoon they had welcomed a galaxy of former stars whose value on the current transfer market would have run into hundreds of thousands, if not millions, of pounds, and the present side were champions. Who could have asked for more? It was a great day for Derby County.

Derby County: Boulton; Thomas, Nish, Rioch, McFarland, Todd, Newton, Gemmill, Davies, Hector, Lee(Hinton).
Carlisle United: Ross; Carr, Spearitt, O'Neill, Green, Parker, Martin, Train, F.Clarke, Laidlaw, Balderstone.
Referee: A.E.Morrissey (Bramhall)
Att: 36,882.

Colin Boulton and Roger Davies have a tight grip on the trophy as the Rams go on a lap of honour.

Rams Charity Display A Great Boost For Football

Saturday, 9 August 1975

Derby County 2   West Ham United 0

ON a sweltering August day in 1975, Derby County returned to Wembley Stadium for the first time since the club won the FA Cup, almost 30 years earlier, and took the FA Charity Shield with a display of football that proved a marvellous pipe-opener to the season which lay ahead.

The Rams, League champions, met West Ham, holders of the FA Cup, in a game which went some way to restoring the image of English football. The previous season, Leeds United and Liverpool had met in an ill-tempered game — the first Charity Shield match to be staged at Wembley — but Derby and West Ham wiped out the memory of that bitter afternoon with a match that displayed all that was best about the game of soccer.

For Rams skipper Roy McFarland it was a testing afternoon. Fifteen months earlier he had severed an Achilles' tendon playing for England against Northern Ireland on the same pitch. He came through this match with a goal to his credit which capped an absolutely brilliant performance at the centre of the Derby defence.

Said McFarland: "A lot of people tried to build it up. But to me it was just another game. I've played at Wembley often enough and I wasn't injured because of the pitch. I just fell awkwardly. It could have happened anywhere."

West Ham were without Billy Bonds, who was out with a groin injury, but the Rams fielded their star signing, Charlie George, the brilliant attacking midfielder who Dave Mackay had bought from Arsenal for £100,000 the previous month.

Rams new boy Charlie George sees his header pushed over by Mervyn Day in the 1975 Charity Shield game.

The Rams were already well in command when they took the lead after 20 minutes. George found Hector on the right with a magnificent pass and the Rams striker cut in to shoot past Mervyn Day, who was not all that well positioned, and into the far corner.

The Hammers came close on two occaisons — Holland's header grazed the top of Boulton's bar and then the Rams 'keeper turned over a header from Jennings — before Derby scored their second two minutes before half-time.

Nish took a corner, Lee headed the ball down to Hector and after his back heel bounced back off Day, McFarland beat all comers to force the ball over the line. The

Charity Shield was already on its way back to the Baseball Ground.

Charlie George had enjoyed a fine game. Even though it was his challenge on the Day which had ruled out an earlier 'goal' from Rioch, and even though he might have passed to Lee instead of chipping a shot over the bar after Tommy Taylor's remarkably slack pass had set him up, George had shown the spirit of adventure which would endear him to Rams supporters and result in him being voted Player of the Year at the end of the season.

Near the end, Lee smashed a shot against the West Ham post but the Londoners, one of the most attractive teams in the country, had by then already been established as having

Roy McFarland hammers home Derby's second goal after the Hammers failed to clear David Nish's corner.

Roy McFarland holds aloft the FA Charity Shield which he has just received from UEFA president Dr Artemio Franchi.

only a supporting role in this showpiece. It may only have been a friendly, but the game gave Rams fans a wonderful day out at Wembley, a first sight of their latest hero in a Derby shirt, and the promise that the season ahead would be full of good football.

Derby County: Boulton; Thomas, Nish, Rioch, McFarland, Todd, Newton, Gemmill, Lee, Hector, George.

West Ham United: Day; McDowell, Lampard, Holland, T.Taylor, Lock, A.Taylor, Paddon, Jennings(Coleman), Brooking, Robson.

Referee: G.C.Kew (Amsterdam)

Att: 59,000.

Rams Scaled New Heights in European Classic

Wednesday, 22 October 1975

Derby County 4   **Real Madrid 1**

WHEN Real Madrid were winning the European Cup for the first few years of the competition's existence, Derby County were struggling back from the Third Division North and then trying to re-establish themselves in the Second in what was a mediocre era in the club's history. Certainly, the gap between the clubs could hardly have been greater and the suggestion that Derby would one day meet the Spanish champions in European competition would have been greeted with derision.

But 20 years after Real recorded the first of five successive European Cup Final victories, the Rams not only qualified to meet them as English champions, they went on to produce a magnificent performance at the Baseball Ground to destroy the Spanish giants with a classic display. It was, said the *Derby Evening Telegraph's* Gerald Mortimer, 'a victory of startling brilliance'.

What was even more heartening was that Real Madrid were a much better side than the Benfica team well beaten at Derby three years earlier. Indeed, Real played quite brilliantly in patches, but the Rams played brilliantly throughout.

The days of visits to Accrington, Gateshead and Crewe in the old Northern Section seemed a million years away as Derby tore into the Spaniards from the start to take the lead after only ten minutes.

Colin Todd swept out an astonishing pass to David Nish on the other side of the pitch and then Archie Gemmill sent in a low, hard centre. Charlie George was running across the face of the goal and his first-time left-foot shot left Miguel Angel with no chance.

Todd was singled out by Gerald Mortimer:

Charlie George (11) gives Derby the lead over Real Madrid with his wonder goal.

George sends Real Madrid 'keeper Miguel Angel the wrong way and converts the penalty for Derby's fourth goal.

'Todd, faultless at the back, exciting when he moved forward, has never played better. Indeed, I doubt if any defender in the history of the game can have played substantially more effectively than Todd.'

Seven minutes later the Rams were 2-0 ahead and George was again the scorer. Lee attacked the ball, driving hard into the Real penalty area. Camacho panicked, bowled Lee over, and up stepped George to hammer the spot-kick past Angel.

Real had been a disorganised side, but instead of capitulating, they pulled themselves together and drew a goal back after 25 minutes when Amancio chipped in a perfect pass and Pirri chested the ball down before beating Boulton neatly.

Real were now buzzing and the Rams

Goalkeeper Colin Boulton cannot conceal his delight as the Rams take a 4-1 lead over the Spanish champions.

certainly needed another goal. It came two minutes before half-time when McFarland laid the ball off to Nish, who whipped in a shot under Angel's body to make it 3-1 to the Rams.

In the second half, Angel made amends for that slip. He stopped a ferocious free-kick from Bruce Rioch and then twice saved well from Lee, first holding a free-kick and then turning a header over the bar.

Back at the other end, Real might have reduced the deficit to a single goal again when Pirri looked to have scored a fine goal but was denied by the flag of Russian linesman Bakhramov, the man who had signalled that Geoff Hurst's controversial goal in the 1966 World Cup Final had crossed the line.

Real protested even more fiercely when the Russian referee awarded the Rams a penalty after Netzer had pulled down Kevin Hector with 12 minutes remaining. Again, George struck the kick firmly into the back of the Real net.

So, Charlie George finished with a hat-trick, but his overall contribution had been even greater than that. His running and passing had stamped an indelible image in the minds of those who witnessed this.

Gerald Mortimer commented: 'Derby County are good enough to win the European Cup. That much they announced last night with a victory of startling brilliance over Real Madrid. And they can win it the way Dave Mackay would want: gloriously with flair and surging football that tears at the guts of continental teams.'

But he also warned: ' . . . .the feeling is that the tie is by no means over yet. In their own Eastadio Santiago Bernabéau, Real could still make Derby sweat it out . . . .'

And so it proved. In Madrid, without the suspended Francis Lee, the Rams went down 5-1. It was a bitter disappointment, but nothing could take away the memory of the night that Real Madrid came second-best at the Baseball Ground.

Derby County: Boulton; Thomas, Nish, Rioch, McFarland, Todd, Newton, Gemmill, Lee, Hector(Bourne), George(Davies).
Real Madrid: Miguel Angel; Sol, Rubinan, Pirri, Camacho, Velazquez, Amancio, Breitner, Del Bosque, Netzer, Roberto Martinez.
Referee: A.Ivonhal (USSR)   *Att: 34,839.*

The Good, The Bad And The Ugly

Saturday, 1 November 1975

Derby County 3   **Leeds United 2**

THIS game should be remembered for the magnificent goal which substitute Roger Davies scored to earn League champions Derby County a memorable victory over Leeds United at the Baseball Ground.

Instead, it will almost certainly go down in people's memories for the ugly brawl which resulted in Derby's Francis Lee and Leeds' Norman Hunter both being sent-off. That cast a shadow over the afternoon, yet the Rams' victory over a Leeds side who were once the great masters of English football was a glorious affair and should be remembered as such.

Leeds, it was, who took the lead after only 11 minutes when the Rams defence got itself into a pickle and Trevor Cherry rose unchallenged to head Peter Lorimer's corner into the net after Boulton had saved one of Lorimer's thunderbolt free-kicks.

Then the Rams woke up to the fact that they were facing a team like Leeds and they equalised in the 24th minute, thanks initially to Colin Todd's immense power. Todd won tackles against Bremner and Lorimer before switching the ball to Charlie George on the right. George whipped in a savage cross-shot which David Harvey could not hold and Gemmill was first to the ball to scramble it over the line.

By now Bruce Rioch was obviously struggling with an ankle injury and he was replaced by Davies, with Kevin Hector dropping back.

Three minutes before half-time, the Rams took the lead with a dubiously-awarded penalty which was the spark which ignited the Lee-Hunter affair.

Lee bustled past Hunter, then fell in

Charlie George beats David Harvey from the spot after Francis Lee's alleged dive had angered Norman Hunter.

Lee versus Hunter. The infamous brawl with ten players involved in one way or another.

Lee, white-shirted and bloodstained, is led away by Gordon Guthrie with Dave Mackay and Des Anderson behind.

spectacular fashion. Said Gerald Mortimer in the *Derby Evening Telegraph*: 'It had all the appearances of a Lee dive and the television recording did nothing to dispel that impression.'

Bournemouth referee Derek Nippard came racing into the picture — he was hardly on the spot — and gave the penalty which George converted by sending Harvey the wrong way. It was a lead which the Rams perhaps deserved after fighting their way back into the match, but it was a wholly unsatisfactory way to gain it.

Bad feeling was now obviously boiling up between Lee and Hunter and seven minutes into the second half it erupted into violence.

Harvey has no chance as substitute Roger Davies' swerving drive seals victory for the Rams.

Lee got in a shot but Hunter steamed in to clatter him with a tackle. Gerald Mortimer takes up the story: 'Lee retaliated. Hunter hit back with a blow to Lee's lip which caused a cut requiring four stitches. Players from both sides separated them and referee Derek Nippard quite rightly sent both of them off the field.

'As the pair straggled away to the dressing-room, they began another fight and had to be forcibly separated, although Billy Bremner seemed keen to have a dig on his own behalf.

'For two such experienced players, it was ridiculous behaviour but in matches in matches between Derby and Leeds there is always a simmering undercurrent of passion, a legacy of the hostility which existed when Brian Clough and Don Revie were the managers.'

After Lee and Hunter departed, Leeds regained control, although Nish could count himself unlucky when his delicate chip bounced off the bar and out of danger with Harvey nowhere.

It was no surprise when Leeds drew level with 17 minutes remaining. A short corner on their left saw Frank Gray slam Bremner's pass into the goalmouth, where Duncan McKenize stabbed his shot high past Boulton.

A Leeds victory was by no means impos-

sible but the Rams got back in control and Hector and Todd brought good saves out of Harvey before Davies scored his wonder goal.

Again it was Todd, driving forward, who started things, but it was Davies — still waiting for his first full League outing since a cartilage operation the previous August — who finished it off in wonderful fashion. The big centre-forward got inside the Leeds defence before swerving a left-foot shot into the far corner, giving Harvey no earthly chance. The goal sealed the Rams' first win over Leeds at the Baseball Ground since April 1972.

Lee's sending-off meant that he missed the following Wednesday's European Cup second-leg match against Real Madrid. Both men were charged by the FA with bringing the game into disrepute: Lee was fined £200 and banned for four games; Hunter was cleared.

Derby County: Boulton; Webster, Nish, Rioch(Davies), Thomas, Todd, Newton, Gemmill, Lee, Hector, George.
Leeds United: Harvey; Reaney, F.Gray, Bremner, Cherry, Hunter, Lorimer, Clarke, McKenzie, Yorath, Madeley.
Referee: D.R.G.Nippard (Bournemouth)
Att: 33,107.

Magnificent Rams Into FA Cup Semi-Final

Saturday, 6 March 1976

Derby County 4   Newcastle United 2

NOT since 1948 had Derby County fought their way through to the semi-finals of the FA Cup. Then, they were unlucky enough to meet a rampant Manchester United and, with the Rams facing something of a goalkeeping crisis, it was United who went through and on to beat Blackpool in one of the best-ever Wembley Finals.

All of this, of course, was academic some 28 years later, when the Rams faced Newcastle United in the sixth round of the Cup. But supporters couldn't help but look back — and forward, wondering if this was to be their club's year after so much time in the Cup wilderness.

And after their performance in this quarter-final against the Magpies at the Baseball Ground, those same fans couldn't be blamed for thinking that perhaps 1976 — 30 years after the Rams' only FA Cup Final victory — was going to herald a second Wembley triumph.

For Derby County were absolutely brilliant against Newcastle. The *Derby Evening Telegraph's* Gerald Mortimer summed it up perfectly as an 'afternoon with vivid goals and patches of football clothed in imperial purple'.

True, Newcastle were depleted through injury and illness, but they kept on battling and if the impression was that the Rams had simply brushed them aside, one had to remember that there were spells when they caused Derby some anxious moments.

The first two goals belonged to Bruce Rioch, refreshed after a two-match suspension. His goals came inside the first 16 minutes and set the scene for the rest of the afternoon.

The game was only four minutes old when Rioch first struck. Rod Thomas won the ball from Malcolm Macdonald and then Rioch switched it out to Kevin Hector on the right

and kept on running, so that when Hector's cross was eventually laid off by Charlie George, Rioch was there to finish the attack by forcing the ball past Eddie Edgar, making what proved to be his only senior appearance in Newcastle's goal.

Twelve minutes later, Rioch struck again. George was felled just outside the Newcastle penalty area. Rioch waited, hands on hips, while referee Ken Burns sorted out the Magpies' defensive wall, then hit a perfect free-kick into the top corner. Poor Edgar must have pondered on just what a difficult game this was in the top flight. For Rioch it was his sixth goal in his last six appearances

In between these latest two, Malcolm Macdonald had the ball in the net for Newcastle but referee Burns ruled that he had fouled Graham Moseley, who appeared to have the ball knocked out of his hands.

After 21 minutes, however, Alan Gowling brought life back into the tie when a cross from Blackhall rebounded obligingly off George and the former Manchester United player— who had been confined to bed all week suffering from bronchitis — beat Moseley at the near post.

In the 64th minute, the Rams scored their third goal and the 13th FA Cup semi-final appearance in their history beckoned. Macdonald headed out a corner from Nish, straight to Henry Newton who steadied himself before hammering a vicious swerving shot past Edgar from outside the penalty area.

With 15 minutes to go, Newton limped off to be replaced by Roger Davies who missed two easy chances before Charlie George put the outcome of the tie beyond any doubt.

George had headed on Moseley's long kick to Hector, who simply destroyed the Newcastle defence with a cheeky back-heel, straight into the path of George who tucked away his shot.

Newcastle grabbed another goal when Gowling, always looking to sniff out a chance even in the most hopeless of causes, diverted Cassidy's effort over the line after 80 minutes.

The Magpies had been without the influential Tommy Craig in midfield and, of course, goalkeeper Mike Mahoney was also missing, whereas the Rams had Rioch back and were also heartened by the news that Welsh

The net bulges as Bruce Rioch, out of picture, hammers an unstoppable free-kick past Eddie Edgar.

Another view of Rioch's goal with poor Edgar, in his only senior appearance for Newcastle, well beaten.

Charlie George tucks away the Rams' fourth goal after a cheeky one-two with Kevin Hector.

international winger Leighton James was fit. But the Derby display had been such that it is doubtful whether even a full-strength Newcastle could have lived with them.

Alas, the Rams' Cup challenge was almost over. History repeated itself when they were again drawn against Manchester United in the semi-final — as in 1948, at Hillsborough — and again United it was who marched on to Wembley, although this time the defeat was no quite as emphatic and the Rams might have felt a little aggrieved at not at least forcing a draw.

Derby County: Moseley; Thomas, Nish, Rioch, McFarland, Todd, Newton(Davies), Gemmill, Hector, George, James.
Newcastle United: Edgar; Blackhall, Kennedy, Barrowclough, Keeley, Howard, Burns, Cassidy, Macdonald, Gowling, Hudson.
Referee: K.H.Burns (Dudley)   *Att: 38,362.*

Lee Signs Off With Two Goals To Sink Ipswich

Saturday, 24 April 1976

Ipswich Town 2   Derby County 6

BY the time the last Saturday of the 1975-76 season came around, Derby County knew that they had been unable to retain the League championship. Liverpool, with QPR and Manchester United snapping at their heels, had been on course to regain it. So the Rams' visit to Portman Road was hardly a significant affair as their last hope had vanished over Easter, when Leicester held them to a draw seven days earlier, to be followed by two midweek defeats.

The Rams had midfielder Jeff King, signed from Albion Rovers for £7,000 in April 1974, making his debut but one great name signing off in Derby's colours was Francis Lee, who was to retire after this, his 500th League appearance.

Rams midfielder Bruce Rioch always had an eye for goal and in this game he played as an out-and-out striker, but even he could not have imagined just how successful he would be in that role as the afternoon wore on.

The Rams began confidently, stringing together several moves with a series of lovely passes. It soon paid dividends, for Derby took the lead after only seven minutes when Todd, playing in midfield for the first time that season, worked his way down to the byline before pulling the ball back for Kevin Hector to tap it into the empty net.

The Rams increased their lead after 11 minutes when Todd and Lee again linked well down the middle before finding King, who appeared to fall over Mick Mills. The referee pointed to the spot and Rioch came forward to blast the ball into the bottom corner for his 13th League goal of the season.

Ipswich pulled a goal back only three minutes later when Burley threaded the ball into the area and Lambert kept a cool head to slide it past Graham Moseley.

In the next moment, however, the Rams had restored their two-goal lead when Rioch fastened on to a Newton pass and cooly drove the ball past the advancing Cooper.

Amazingly, Ipswich made it 3-2 — and the game was still less than 20 minutes old. A terrible back-pass from Webster set up Whymark who scored from close range.

The Rams might have scored a fourth goal straight away, but both Gemmill and Lee failed to get in their shots as the Ipswich defence struggled to regroup.

And two minutes before half-time, Hector missed a great chance when Hunter misjudged the bounce of the ball but the Rams striker, completely clear, headed straight to Cooper.

The second half opened in sensational fashion when an awkwardly bouncing ball hit Roy McFarland on the arm and Mr Walters gave the second penalty-kick of the game. This time, however, Trevor Whymark casually side-footed the ball against a post.

That would have put Ipswich back on level terms but after Hector blazed over the bar following some brilliant work from debutant King, the same player put the Rams 4-2 ahead. Hector calmly chested the ball down and rolled it wide of Cooper.

Still Ipswich might have dragged themselves back into contention but first Moseley, after a bad mistake, recovered well to snatch the ball from Lambert, then Bertschin's shot cannoned to safety off Webster, and finally McFarland twice blocked shots before limping off injured to be replaced by Davies.

The stage was now set for Francis Lee to sign off in style with goals in the 89th and 90th minute. It was a fitting way to end a glorious career and a fine ending to the Rams' season which saw them finish in fourth place.

If this, Lee's last season, had been marred by the ugly sending-off incident involving Leeds United's Norman Hunter, it certainly did nothing to overshadow his great contribution to football. The Rams would have fond memories of his bustling style which helped them win a second League championship. Indeed, there were many who felt that he could have gone on for at least another season in Derby's colours.

Ipswich Town: Cooper; Burley, Mills, Sharkey, Hunter, Peddelty, Osborne(John-

Francis Lee, signed off with two goals in the dying moments of his 500th and final League game.

son), Talbot, Bertschin, Whymark, Lambert.

Derby County: Moseley; Webster, Newton, Rioch, McFarland(Davies), Todd, Powell, Gemmill, Lee, Hector, King.

Referee: P.Walters (Bridgwater)   Att: 26,971.

Charlie George heads goalwards as the Rams swamp League of Ireland club, Finn Harps.

Irish Reel As The Rams Hit Twelve

Wednesday, 15 September 1976

Derby County 12   **Finn Harps 0**

DERBY County made history when they destroyed League of Ireland club Finn Harps in this UEFA Cup first-round first-leg game at the Baseball Ground. The 12-goal mauling saw the Rams pass their record highest score, set in the last century, and they were only one goal short of equalling the record for this particular competition.

It goes without saying that this was an utterly professional performance from a Derby County side who were heads, shoulders and the rest above their Irish part-time counterparts, although Bruce Rioch said afterwards: 'It doesn't matter they lost 12-0.

What matters is that they are in the competition and they turned up to compete.'

The Rams were 9-0 up at half-time, added three more in the second half and hit the woodwork on several other occasions. And Kevin Hector equalled Roger Davies' feat of the previous year by scoring five goals in a single match.

The goals came like this: After five minutes, Charlie George evaded a tackle before pushing the ball through to Hector, who shot into the far corner of Murray's goal.

Inside 11 minutes George again laid on a goal, this time working a lovely pass through for Rioch to slam the ball just inside the left-hand post with Murray again helpless to do anything about it.

Eight minutes later it was 3-0. Gemmill hit the post with a great shot from well outside the penalty area and Leighton James collected the rebound, cut in from the left and saw his shot deflected in.

In the 21st minute, Hector and Gemmill

Kevin Hector scores one of his five goals against the Irish club to propel himself into the record books.

combined before Hector chested down Rioch's cross and jabbed the ball home.

Two minutes later it was 5-0. Gemmill robbed Stephenson of Murray's throw and played a square pass to George who had all the time in the world to hammer the ball home.

Before the half-hour mark the Rams had seven goals in the bag. First George headed in James' centre off the bar, following up to nod in the ball in again, just to make sure. Then Gemmill was again involved before James curled a shot past Murray.

In the 36th minute, Hector made it 8-0 when James cut out a slack back-pass and the Rams striker got the ball in the net from the tightest of angles.

Five minutes before the break, Murray was pulled up for taking too many steps and when Gemmill tapped the free-kick to George, his shot bounced off the goalkeeper's chest before Hector ran in his fourth goal of the evening.

Ten minutes into the second half, Hector scored his fifth and put the Rams into double-figures. George, Rioch and Gemmill all had a hand in the goal before Hector finished it off.

It was 11-0 after 71 minutes when Jeff King came through, took a return pass from Hector and then crossed for James to complete his hat-trick.

The fun ended in the 77th minute when Tony Macken, enjoying himself immensely against his fellow Irishmen, found Gemmill from inside his own penalty area. The little Scot sent George running through he and walloped home Derby's 12th and last.

In the *Derby Evening Telegraph*, Gerald Mortimer said: 'The Rams were supremely professional, utterly ruthless. Dave Mackay spent Monday afternoon talking to his first-team players and trying to make sure that they approached this week's games in the right frame of mind.

'What he saw at the Baseball Ground last night cheered him immensely.

George has all the time in the world to score Derby's fifth. They went on to collect a round dozen.

'The easy thing is to say that Finn Harps were hopeless and that Derby did no more than was necessary.

'Yet, 24 hours earlier, I watched Liverpool struggle to beat Crusaders of Belfast, a team of similar standard, 2-0 in the European Cup. Crusaders might have defended more intelligently than Harps, but they were no more skilful.'

Said Dave Mackay: 'It's a tremendous feat to score 12 against any team. But the great thing is I have the players down in the dressing-room who are absolutely exhausted. We're 9-0 up at half-time, we've won 12-0 and they've given absolutely everything to keep up the pace until the final whistle.'

Derby won the second leg 4-1, but in the next round they went out to AEK Athens and Dave Mackay was on his way out of the Baseball Ground.

Derby County: Moseley; Thomas, Nish, Rioch, McFarland, Todd(King), Macken, Gemmill, Hector, George, James.
Finn Harps: Murray; McDowell, Hutton, T.O'Doherty, Sheridan, Stephenson, D.O'Doherty(Logan), Harkin, Bradley(Mahon), Healey, Carlyle.
Referee: A.Quedeville (Luxembourg)
Att: 13,353.

Bruce Rioch is first to the ball to steer home his second goal in the 8-2 thrashing of Spurs.

Superb Rams Peaked In Amazing Spell

Saturday, 16 October 1976

Derby County 8　　Tottenham Hotspur 2

'DERBY County treated their supporters to a quarter of an hour of dazzling virtuosity such as they will be lucky to see equalled in their watching lives. During that second-half spell, the Rams scored five goals and not only Tottenham Hotspur but the very fabric of the Baseball Ground reeled before a display of football genius.'

That was how Gerald Mortimer began his Monday evening report in the *Derby Evening Telegraph* after the Rams had demolished a poor Tottenham side to record Derby's highest score in domestic competition for 42 years.

At the end of the season Tottenham would finish bottom of the table to end a 26-year run in the First Division, but that should not in any way diminish the Rams' performance on an afternoon when they ended a run of eight League games without a win. Indeed, Derby's previous League game had been nothing short of a disaster when they lost 5-1 at Birmingham. So this victory against Spurs was not only remarkable — it was very welcome.

The game was a personal triumph for Bruce Rioch, who scored four of the Rams' goals, his shooting verging on violence. Charlie George, too, was absolutely magnificent, his passing quite breathtaking. Leighton James went past defenders as though they did not exist and Roy McFarland underlined that he was the best centre-half in England.

It was also pleasing to see Tony Macken, a signing from League of Ireland club, Waterford, in August 1974, stamping his authority on the game.

Charlie George attempts a lobbed shot during the demolition of Tottenham.

The Rams took the lead after only four minutes when George hammered in a cross-shot from James' centre. A minute later it was 2-0 after George left the Tottenham defence groping with a stunning 40-yard pass for Rioch to steam in and fire home.

After 25 minutes, Tottenham pulled a goal back through Steve Perryman's long-range effort, but inside ten minutes the Rams were back in front by two goals. McFarland's long free-kick bounced off George and there was Rioch to steer in his second goal.

Four minutes before half-time, Tottenham again clawed their way back, this time when Osgood scored from the penalty-spot after Macken had brought down Naylor.

It had been an encouraging first-half for the Rams, but in the second half they simply ran riot in an astonishing 15-minute spell, beginning in the 59th minute when Rod Thomas scored his first goal for Derby after the ball had rebounded to him off Conn.

Four minutes later came the most spectacular goal of the game when James went away after a quick throw by Powell. The Welsh winger drove in his centre and there was Rioch, launching himself to power a bullet-like header past the helpless Pat Jennings.

George made it 6-2 with a 68th minute penalty, after Perryman had tripped Gemmill, and a minute later Colin Todd scored the Rams' seventh after James set him up.

The breathtaking spell ended in the 74th minute when Rioch scored his fourth goal. James centred, George saw his shot half blocked and there was Rioch, following up to thump the ball into the roof of the Tottenham net.

Remarkably, it was to be Rioch's last goal for the Rams for a while because in December he was sold to Everton for £180,000, by new manager Colin Murphy. In November, Dave Mackay, troubled by rumours around town that the team lacked discipline, and dogged by unrest in the boardroom, asked the Derby directors for a vote of confidence and found instead that they looked awkwardly at their feet. He was the second manager to lose his

George makes it 6-2 from the penalty spot, sending Pat Jennings the wrong way.

job not long after steering the Rams to a League championship. Rioch, of course, would be back in Derby's colours before long.

After this defeat — their first-ever eight-goal drubbing — the Tottenham players were kept in their dressing-room as manager Keith Burkinshaw conducted an 80-minute post mortem on what had gone wrong. For the Rams it was their biggest domestic win in 42 years, since they hammered nine goals past West Brom in December 1934.

Of course, a month before beating Spurs, the Rams had established a club record with 12 goals against Finn Harps in the UEFA Cup. Amidst all the turmoil at the Baseball Ground there were still some exciting times on the pitch.

Derby County: Moseley; Thomas, Nish, Macken, McFarland, Todd, Powell, Gemmill, Rioch, George, James.
Tottenham Hotspur: Jennings; Naylor, Osgood, Hoddle, Young, Pratt, Conn, Perryman, Moores, Jones, Taylor.
Referee: C.L.Newsome (Broseley, Salop)
Att: 24,216.

Decimated Derby Routed Title Chasing City

Saturday, 30 April 1977

Derby County 4   Manchester City 0

WHEN Manchester City arrived at the Baseball Ground on the last day of April 1977, they had just won three successive League games and were right back in contention for the First Division title. The Rams, on the other hand, had taken only three points from their previous five games, were in danger of going down and, because of injury, fielded only one recognised striker, albeit the great Kevin Hector.

City, then, could have been forgiven for feeling confident that their title challenge would still be on the roll after their trip to Derby, but somehow the Rams conjured up an exhilarating display to take both points as City lost their heads — they had four men cautioned and Kidd sent off — and there was even a moment of high farce when referee John Yates, in his last First Division game before retiring, 'lost' a penalty spot in the Baseball Ground mud.

Although Colin Boulton returned in the Rams' goal after missing one game with a thumb injury, Derby were without Leighton James, Charlie George and Derek Hales, all on the injured list. So manager Colin Murphy shuffled his pack: Peter Daniel played in the back four, Colin Todd went into midfield and Gerry Daly played as a spare man between the midfield and strikers Hector and Archie Gemmill.

It was Gemmill who proved to be the star of the show with a brilliant performance, his display as a front runner underlining what a magnificent footballer he was. Indeed, the whole Rams showing made one wonder just how they had managed to get themselves into

Archie Gemmill gives Derby the lead over Manchester City with his first goal of the season.

trouble in what the *Derby Evening Telegraph's* Gerald Mortimer called 'this bungled season'.

The Rams battled for every ball, won most of them and dominated the first half so much that Boulton was hardly bothered at all.

Early in the second half, though, he had to make a brilliant save from Doyle and then react quickly to beat out a header from Kidd.

Those saves kept Derby in the game and after 67 minutes they took the lead to signal the start of a remarkable spell. Hector and Daly exchanged passes and then it was left to Gemmill to score his first goal of the season, his effort going in off a post.

Within five minutes the Rams were 2-0 ahead and this time it was the turn of Peter Daniel to score. Steve Powell headed Gemmill's corner back into the area and then David Langan slammed the ball across the face of the goal for the lunging Daniel to turn it over the line.

Hector, Gemmill and Kidd all went into

the referee's notebook, Kidd for kicking Hector from behind, and that brought about the Rams' third goal after 79 minutes. Gemmill lifted the free-kick into the goalmouth, Corrigan could not hold Daly's volley and there was Hector, first to the loose ball, to rattle in his shot.

Soon afterwards, Kidd was dismissed — not surprising since he had spent most of the period after the interval looking for trouble — and then came the Affair of the Missing Penalty Spot. Owen was adjudged to have brought down Gemmill — although it looked as if he was simply trying to get out of the way when Gemmill went tumbling — and when referee Yates placed the ball on where he thought the penalty spot ought to be, Corrigan complained so furiously that he went into the referee's notebook.

Eventually, Mr Yates called out Rams groundsman Bob Smith, armed with tape measure, bucket of white paint and brush. The spot duly restored, Daly kept his 100 per

Peter Daniel lunges in to turn David Langan's cross past Joe Corrigan.

Rams groundsman Bob Smith and City goalkeeper Joe Corrigan discuss the merits of Smith's paintbrush while referee John Yates measures up the penalty spot.

Gerry Daly fires home the eventual kick, although Corrigan guessed the right way.

cent record from penalties, even though Corrigan guessed the right way.

This was easily the most convincing win of Colin Murphy's short reign as manager of Derby County. As for City, they finished runners-up, one point behind Liverpool, and created a club record for a 42-match season by conceding only 34 goals, four of which had come in that short spell at the Baseball Ground.

Derby County: Boulton; Langan, Webster, Daly, McFarland, Todd, Powell, Gemmill, Daniel, Hector, Newton.
Manchester City: Corrigan; Clements, Donachie, Booth, Watson, Doyle, Barnes, Kidd, Royle(Power), Owen, Keegan.
Referee: K.J.Yates (Redditch)   Att: 29,127.

Charlie Is The Darling As Liverpool Are Beaten

Saturday, 29 March 1978

Derby County 4   **Liverpool 2**

CHARLIE George inspired the Rams back to top form against European champions, Liverpool, after the critics had slammed Derby for their dismal showing against Newcastle only four days earlier. Then, the Rams had been held to a 1-1 draw at the Baseball Ground and that had followed a goalless home draw against Forest and convincing defeats at Old Trafford and Ayresome Park. But against the Merseysiders, who were challenging for yet another First Division title, everything came right for Derby.

Indeed, at one stage the Rams were four goals up and only two late strikes for the Reds made the win appear less comprehensive than it was. The victory was important for Derby's confidence, because what with the FA Cup and some bad weather interrupting their fixtures, they had not won in the League since 2 January, when a George hat-trick gave them a 4-2 win over Coventry at the Baseball Ground.

Liverpool stood fifth in the table and were on their way to winning another European Cup Final. They were also one week away from a League Cup Final against Nottingham Forest. But it was Derby who took the lead after 27 minutes and the scorer was Andy Crawford, a former Baseball Ground apprentice who marked his League debut in splendid fashion.

The move which led to the goal began at the other end of the pitch with a Liverpool corner. George, back to support his defence, headed clear and then followed up to rob Emlyn Hughes and send Terry Curran away. Curran's cross was blocked but David Langan eventually got the ball over and Crawford bustled in to nip the ball over the line just inside a post.

George and Curran both shot over and then Steve Ogrizovic, making his League debut for Liverpool in place of the injured Ray Clemence who was missing his first League game in 232 matches, saved a shot from Don Masson.

A minute after the interval, Derby went 2-0 in front when Steve Powell hit in a low centre and George threw a dummy which sent the Liverpool defence into disarray. The ball found Daly, who curved a great shot into the back of Ogrizovic's net. It was the Irishman's goal all right, but George deserved most of the credit for a brilliant piece of individualism.

In the *Derby Evening Telegraph*, Gerald Mortimer told readers: 'By now George was running riot and after Case had been booked for a foul on Masson, scored a thrilling goal in the 64th minute. Daly headed on Middleton's long kick and George played a one-two with young Crawford. The ball came back to him just right and Charlie lashed a brilliant shot in off the near post. It was a vivid goal and crowd, directors and managers joined the celebrations.'

In a season of few goals at the Baseball Ground, the team with the second-best defensive record were all at sea as Derby swept forward again and six minutes later it was 4-0 when Steve Buckley crossed, George dummied again and Crawford helped it on for Daly to score.

Liverpool's so-called 'supersub', David Fairclough, scored a minute after replacing McDermott, and Kenny Dalglish, given plenty of space, hit a second right near the end, but the final scoreline did not reflect the Rams' superiority on the night. Indeed, in between the two Liverpool goals, Langan had seen his wickedly swerving shot hit the post.

The Rams had enjoyed a night to savour and even the unpopular John Middleton had a rare respite from the barracking he had been receiving from Derby supporters who could not forgive new boss Tommy Docherty for banishing Colin Boulton.

The fans were not the only ones who didn't seem to appreciate Docherty. Bruce Rioch, who had rejoined Derby from Everton, had a spectacular public row with the manager and was fined two weeks' wages and transfer-listed because of it, although bad feeling had been simmering for some time.

Gerry Daly (left) scored twice against Liverpool but Charlie George (right) was the real star of the night.

This victory was the last time Derby County beat Liverpool and in 12 League games since then, the Merseysiders have won 11 and scored 33 goals to the Rams' three.

Derby County: Middleton; Langan, Buckley, Powell, McFarland, Daniel, Curran, Daly, Masson, George, Crawford.
Liverpool: Orgrizovic; Neal, Smith, Hansen, Kennedy, Hughes, Dalglish, McDermott (Fairclough), Heighway, Souness, Case.
Referee: A.F.Jenkins (Scunthorpe)
                                    Att: 23,413.

Going Down — But Kings For The Day

Saturday, 24 November 1979

Derby County 4   Nottingham Forest 1

BETWEEN 21 April and 4 September 1979, Derby County played a total of 854 minutes' League and League Cup football without scoring a goal. Steve Buckley's 23rd-minute goal against Arsenal towards the end of the 1978-79 season was followed by three goalless games and then a further five at the beginning of 1979-80 before Andy Crawford scored in the 67th minute of a League Cup tie at Middlesbrough.

The writing, then, was on the wall and as the season unfolded, it was clear that the Rams would struggle to retain their place in the First Division. Indeed, it was a place which they ultimately lost, finishing 21st to

go down with Bolton Wanderers and Bristol City.

Some 16 miles up the road at Nottingham, meanwhile, Brian Clough's Forest were riding high as European champions, a title they were to retain the following year, and they also had the League Cup. So when Forest arrived at the Baseball Ground for the fiercest of East Midlands derby fixtures, the Rams were on a low, their biggest rivals on an all-time high.

Rams supporters had suffered plenty in the previous four years, the glory days of the Clough-Taylor regime, whilst not so far away, seeming light years from the days of background turmoil and poor results that everyone at the Baseball Ground was now enduring. No wonder, then, that this result against Forest still shines like a beacon in a fog of misery.

The *Derby Evening Telegraph's* Gerald Mortimer takes up the story: 'All the pre-match caution about Derby's prospects for this meeting with their local rivals was swept

Derby defend a Forest corner. Left to right are John Duncan, Larry Lloyd, Dave Needham and Steve Emery.

The Rams celebrate Daly's first goal. Left to right are David Webb, Keith Osgood, Roger Davies, Daly and Barry Powell.

away in a delerious burst of goals in the first half.

'Three times in the space of four minutes, the world's best goalkeeper was left to pick the ball out of the net after Derby had taken ruthless advantage of defensive errors.'

Forest did most of the early attacking but in the 13th minute, the Rams took the lead when Peter Shilton, under no great pressure, dropped a Buckley cross and Gerry Daly, back after a long absence because of injury, was ready to slam the ball into the net.

It was a dream start for the Rams and there was even better to follow as Forest's rearguard just fell apart. Almost from the restart, Daly sent a perfect curved pass to Langan and then Davies did well to get in a cross from the right. Clark hit it back across goal, Langan put in another cross and when Shilton could only palm the ball on, John Duncan headed the ball into the net from an angle.

After 17 minutes it was 3-0 when Gray messed up a back-pass and Steve Emery, in

only his 11th First Division appearance, looked like a veteran as he snapped up the chance to steer the ball wide of Shilton and over the line.

By now, the majority of the near-28,000 crowd were in raptures. The Rams had turned the game right on its head. If Forest had stormed into a 3-0 lead, then no-one would have been surprised. But Derby? It took some believing.

One factor had to be taken into account, however. Even though Forest were now staring their third successive defeat in the face, there were still 73 minutes to play and whatever the Rams did, they dared not relax. Sure enough, in the first 20 minutes after the interval Forest looked dangerous and when John Robertson pulled back a goal from the penalty spot after Daly brought down Mills, there were a few shivers.

But the Rams got back into it and after Duncan had seen his header saved by Shilton, after a stunning pass by Clark had set it up,

John Robertson, later to join Derby, pulls back a goal from the penalty spot.

John Duncan, scorer of two goals in the memorable win over Nottingham Forest, tussles with Dave Needham. The other Forest player is Frank Gray.

the centre-forward scored Derby's fourth goal in the 77th minute. After a foul by Needham, Buckley curled in another free-kick and Duncan beat Shilton with a brilliant diving header.

'Duncan has never played better since his move from Tottenham,' wrote Gerald Mortimer. 'He took his goals in masterly fashion and, like Davies, worked so hard to pull the Forest defence around and keep the ball moving.'

This was certainly a swan song for the Rams. They had to wait another 13 matches before winning again — a 2-1 victory over Spurs on 23 February — and by then they were deep in touble and were relegated despite remaining unbeaten at home from 2 February.

None of the scorers against Forest found the net again that season. Indeed, both Daly and Duncan, beset by injuries, never scored a League goal for the Rams again.

Derby County: McKellar; Langan, Buckley, Daly(Emson), Webb, Osgood, Emery, B.Powell, Duncan, Davies, Clark.
Nottingham Forest: Shilton; Anderson, Gray, McGovern, Lloyd, Needham, O'Neill, Mills, Birtles, Francis, Robertson.
Referee: M.G.Peck (Doncaster)   Att: 27,729.

Pre-match presentation to Kevin Hector, who retired after the win over Watford.

Survival — And The End Of A Great Career

Saturday, 15 May 1982

Derby County 3   Watford 2

THEY came to see if Derby County could gain a point to ensure the Rams survival in the Second Division. And they came to witness the end of a truly great career as one of the biggest names in the club's history bowed out after a record number of appearances and a magnicent haul of goals.

They saw both and more, for not only did the Rams win this vital last game of the season against already-promoted Watford, they did it with a goal scored by Kevin Hector in his 589th senior appearance for Derby County. Only a superstar could have signed off in such

Kevin Wilson hits his penalty straight at Steve Sherwood so it is still 0-0.

memorable fashion. And Kevin Hector was certainly that.

It was also Hector's 201st goal for the club in all senior competitions and there had been many memorable ones along the way. But as the player said afterwards: "This has made sure we stayed up, so it has to rank as the most important."

The Rams went into the match knowing that salvation, if it were at hand, lay firmly with themselves. They dared not rely on other results and in the end, when it was learned that Shrewsbury had drawn at Leicester and Cardiff had triumphed at Grimsby, the Rams certainly needed something from their game against Graham Taylor's team.

Derby certainly went to their task with some handicaps. Frank Sheridan was missing, suspended for the second time that season, and also sidelined through injury were Charlie George, Steve Powell and Barry Powell. Like Hector, George had returned for a second spell with the Rams, although both

players found themselves in conditions far removed from their earlier, highly successful days at the Baseball Ground.

Nerves, already taut, were stretched even further when the Rams missed an early penalty. Kevin Wilson outpaced Terry as they ran after a long pass from Paul Emson. Sherwood blocked the shot but when Bolton gave Hill a nudge in the back, referee George Tyson pointed to the spot. Wilson must have wanted the ground to open up and swallow him when he hammered the spot-kick straight at the goalkeeper. His miss could have consigned the Rams to Division Three, even though there was still plenty to play for.

Wilson would have felt better in the 39th minute when the Rams took the lead. Swindlehurst brought the ball forward down the right and then played it inside for Steve Buckley to bend a magnificent shot into the far corner of the net.

Buckley, a forward when he was playing in local non-League football, had scored some

Watford goalkeeper Steve Sherwood surveys the damage after Steve Buckley's spectacular effort.

spectacular goals from full-back for the Rams. He said afterwards: "This was the best and certainly the most important."

The Rams were in front but there was still plenty of high drama to come and when Nigel Callaghan — later to join Derby — was tripped, Luther Blissett sent Yakka Banovic the wrong way from the spot.

Four minutes later, Skivington was pulled up some eight yards outside the penalty area and then booked for disputing the decision. From the free-kick, Bolton saw an opening and hammered his shot through a badly positioned defensive wall and into the net. Derby were now 2-1 adrift and relegation loomed large.

Rams manager John Newman, who had stepped up to succeed Colin Addison the previous January, said afterwards: "I turned to Charlie George and told him that if we didn't score within five minutes of that goal, we'd be dead."

In fact, it took four minutes for the Rams to draw level again. Emson went off on a long run before switching the ball back inside to Wilson. He turned and shot, and although the ball deflected off Rostron, it still finished up in the back of the net. Wilson claimed the goal, the club backed him up and he ended the season as the Rams' leading scorer with nine League goals.

The Rams now looked safe but Wilson was not finished and a neat turn and a good centre left Kevin Hector to rise and steer a header past Sherwood for the winning goal. What a wonderful way it was to finish such a glorious career. Even though Banovic was called upon to make two fine saves from Blissett, it was Hector's goal which remained the indelible image of the afternoon.

Derby County: Banovic; Barton, Buckley, Attley, Skivington, McAlle, Hector, Wilson, Hill, Swindlehurst, Emson.
Watford: Sherwood; Rice, Rostron, Taylor, Terry, Bolton, Callaghan, Blissett, Armstrong, Lohman(Johnson), Barnes.
Referee: G.M.Tyson (Sunderland)

Att: 14,946.

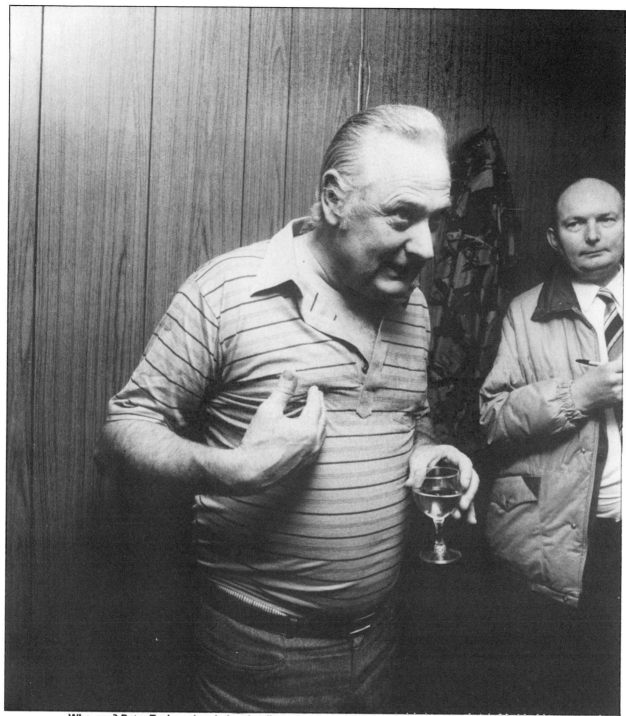

Who, me? Peter Taylor, glass in hand, talks to the Press after the Rams' great Cup win over Forest.

An Afternoon To Savour As Forest Are Knocked Out

Saturday, 8 January 1983

Derby County 2   Nottingham Forest 0

TWO months into the 1982-83 season, things looked so bleak at the Baseball Ground.

Attendances had dropped below 10,000, relegation was a very real prospect. Then came the arrival of new chairman Mike Watterson, the Chesterfield-based snooker millionaire, and the return of Peter Taylor as manager.

But even their appearance didn't stem the flow of bad results. Indeed, after winning at home to Chelsea on 8 September, the Rams had to wait until 4 December for their next League win. And by the time the third round

Archie Gemmill hits his free-kick around the Forest defensive wall to set up a sensational victory.

Steve Sutton cannot get his fingertips to Gemmill's effort and the Rams are on the way.

of the FA Cup came round in this, the second season of three points for a League win, Derby had taken only 19 points from 23 matches and were 22nd in the Second Division.

The Cup draw paired the Rams with their fiercest rivals, Nottingham Forest, still managed by Brian Clough and still riding high in the First Division, albeit with their greatest glory days just behind them. Inevitably, the media billed the tie as 'Clough v Taylor', although both men did their best to play that down. "It's just another game," said Taylor, but Derby fans knew different.

The build-up ensured an electric atmos-phere from a full-house and with a police helicopter circling overhead to moniter the traffic and any problems from a potentially volatile clash, almost 29,000 fans swarmed towards Baseball Ground on this January Saturday

Clough sprung a surprise by leaving out former Rams favourite Colin Todd, but Derby included Archie Gemmill, who had starred with Todd at Derby, then gone on to further successes with Forest before returning to the Baseball Ground via Birmingham and Wigan. A 'current' Forest player in the Rams ranks was midfielder Gary Mills, on loan from

Andy Hill knocks Mick Brolly's through ball past Sutton and the game is in the bag for Derby County.

NASL club Seattle Sounders but still a Forest player under the complicated procedure involving the two competitions. Forest included two players, Steve Sutton and John Robertson, who would later sign for Derby.

Spennymoor referee George Courtney got the game under way and in an atmosphere that bubbled and crackled, the Rams gave as good as they got and certainly did not look outclassed during the first 45 minutes.

Gemmill soon stamped his authority and the stark truth was that Forest did not have a midfield player in his class. The Rams' central defenders, George Foster and John McAlle, had suffered plenty of criticism that season, but neither put a foot wrong and Mills was also a revelation in shutting out John Robertson, thus denying Birtles and Wallace the service they wanted.

Up front, the Rams' two young strikers, Kevin Wilson and Andy Hill, created plenty of problems for the Forest defence, although neither would have been included if Bobby Davison and John Richards had not been cup-tied.

In the second half, the Rams still looked value for money and after 63 minutes they took the lead in spectacular fashion. Wilson grazed a post with a volley and then big Willie Young brought him down outside the penalty area. Swindlehurst ran over the ball and it was left for Gemmill to curl a beautiful free-kick over the wall and into the net. It was a magnificent goal and fitting that it should be scored by Gemmill, the man of the match who left the field to a standing ovation after damaging a hamstring.

Near the end, Derby made certain when Mick Brolly broke down the right before releasing the ball at just the right moment for Hill to steer it past Sutton. It, too, was a brilliantly-taken goal, the young Rams striker allowing Sutton to advance before slipping the ball into the net.

It was a victory which left Rams supporters smiling for the whole of the next week and the Cup run extended to another home win, over Chelsea, before Manchester United won 1-0 at the Baseball Ground in the fifth round.

A week after their victory over Forest, the Rams lost at Carlisle but then embarked upon a remarkable 15-match unbeaten run which saw them finish 13th, a position which had seemed utterly out of their grasp only a few weeks earlier. The season ended with a controversial match against Fulham, when a crowd invasion meant that the last 78 seconds could not be played. The Rams were winning 1-0 and Fulham, who might have been promoted had they won, appealed in vain. After the run-in to the 1982-83 season, it seemed that Peter Taylor had turned the situation around. Alas, he had not and eventually into the Baseball Ground came a man called Arthur Cox.

Derby County: Cherry; Barton, Attley, Gemmill(Dalziel), Foster, McAlle, Brolly, Wilson, Hill, Swindlehurst, Mills.
Nottingham Forest: Sutton; Swain, Bowyer, Gunn, Young, Walsh, Proctor, Wallace, Birtles, Hodge, Robertson(Davenport).
Referee: G.Courtney (Spennymoor)

Att: 28,494.

Garner's Hat-Trick Makes History

Saturday, 7 April 1984

Derby County 3   Crystal Palace 0

THE second half of the 1983-84 season must go down as the most traumatic period in Derby County's history. On one day alone in mid-March, the Rams were knocked out of the FA Cup by Third Division Plymouth, when an error by goalkeeper Steve Cherry helped deny bankrupt Derby a money-spinning semi-final appearance; and Robert Maxwell temporarily withdrew his support as the club faced a winding-up order. Moreover, Derby looked doomed to relegation.

Later events proved that Maxwell's involvement with Derby County had not been quite as beneficial as many had hoped, but the fact remained that his appearance in 1984 almost certainly saved the club from going to the wall. Eventually the Rams were saved — 'at one minute to midnight' as Stuart Webb put it — but results did not improve, manager Peter Taylor was sacked and former Rams star Roy McFarland, Taylor's assistant, was given charge until the end of the season.

His immediate task looked was clear enough — to keep Derby County up — but it looked impossible. McFarland had two years of his existing contract still to run but in reality he knew that he had nine games to turn around the Rams' fortunes. The deficit was enormous, the time too short, but McFarland set off for his first match in charge — a home to Crystal Palace — by telling the players: "I'm going to be greedy and ask you to play for me."

McFarland decided to try for a settled team in a bid to bring some stability to this season of great uncertainty. First, though, he brought in Andy Garner at centre-forward. Garner, barely 18, was a Derbyshire lad, born at Stonebroom, and had joined the Rams as an apprentice. He had made his senior debut in the excellent FA Cup fifth-round victory over Norwich City at the Baseball Ground only seven weeks earlier. Now McFarland preferred him to Kevin Wilson, who was left on the substitute's bench.

Palace were eight points ahead of the Rams, so victory would be vital if Derby were to close the gap on the clubs in front. But then the scenario was depressingly familiar to Rams fans, who for most of the season had seen their side locked in relegation battles that they just had to win.

Besides the inclusion of Garner, McFarland made other changes — "I was looking for a mix of young legs and old heads," he said — and another youngster given his chance was Steve Devine (19), a former Wolves apprentice. Chesterfield-born Graham Harbey, also 19, was recalled as the Rams set out on a mission impossible.

Palace were a poor side, but then plenty of mediocre teams had taken the spoils from the Baseball Ground that season. This time, though, it was different and after only 77 seconds the Rams went ahead and Garner was the scorer.

Archie Gemmill — restored to the team after being discarded by Peter Taylor with the words, "Archie, your legs have gone!" — won the ball and laid it off to Bobby Davison. His shot was off target, but as Palace goalkeeper George Wood followed it, Steve Buckley got the ball back into the danger zone and Garner had time to turn and tuck away his shot.

The goal settled Derby's nerves straight away and they began to dominate proceedings. After 30 minutes, Garner struck again. He evaded two tackles before giving the ball to Davison, whose cross was volleyed in by John Robertson. The shot would probably have gone wide but Garner reacted quickly to run in his second goal of the afternoon.

Eleven minutes into the second half, Garner became the youngest player to score a senior hat-trick for Derby County. And the goal was the pick of the bunch. The youngster accepted a quick throw on the right from Robertson and then turned brilliantly to leave the Palace defence foundering before he slid in his shot at the far post.

Garner completed an eventful afternoon by being booked for failing to retreat ten yards at a free-kick. It was a silly booking by referee

Andy Garner, probably the youngest player to score a senior hat-trick for the Rams, runs in his second goal against Palace.

Bobby Davison looks on as Garner scores another of his hat-trick goals.

Peter Willis, who did not have the best of matches.

Alas, the match did not herald the turna-round everyone hoped for. The Rams won another three games but it was not enough and they went down to the Third Division. Garner's historic hat-trick had not sparked a revival after all.

Derby County: Cherry; Burns, Buckley, Gemmill, Watson, Powell, Devine, Davison, Garner, Harbey(Wilson), Robertson.
Crystal Palace: Wood; Locke, Murphy, Cummins, Cannon, Gilbert, McCulloch, Evans(Barber), Hughton, Nicholas, Hilaire.
Referee: P.N.Willis (Meadowfield)
Att: 10,903.

Rams Hit Five As Cox's Team Takes Shape

Saturday, 29 December 1984

Swansea City 1   Derby County 5

DERBY County's first season of Third Division football for 27 years saw the Rams with a new manager in the shape of Arthur Cox, the former Chesterfield boss who had sensationally quit Newcastle United, the club he had just guided back to Division One. Roy McFarland had agreed to stay on as Cox's assistant and the pair set off in search of the blend that would bring about a revival in Derby County's fortunes.

Cox was soon busy, signing Rob Hindmarch from Sunderland, Eric Steele and Charlie Palmer from Watford, Paul Richardson from Nuneaton Borough, Kevin Taylor from Sheffield Wednesday, Floyd Streete from S C Cambur and Mickey Lewis from West Brom. Kevin Wilson, restored to the side, began the season well and scored 13 goals in 14 League and Milk Cup games before suffering a broken arm against Plymouth in October. Thereafter, the burden fell mainly on Bobby Davison and he responded magnificently to finish the season with 24 League goals, the best since Ray Straw's record-equalling 37 in 1956-57, Derby's last season in the old Third Division North.

By the end of the year, Arthur Cox's new-look team was taking shape and when the Rams visited Swansea City just after Christmas, the Welsh club were unfortunate to be the ones who met the full force of Cox's rampant Rams.

In the *Derby Evening Telegraph*, Gerald Mortimer said: 'Devastating finishing brought Derby County their most convincing

Bobby Davison (far right, dark shirt) chips the ball over Jimmy Rimmer's head for Derby's opener at Vetch Field – 'a goal to grace any stadium in the world.'.

Rimmer is beaten for a second time, this one from Kevin Wilson's looping header, his last goal for the Rams.

away win for more than eight years as they hammered five goals past Swansea City at a rain-sodden Vetch Field on Saturday.

'The clouds sat low over Swansea, rain belted down and the mud down the middle made running hard work.

'But the Rams had learned from their mistakes against Newport in similar conditions and ran riot in the last half-hour. After the disappointment at Gillingham on Boxing Day, Derby were back on course.'

Indeed, not since Francis Lee signed off with two goals in the Rams' six-goal win at Ipswich on the last day of the 1975-76 season had Derby achieved anything like this away from the Baseball Ground.

The Rams got under way after ten minutes when Davison accepted a through pass from Taylor, checked inside David Cole and then beat Jimmy Rimmer with a chip which, as Gerald Mortimer said, 'would have graced any stadium in the world.'

Swansea lost Pat McQuillan, who broke a leg in an accidental collision with Palmer, before Wilson, back after a ten-week lay-off, made it 2-0 after 35 minutes when he sent the ball looping past Rimmer with a glancing header from Garner's cross. It was Wilson's 14th goal of the season for the Rams — and his last for the club as he was transferred to Ipswich Town for £150,000 in January.

After 59 minutes, Swansea pulled a goal back when Palmer was adjudged to have fouled Dean Saunders. The man who was to become such a star at Derby missed with his first kick, but Streete had foolishly strayed into the area and Saunders made no mistake with his second chance.

Davison and Wilson were causing the Swansea defence plenty of headaches and after Davison was brought down by Cole, Steve Buckley curved home a high-class free-kick for the second time in four days to restore the Rams' two-goal advantage

Andy Garner rams the ball home at the second attempt in appalling conditions at Swansea. The rain poured down and heavy mud made good football almost impossible, yet the Rams ran riot in the last half-hour.

Wilson set up the fourth after 73 minutes, worrying Rimmer who could not then prevent Garner from ramming the ball home at the second attempt. Then Rimmer saved from Wilson and Davison before Palmer swept home the Rams fifth with nine minutes remaining, after the 'keeper had collided with Davison.

Asked Gerald Mortimer: 'Derby left the most troubled year in their history with fine flourish. Dare we hope for better days ahead?'

Some significant signings, financed by the sale of Kevin Wilson, meant that we could.

Swansea City: Rimmer; Marustik, McQuillan(Evans), Cole, Stevenson, D.Lewis, Saunders, P.Williams, Mardenborough, Richards, Pascoe.
Derby County: Steele; Palmer, Buckley, Richardson, Streete, Pratley, K.Taylor, Wilson, Davison(Biggins), M.Lewis, Garner.
Referee: D.A.Hedges (Oxford)   Att: 5,187.

Imps Swallowed Up In Rams Goal Feast

Saturday, 9 November 1985

Derby County 7   Lincoln City 0

BEFORE the 1985-86 season began, Rams manager Arthur Cox further strengthened his squad with the signings of Mark Wallington (from Leicester for £25,000), Ross MacLaren (Shrewsbury, £67,000), Jeff Chandler (Bolton, £38,000) and Steve McLaren (Hull, £70,000). They joined three major signings in Trevor Christie, who had recently helped Notts County into Division One, Gary Micklewhite, from First Division Queen's Park Rangers for £80,000, and Welsh Under-23 international Geraint Williams, from Bristol Rovers for £40,000.

Of the major players when Cox arrived, only Buckley, Davison, Blades, Harbey and Pratley remained. Steve Powell was to stay another season but he had played his last first-team game.

The Rams began their second season in Division Three in fine style, losing only three League games out of their first 25. Everyone was making a contribution and when Lincoln City visited the Baseball Ground in early November, they found the Rams in devastating form. Derby ran in seven goals without reply, five different players got on the scoresheet and, if we hadn't known it before, the Rams were confirmed as one of the major powers in the Third Division.

Watching from the stand was former England player John Gregory, signed from

Jeff Chandler, collecting a pass from Geraint Williams, cut inside before swerving in this shot to put Derby ahead.

Queen's Park Rangers for £100,000, his transfer finalised that very day. Gregory was about to join up again with his former Loftus Road teammate Gary Micklewhite. But for the moment he could only sit and admire.

Lincoln were without five regulars through injury but they held their own until just before half-time. Soon afterwards, the points were in the bag for Derby as they steamed into a 4-0 lead.

Chandler had put the Rams ahead after 13 minutes with a classy goal. The Irish international took an excellent crossfield pass from Geraint Williams and jinked inside to curve a magnificent shot into the top corner of Judge's net.

Chandler almost scored a repeat of that goal but this time his effort hit a post and rebounded awkwardly to Micklewhite, so as the interval approached there was the feeling that the Rams had not yet done nearly enough to consider the points theirs. All that was to change, however, in the next few minutes.

Two minutes before half-time, Derby went

Bobby Davison falls after sending Chandler's cross into the Lincoln net for Derby's second.

Gary Micklewhite steers the ball past Judge for Derby's third goal after 48 minutes.

Micklewhite (7) hits the Rams' sixth goal after a perfect centre from Chandler.

two goals ahead and this time Chandler was the architect. His first centre was scrambled away but came back to him via Micklewhite. The Irishman sent in a low cross and Bobby Davison headed home his 12th goal of the season.

Three minutes after half-time, the Rams were 3-0 ahead. Davison headed on Chandler's centre, Christie headed it down and there was Micklewhite to place his shot well clear of Judge, who was on loan from Oxford United for two games.

Two minutes later, the unselfish Christie helped set up a fourth goal, laying back Ross MacLaren's free-kick to the same player. From MacLaren's cross, Rob Hindmarch steered home a powerful header.

After 62 minutes it was Hindmarch again to make it 5-0, lunging in after Christie had headed down a free-kick. In 115 League games for Sunderland, Hindmarch had managed only two goals. Now he had scored four in

his last two games for the Rams, having netted twice in a 3-3 draw at Brentford three days earlier.

After 73 minutes, Micklewhite struck Derby's sixth, from a perfect low centre from Chandler, and with five minutes remaining, Garner tucked away a header from Chandler's cross after Micklewhite had begun the move.

Chandler had enjoyed a brilliant game, the Rams were riding high — and there was still John Gregory to come.

Derby County: Wallington; Blades, Buckley, Williams, Hindmarch, MacLaren, Micklewhite, Christie, Davison(Harbey), Garner, Chandler.
Lincoln City: Judge; McNeill, McCarrick (Cooper), Redfearn, Strodder, G.Richards, Measham, Turner, Latchford, Ward, McGinley.
Referee: J.Lovatt (Crewe)   Att: 10,560.

Cheers! The Rams have just beaten Sheffield United in an FA Cup thriller at Bramall Lane.

Rams Blunt The Blades In FA Cup Thriller

Saturday, 25 January 1986

Sheffield United 0   Derby County 1

DERBY County took a day off from their promotion battle to continue a promising FA Cup run with this fine victory over troubled Second Division club Sheffield United at a frosty Bramall Lane. Some 9,000 Rams supporters urged on their side, in contrast to the barracking that Blades manager Ian Porterfield and chairman Reg Brearley received from disgruntled home supporters.

The Rams' Cup trail began with a 5-1 home romp over Fourth Division Crewe before non-

League Telford United paid their second visit to Derby in three seasons and were beaten 6-1. Then came a replay win over fellow Third Division side Gillingham before the Rams were drawn at Sheffield.

With a Cup run developing and with bad weather interrupting their programme, the Rams had some catching up to do in their League fixtures, but on this day thoughts of a return to the Second Division were temporarily put aside.

Only three days earlier, the Rams had gone down 2-0 to Gillingham in a Freight/Rover Trophy preliminary round match before less than 4,000 fans at the Baseball Ground. Now, the contrast could not have been greater as they were roared on by twice as many on an opponent's ground.

Although the day was sunny, the pitch was rock-hard — at neighbouring Hillsborough,

Rob Hindmarch slides in to score the only goal of the game at Bramall Lane past the diving John Burridge.

in the match between Wednesday and Orient, the toss for ends was carried out in the dressing-room because of the state of the pitch! — and tackling, passing, even standing up, proved difficult manouevres.

The Rams soon got to grips with the conditions, however, and adapted better than United, although the home side gave them an early shock when Ray Lewington took advantage of a slack clearance to hammer the ball into the net. Thankfully, the linesman's flag was raised for offside against either Peter Withe or Keith Edwards.

Then Mark Wallington, although on the wrong foot, managed to make a fine save from Edwards, but overall Derby were taking the game to United and Andy Garner, who had suffered a nightmare game against Gillingham, saw a shot and then a header go close.

The conditions probably robbed the Rams when a low cross from Jeff Chandler flew across the face of the United goal, but neither Garner nor John Gregory could adjust their footing to take advantage.

After 34 minutes, however, the Rams took the lead. Peter Withe, who had found his way into the referee's notebook after only 12 minutes, was again penalised and the Rams then unveiled a neat free-kick routine worked out on the Raynesway training ground. There was a knot of three Derby players around the ball which finished up with Gregory. The former England player sent over a teasing centre and Rob Hindmarch, over by the far post, came in to steer the ball past John Burridge.

It proved to be the only goal of the game and made Hindmarch a Cup hero, for the weekend at least, but just as important was the way he kept a tight reign of Withe. Indeed, the former England centre-forward was hardly given a kick all afternoon.

After Hindmarch's goal, the Rams never looked like being beaten and they might have had more, particularly when Trevor Christie beat Burridge with a header which came back off the crossbar with the United 'keeper well beaten. Jeff Chandler had laid on the cross for that chance and the Republic of Ireland international enjoyed his best game for several weeks.

Geraint Williams, too, was back to his best — he was cautioned near the end, a few moments after United's Foley had gone into the book — and John Gregory was superb in midfield, settling things down and largely running the Rams' show.

In the later stages, when attacker Mel Eves replaced former England defender Phil Thompson, they were called upon to defend and were equal to that task, too. Ross

John Gregory, superb in midfield as the Rams beat Sheffield United to score an FA Cup shock.

MacLaren was magnificent, Paul Blades and Steve Buckley so confident on a difficult surface.

It was a great day for Derby County and the club's supporters, who looked forward to the next round with some relish. Coincidentally, it took them back to Sheffield and Hillsborough via a Baseball Ground game that was postponed several times. In the second game the Owls went through 2-0 and Derby's thoughts now concentrated on promotion.

Sheffield United: Burridge; P.Smith, Kenworthy, Thompson(Eves), Stancliffe, McNaught, Morris, Edwards, Withe, Lewington, Foley.
Derby County: Wallington; Blades, Buckley, Williams, Hindmarch, MacLaren, Micklewhite, Christie, Garner, Gregory, Chandler.
Referee: T.Fitzharris (Bolton)   Att: 22,658.

Rams players and management staff pictured in 1986 after they had won back their place in the Second Division.

The End Of A Nightmare

Friday, 9 May 1986

Derby County 2　　　Rotherham United 1

VICTORY at Swansea, by three goals to nil, on the first Tuesday of May 1986, left Derby County with a clear path back to the Second Division. With two games to play, the Rams needed two points to be sure. They won them in the first of those games, at home to Rotherham United when a Friday night crowd of 21,036 was the best Third Division attendance of the season.

Those fans witnessed the end of a nightmare. Just over two years earlier, Derby County, doomed to relegation, had been on the verge of going out of business altogether. And even before then, the Baseball Ground had become a depressing place, the glorious European nights under Brian Clough, the great domestic victories over the likes of Liverpool, Spurs, Leeds, Manchester United and Arsenal seeming so long ago.

Now the club had been saved, Arthur Cox had arrested the decline and was bringing the Rams back.

That Rotherham had a poor record was somewhat academic, for they came determined to make Derby fight every inch of the way, as, indeed, many teams had played above themselves at the Baseball Ground that season.

And for 77 minutes, the Millers achieved a great deal, soaking up punishment as the Rams battered away at them, with Kevan Smith and Mike Pickering winning many balls in the air. During that time, however, Derby might still have taken the lead: Gary Micklewhite went through the middle and then tried a centre when he looked well-placed to shoot; and at the start of the second half, Chandler was chasing a badly-hit back-pass when he was felled. Calls for a penalty were turned down, but it looked a legitmate claim.

Rotherham were certainly giving nothing away at the back and they had John Dungworth and Mike Gooding booked, the latter for a scything tackle on Trevor Christie.

With 13 minutes remaining and tension high, Christie had a hand in the goal which

Trevor Christie scores from the penalty spot to give Derby victory over Rotherham and a place in Division Two.

sents hearts racing and hopes soaring. Ross MacLaren hit a superb clearance and Christie dummied over the ball. Twenty-one-year-old Phil Gee, a signing from Gresley Rovers, had come on for the injured Geraint Williams after 36 minutes. Gee took the ball in his stride and was away. He looked as if he might have been offside, but the flag stayed down and Gee raced on before beating O'Hanlon for his first senior goal for the club.

Two minutes later, however, Rotherham were level. A bad pass by Steve Buckley left Rob Hindmarch with only two options — to allow Gooding through or bring him down. Hindmarch chose the latter course and after the Rams defender had gone into the referee's book, Mark Wallington failed to assert himself over Andy Barnsley's free-kick and Trusson walloped home the loose ball.

There were only six minutes left when Derby regained the lead and with it their place in the Second Division. Bobby Davison, who had taken over Williams' place on the right of midfield after the Welshman had gone off with an ankle injury, was tripped on the edge of the penalty area by Dungworth. The Rotherham player had already been booked, so off he went before MacLaren hammered in a shot from the free-kick which was tapped to him.

The ball was on its way to Kelham O'Hanlon in the Rotherham goal when Chandler was elbowed in the face by Dean Emerson and for the fifth time in four games, Derby were awarded a penalty.

Earlier in the season, Christie, Buckley, Chandler and MacLaren had all missed from the spot, but now Christie, enjoying one of his best games for the Rams, was happy to step up. He cracked his shot to O'Hanlon's right, the ball bulged the back of the net and the release of tension was almost tangible.

Still there was time for a few thousand hearts to flutter as Chandler got in a mess when trying to pass back and then in injury time, Gregory appeared to trip Alan Birch in the penalty area but the referee ignored Rotherham's appeals.

The Rams had one match to play, at Darlington the following Monday when victory would give Derby a club record 11 away wins in a season and ensure that they finished runners-up to champions Reading. The Quakers spoiled the party by winning 2-1, but Derby County, finishing third, were on the way back.

Derby County: Wallington; Palmer, Buckley, Williams(Gee), Hindmarch, MacLaren, Micklewhite, Christie, Davison, Gregory, Chandler.
Rotherham United: O'Hanlon; Barnsley, Dungworth, Gooding, Smith, Pickering, Birch, Emerson, Trusson, Simmons, Pugh.
Referee: T.Fitzharris (Bolton)   Att: 21,036.

Back in the big time. Everyone seems to have come out to celebrate the Rams' return to Division One.

A Dream Fulfilled — Back To The First

Saturday, 2 May 1987

Derby County 2   Leeds United 1

ON 18 March 1987, Derby County beat Blackburn Rovers 3-2 at the Baseball Ground to move to the top of the Second Division, where they remained for the rest of the season. They were crowned champions after beating Plymouth Argyle 4-2 on the very last day of a wonderfully entertaining campaign, but the vital result had come seven days earlier, when this victory over Leeds United confirmed promotion. The title was simply the icing on the cake.

Once again, Arthur Cox had strengthened his squad. This time his signings included two full-backs, Mel Sage from Gillingham for £60,000, and Michael Forsyth, who had been signed from West Brom the previous March. Mark Lillis came from Manchester City for £200,000 (with Trevor Christie, valued at £100,000, going to Maine Road as part of that deal), and Steve Cross from Shrewsbury for £60,000.

And in January, Cox brought Watford winger Nigel Callaghan to the Baseball Ground for £140,000.

But the real star of the season had cost only £5,000. Phil Gee, one time painter and decorator from the Walsall area, came into the Rams side in early September after Lillis was injured. He ended the season with 15 League goals, second only to Bobby Davison who had 19, and was one of the darlings of the Baseball Ground crowd as it dawned that promotion was a real possibility.

The Rams took the field against Leeds knowing that a draw would ensure their re-

Phil Gee runs through to crack in a low shot which gave Derby the lead over Leeds United.

appearance in the First Division. They did better than that and it was sweet that the triumph should come against Leeds, their one-time bitter enemies from the 1970s.

For the first 45 minutes the Rams utterly dominated Leeds, who indulged in plenty of passing back to goalkeeper Mervyn Day. Nigel Callaghan, enjoying his best game since moving from Vicarage Road, had the measure of Neil Aspin and Gee and Davison were giving Ashurst and Ormsby a torrid afternoon.

After 17 minutes, the influential John Gregory fed Gee and off he went, driving straight for goal with David Rennie flagging in his wake. Day left his near post exposed and Gee needed no second bidding to drill his shot low into that corner of the net.

Nine minutes later, Davison added a second and the Rams' place in Division One was booked. Callaghan, cutting inside, found Gary Micklewhite on the right. His centre teased Day into hesitating but Davison, back after injuring knee ligaments, did not bother to wait, instead sending a glancing header into the net.

Six minutes into the second half, Leeds pulled a goal back when Ashurst headed in

Bobby Davison gets in a challenge as goalkeeper Mervyn Day attempts a clearance. Davison scored the Rams' second with a header after Day hesitated.

Sheridan's corner and then a rare lapse by Eric Steele gave away a corner before the 'keeper redeemed himself by holding on to the slippery ball as rain teemed down. It was a superb catch and said as much for Steele's character as for his skill.

But this was an all-round performance with Geraint Williams keeping things moving in midfield, where John Gregory collected the ball and stroked passes around. Hindmarch was again excellent at the back and MacLaren and Forsyth did their respective jobs well. Down the right flank, Micklewhite did plenty of raiding and, of course, Davison and Gee tucked away the goals.

Gerald Mortimer summed up the scenes:

Thanks fans! Nigel Callaghan applauds the crowd as Derby leave the field. Geraint Williams discusses a point with Eric Steele. John Gregory, Paul Blades and Michael Forsyth are the other Rams players.

'Then came the laps of honour, the chances to say thank you to Arthur Cox, Roy McFarland and one of the most genuine groups of players to wear Derby County shirts.

'. . . .Events have proved that Webb's decision to bring in Cox was not only correct but inspired.

'Three years of hard work came to fruition on Saturday, an occasion made all the easier for Cox because in the morning the Rams won the Midland Intermediate League title to go with the MIL Cup. It is a club again, not just a team . . . . '

Derby County: Steele; Blades, Forsyth, Williams, Hindmarch, MacLaren, Micklewhite, Gee, Davison, Gregory, Callaghan.
Leeds United: Day; Aspin, McDonald, Rennie(Edwards), Ashurst, Ormsby, Stiles, Sheridan, Pearson, Baird, Adams.
Referee: M.D.Peck (Kendall)   *Att: 20,087.*

Dino's Debut Sets The Baseball Ground Alight

Saturday, 29 October 1988

Derby County 4   Wimbledon 1

IN October 1988, Derby County broke the million-pound barrier for the first time when they signed striker Dean Saunders from Oxford United. Of course, many claimed that it was simply a case of Robert Maxwell switching money from one pocket to another — after all, he effectively controlled both clubs — but it was still a milestone in the Rams' history.

More important, the signing proved a huge success for Derby. Saunders, a Welsh international, established an immediate rapport with supporters, and until the day he left the Baseball Ground always gave his all in the Rams' cause. And he could not have wished for a better debut, when his goals helped Derby score a rare comprehensive victory over the team almost everybody had learned to dislike, Wimbledon.

The Rams' first season back in Division One had been disappointing, despite some major signings who included England goalkeeper Peter Shilton from Southampton, and centre-half Mark Wright, also from the Saints, who would regain his England place as a Derby player. The Rams finished 15th, with relegation a mathematical possibility until the very last day of the season.

Wimbledon's first ever appearance at the Baseball Ground came early that season when the Dons, a boring team devoted to humping long balls downfield and annoying the opposition with niggling fouls, won 1-0. On their second appearance, however, they were well beaten — and Saunders was the star.

In the *Derby Evening Telegraph*, Gerald Mortimer reported: 'Whether Saunders scored one or two goals (and Arthur Cox credits him with two) is irrelevant to the main point that he galvanised Derby and electrified the supporters, who were still chanting for Dino as they left the Baseball Ground.

'Arthur Cox likened Saunders to Kevin Hector when he signed him, someone to play with Paul Goddard, his John O'Hare. Then he threw in Kevin Keegan for good measure.'

Rob Hindmarch deserved to share top

Paul Goddard watches Dean Saunders' shot beat Segers. The ball came down off the bar but Saunders claimed the goal.

billing with Saunders as the Rams had to defend courageously for the first half-hour. It wasn't that Wimbledon were all that dominant, but they never gave the Derby rearguard any peace, snapping and pushing and make life so difficult. Indeed, they had practically elevated that approach to an art form, although there was precious little artistry about it.

There were relief for Derby, then, when they took the lead after 35 minutes. Hindmarch got the ball upfield. Saunders swept it out to Ted McMinn, signed from Seville for £300,000 the previous February, and when his centre found its way to the opposite flank, Nigel Callaghan switched it back across and Saunders appeared to steer a perfect header in off the near post.

Wimbledon equalised with a brave header from Jones five minutes before half-time, but 17 minutes into the second half, the Rams regained the lead with a classic goal. Saunders held the ball on the right and then Goddard touched on his low centre for Mel Sage to run on to the ball and shoot home his first goal of the season.

Seven minutes later, Saunders collected a loose ball after Goddard had challenged Hans

Segers and this time the Welshman let fly. Segers touched the ball on to the bar and it bounced down. McMinn lashed it into the net but Saunders claimed the goal. It appeared that the ball had gone over the line before coming back into play.

With ten minutes remaining, Gary Micklewhite came on for Callaghan and in the 85th minute he made it 4-1, hammering in McMinn's low centre after the Scotsman had swept past Clement. It was the first time the Rams had scored four League goals since they beat Plymouth to win the Second Division title in May 1987 and it doubled their tally for the season so far. Saunders went on to score six goals in his first five games. That was more than enough to find him a special place in supporters' hearts.

Derby County: Shilton; Sage, Forsyth, Williams, Hindmarch, Blades, McMinn, Saunders, Goddard, Hebberd, Callaghan (Micklewhite).
Wimbledon: Segers; Joseph, Clement, Jones, Young, Scales, Fairweather, Cork(Brooke), Fashanu, Sanchez, Wise.
Referee: L.C.Shapter (Torquay) Att: 15,050.

Saunders is about to celebrate a debut goal as the Rams score a rare big win over Wimbledon.

Super Ted's Two Give Rams The Points At Tottenham

Saturday, 5 November 1988

Tottenham Hotspur 1   Derby County 3

OVER recent years, Derby County's away form has been as good — even better — than that which they have shown at the Baseball Ground. In 1988-89, the Rams' second season back in Division One, they won seven away games, as many as at home, and one the best of those victories came at White Hart Lane early in the season, when Ted McMinn weighed in with his first goals of the campaign and Dean Saunders continued to show the form which had elevated him into the six-figure bracket.

Yet at Tottenham, the Rams had the worst possible start, going behind after only six minutes. The goal was set up by Chris Waddle, who teased full-back Mel Sage before flashing in a low-cross. Paul Stewart escaped the attentions of Mark Wright and flicked the ball confidently past Peter Shilton. It was a fine beginning for Spurs, but the opening stages of the game were scrappy, with misplaced passes and neither side showing any great cohesion. It was Stewart's first goal since his £1.7 million transfer from Manchester City.

The Rams might have gone two down in the 15th minute but when Terry Fenwick got in a powerful header, Shilton dived full length to hold the ball as Waddle came snapping in looking for a chance.

It was Waddle who was causing havoc on the left flank. Inside a minute he hammered a fierce shot just wide and then provided a pin-point centre from which Stewart went close.

After 24 minutes, however, Ted McMinn equalised for Derby. McMinn tricked his way along the by-line, beating two defenders before beating Bobby Mimms with a powerful shot which gave the 'keeper no earthly chance.

The Rams took heart from McMinn's goal and eight minutes later they went near to taking the lead when Paul Goddard took the ball past two half-hearted Spurs tackles before shooting inches over the bar.

By now the Rams were growing in confidence with Mark Wright and Paul Blades winning all the high balls at the heart of their defence. Spurs, meanwhile, were wilting, their confidence rocked, and they had another close shave when Trevor Hebberd, like Saunders a former Oxford player, went close with a long-range effort. Waddle switched wings in a bid to get Spurs back into the game and it was his dazzling footwork which was Derby's biggest worry as the interval approached.

Tottenham got on to the attack in the second half, but the Rams soon regained their rhythm. Saunders and Goddard linked up to send Callaghan away but the former Watford winger had strayed offside and a promising move broke down. Five minutes after the break, Wright caused problems in the Spurs penalty area but Callaghan shot wildly over from 20 yards out.

In the 63rd minute, the Rams took the lead and McMinn was again the scorer. He beat Thomas and Mabbutt, took the ball to the by-line and then squeezed his shot past Mimms for a repeat performance of his first goal.

Twenty minutes from the end Dean Saunders made sure of the points for Derby, brushing aside two Tottenham defenders before moving on to score confidently from the edge of the penalty area. It was a goal which underlined Saunders' quality as a striker in the top flight.

Tottenham were a deflated team, whilst the Rams, further bouyed by Saunders' goal which put the game firmly in their grasp, might have added to their tally before the close. These were good First Division days for Derby County.

Tottenham Hotspur: Mimms; Stevens, Thomas, Fenwick, Fairclough, Mabbutt, Moran, Gascoigne, Waddle, Stewart, Allen.
Derby County: Shilton; Sage, Forsyth, Cross, Wright, Blades, McMinn, Saunders, Goddard, Hebberd, Callaghan.
Referee: G.Courtney (Spennymoor)
Att: 22,868.

McMinn has scored his first goal Wright (5) comes to congratulate him, although Cross offers a restraining hand.

Saunders Wonder Goal Hits Gunners' Title Hopes

Saturday, 13 May 1989

Arsenal 1   Derby County 2

IN a season when the Rams' away form had been quite remarkable, this victory over title-chasing Arsenal — Derby's eighth success on opponents' grounds in 1988-89 — has to rank as their best. And the goal which started it, laid on by Geraint Williams and finished off by Dean Saunders, was one the finest scored by the Rams for many a long day.

The goal was against the general run of play because Arsenal had dominated for much of the game. But for all that it was no less than Derby deserved, for they had battled so hard and a win at Highbury was a difficult proposition at any time. It also showed great character for their more recent away showings had not been too impressive.

In the *Derby Evening Telegraph*, Gerald Mortimer said: 'They had failed miserably to halt the survival thrusts of Luton Town and Charlton Athletic in their two previous away games. At Selhurst Park, three days before they met Arsenal, they could only be called feeble.'

The victory was even more creditable for the fact that the Rams were without the suspended Mark Wright, whilst Ted McMinn was also missing, nursing a groin strain. It meant that Mel Sage returned after five months out of the side, with Paul Blades playing alongside Rob Hindmarch at the centre of defence. Steve Cross replaced McMinn and gave a fine performance. But so did they all: 'There was not a faint heart in Derby's team', said Gerald Mortimer.

Arsenal disappointed in that they played a lot of long balls forward and chased after them, 'rather like an aristocratic Wimbledon,' but Hindmarch and Blades were equal to anything that the Gunners fired at them. Sage, too, was magnificent and Forsyth gave a brave display, at one time being knocked out by Steve Bould's challenge but recovering as two stretchers were brought out.

Smith and Rocastle had chances to put Arsenal ahead but both blazed over the bar before the Rams showed how it should be done in the 29th minute. Williams supplied a superb angled pass and Saunders lashed it home. John Lukic could do nothing as the ball whistled past him to bulge the back of the net.

With Forsyth lying out cold, Shilton had to make a magnificent save from Kevin Richardson's header and in the second half the England 'keeper twice denied Nigel Winterburn with flying saves. It was vintage stuff.

Rocastle and Winterburn were booked as Arsenal grew more irritable and then Smith, with all the goal to aim at, hammered a pass from Paul Merson against the bar.

The Gunners' chances were slipping by and although Saunders missed an equally good chance to extend Derby's lead, in the 76th minute the Rams did go 2-0 in front when Dino got Tony Adams into such a terrible tangle that the centre-half chopped him down. Saunders picked himself up to smash home the penalty and although Smith pulled

Tony Adams brings down Dean Saunders and the Rams are awarded a penalty.

Saunders tucks away the spot-kick and the Rams are 2-0 in front.

Derby County in 1989. Back row (left to right): Roy McFarland (assistant manager), Phil Gee, Nick Pickering, Michael Forsyth, Peter Shilton, Mark Wright, Martin Taylor, Rob Hindmarch, Ted McMinn, Trevor Hebberd, Gordon Guthrie (physiotherapist). Front row: Brian McCord, John Chiedozie, Mel Sage, Paul Blades, Dean Saunders, Arthur Cox (manager), Paul Goddard, Gary Micklewhite, Geraint Williams, Steve Cross, Mark Patterson.

a goal back from Richardson's corner near the end, it was going to be Derby's day.

Micklewhite, who like Hebberd worked so hard in midfield, had a lucky escape when he deflected a pass from Martin Hayes narrowly wide of a Derby post, but the Rams had it sewn up and were the only team to do the double over Arsenal that season. In a thrilling climax to the campaign, the Gunners claimed the title with a last-minute goal at Liverpool, the only other team who could have taken it. The Rams, who finished fifth, had given them a severe shock on the way.

Arsenal: Lukic; Dixon, Winterburn, Thomas, O'Leary, Adams, Rocastle, Richardson, Smith, Bould (Hayes), Merson (Groves).

Derby County: Shilton; Sage, Forsyth, Williams, Blades, Hindmarch, Cross, Saunders, Goddard, Hebberd, Micklewhite.

Referee: G.M.Tyson (Sunderland)

Att: 41,008.

The 'Tin Man' Stars As Rams Find Their Goal Touch

Saturday, 11 November 1989

Derby County 6   Manchester City 0

IAN Maxwell had warned Derby County's annual meeting that if Baseball Ground attendances did not improve, players would have to be sold — a state of affairs far removed from the time when his father was trumpeting the signings of Peter Shilton and Mark Wright and promising great days ahead for the club.

So a crowd of over 19,000 for the visit of Manchester City was quite pleasing, particularly as the ground capacity was governed to some extent by the numbers allowed at the Osmaston End in the wake of the Hillsborough disaster.

More to the point for those fans was the result, a six-goal thrashing of one of the truly 'proper' First Division clubs as the *Derby Evening Telegraph's* Gerald Mortimer liked to call the Maine Road outfit.

It was important, not just for the way the Rams performed and the fact that six goals without reply will always bring joy to supporters, but also because it moved Derby a little closer towards the middle of the table in what was becoming a relegation-haunted season for the club. Had they lost against City, only Sheffield Wednesday would have been below them — and only on goal-difference — and Wednesday were running into form with two successive League wins.

It did not take the Rams long to assert themselves. In the first minute, Dean Saunders forced goalkeeper Andy Dibble into a diving save and Ted McMinn was in inspired form right from the off. Full-back Gary Fleming was booked as he tried to contain McMinn's threat and later in the game the City defender was lucky to remain on the pitch after a terrible tackle on Derby's own version of the flying Scotsman.

Geraint Williams, too, had a blinder, winning the ball in midfield and using it so effectively, while Mel Sage was always available moving down from right-back, and Gary Micklewhite found the service he wanted to make a significant contribution to the afternoon's proceedings.

Mark Wright, too, was in splendid form, secure in his own penalty area and so dangerous in City's. Indeed, it was Wright who opened the scoring in the 14th minute, after both McMinn and Saunders had missed earlier opportunities to put Derby in front with headers.

McMinn swung over a free-kick and Wright steered a powerful header against the bar. When the ball cannoned back to him, the England centre-half hammered it into the net with a fierce left-foot shot.

Three minutes later, Wright was on to another McMinn corner, this time heading it across the face of the City goal for Trevor Hebberd to head back past Dibble.

Clive Allen had two chances in quick succession before McMinn chipped over and Wright sent another header thudding off the woodwork and the Rams went in 2-0 ahead at the interval.

Three minutes into the second half, however, it was 3-0 when Dibble brought down Hebberd and Saunders lashed home the penalty.

Saunders might have bagged the fourth after Micklewwhite sent in a lovely centre, but the Welshman won another penalty when Brian Gayle brought him down as he bored into the City box. Saunders looked offside when he began the run but the flag stayed down, the referee eventually pointed to the spot and Saunders scored his fourth penalty out of five League goals so far that season.

Eleven minutes from the end, Paul Goddard found himself with plenty of space as he chased a through pass from Sage. Goddard had earlier missed from a similar position but this time he went around Dibble to clip the ball into an empty net.

After 82 minutes it was six. McMinn, who had tormented poor Fleming all afternoon, got past him for the umpteenth time before sending in the perfect centre for Micklewhite to score his first goal since the previous January.

Mark Wright puts the Rams ahead against Manchester City after McMinn and Saunders had missed earlier opportunities.

It was just the tonic Derby needed, but poor Ted McMinn — on the verge of a trip to Italy with Scotland for the World Cup, some thought — was badly injured at Tottenham soon after his dazzling display against Manchester City. Gary Micklewhite, too, was soon injured, Paul Goddard surprisingly sold to Millwall for the remarkably high fee of £800,000, and later in the season no less than eight first-teamers were out of action because of injury.

One new face was Mick Harford, from Luton for £480,000, but after climbing as high as seventh at one stage, the Rams slumped, went seven matches without a win and were not safe from relegation until the third last match of the season. Any thoughts that the thrashing of City would herald a revival had

Ted McMinn, who had tormented Gary Fleming all afternoon, cracks in a shot. But the Rams star failed to get on the scoresheet despite Derby hitting six.

been dashed by injuries and the Rams' continuing parlous financial state as the true worth of Maxwell's involvement slowly, very slowly, began to dawn.

Derby County: Shilton; Sage, Forsyth, Williams, Wright, Blades, McMinn, Saun-ders, Goddard, Hebberd, Micklewhite.

Manchester City: Dibble; Fleming(Beckford), Hinchcliffe, Bishop, Gayle, Redmond, White, Oldfield, Allen, McNab, Brightwell (Fashanu).

Referee: A.N.Buksh (London)   *Att: 19,239.*

Harford's Hat-Trick Destroys Sunderland

Wednesday, 31 October 1990

Derby County 6   **Sunderland 0**

THE start of the 1990-91 season was a dreadful time for Derby County. Robert Maxwell, the man hailed as the saviour who would not only guarantee survival but also successes not seen since the great days of Brian Clough, announced that the club was up for sale, having lost interest in it some time before. And the Rams had to wait two months for their first League win so that by the end of October they were battling against relegation.

Thus, when fellow First Division strugglers Sunderland arrived at the Baseball Ground for a third-round Rumbelows League Cup tie on Halloween Night, it was difficult to put aside the nightmare into which Derby County were descending.

But by the end of the evening, Rams fans had something else to think about, at least in the very short term, because their team had pulled out a top-drawer performance to record Derby's biggest ever score in the League Cup, in any of its sponsored guises.

The obvious star of this particular show was Sunderland-born Mick Harford, who grabbed a hat-trick against his home-town club, but there were plenty of other candidates in a fine all-round performance as the Rams literally tore Sunderland, whose back four were absolutely dreadful, to pieces. Most heartening, of course, was the fact that Derby had hit six goals and Dean Saunders, upon who they had placed such a heavy burden to score, was not on the sheet, although it was his ability to turn in tight positions which caused the Sunderland defence so many problems upon which others capitalised.

He could have scored the Rams' sixth goal, as it happened, but instead chose to lay it on for 20-year-old Craig Ramage, a youngster making his way in the game and in need of a little confidence booster. It said much of Saunders that he was prepared to act in such an unselfish way.

The Rams, who had scored only eight goals in their previous 12 games, opened their account after eight minutes when Tony Norman turned over a Saunders shot and from the corner, Micklewhite sent over a perfect cross for Harford to climb high and beat the goalkeeper with a good old-fashioned header.

Three minutes later, the Rams were two up when Harford caught Anthony Smith in possession. Harford set Micklewhite off and Bennett, trying to clear a low cross, succeeded only in turning the ball into his own net.

Sunderland had a couple of chances to drag themselves back into the game before it was put completely beyond their grasp in the 35th minute. Another fine cross from Micklewhite was again met by Harford who sent another header goalwards, this time into the top corner.

Nick Pickering went close before Harford completed his hat-trick. Yet again Micklewhite was involved, teasing in another centre. The Wearsiders' defence could not cope and John Kay chested the ball down into the path of Harford, who had run intelligently into position with uncappy anticipation as the ball came over. This time the big striker hammered it home. After six months without a goal before the previous Saturday, Harford had certainly come good in spectacular fashion.

Five minutes into the second half, Ramage made it 5-0 after a lovely passing move between several Rams players. They teased the ball around until the opening appeared and then Michael Forsyth supplied the final pass.

The sixth goal came after 66 minutes when Saunders left substitute Richard Ord tackling thin air. Saunders gave up his chance to get his name on the scoresheet, instead teeing-up Ramage for the youngster's second of the night.

In the *Derby Evening Telegraph*, Gerald Mortimer wrote: 'Harford rightly grabbed the glory . . . .but there were plenty of others demanding a share.

'Gary Micklewhite for one. He was involved in all four first-half goals and was close to the most spectacular of the night near the end.

Mick Harford celebrates a hat-trick goal against his home-town club as the Rams enjoy a six-goal romp.

'Craig Ramage scored twice in the second half to cap his most assured performance so far and Geraint Williams was absolutely brilliant in midfield.

'I have not seen Williams run a game as completely as he did against Sunderland. He linked superbly with Micklewhite and was constantly demanding the ball. If one of his moves broke down, he wanted instantly to try again.'

It had been a good week for Roy McFarland, in charge while Arthur Cox recovered from a nose operation. The Rams had gained their first League win the previous Saturday, against Southampton, and the following Saturday they beat Luton 2-1. It was all a rare treat for the fans.

Derby County: Shilton; Sage, Cross, G.Williams, Wright, Forsyth, Micklewhite, Saunders, Harford, Ramage, Pickering.
Sunderland: Norman; Kay, Smith(Cullen), Bennett(Ord), Ball, Owers, Bracewell, Armstrong, Davenport, Gabbiadini, Hardyman.
Referee: K.S.Hackett (Sheffield) Att: 16,422.

Saunders Strike Stuns Cloughie's Forest

Saturday, 24 November 1990

Derby County 2   Nottingham Forest 1

'DERBY County's glorious victory over Nottingham Forest, capped by a magnificent goal from Dean Saunders, sent most of the season's best Baseball Ground crowd spilling happily into the streets on Saturday,' Gerald Mortimer told *Derby Evening Telegraph* readers after this rare League win over the Rams' closest rivals.

It was certainly a memorable victory, for Forest had dominated East Midlands football since Brian Clough's move there from Derby via Brighton and Leeds in the mid-1970s, the City Ground club taking over from the Rams as the region's pace setters.

Yet Derby went into the game against Forest — albeit a Clough side not experiencing one its better starts to a season — with plenty of problems. There was more background unrest as Robert Maxwell began sounding off again, and Arthur Cox also had injury worries with Sage and Cross ruled out and Geraint Williams having to leave the field after only eight minutes when he injured a knee in his 100th consecutive senior appearance.

Craig Ramage, left out of the side after the Rams' 3-0 defeat at Leeds a week earlier, came on for Williams and went on to play a major part Derby's victory, when he equalised Steve Chettle's 15th-minute goal for Forest.

Chettle first hammered a shot against Shilton's post and the ball was crambled away for a corner which Stuart Pearce put in from the left. Nigel Clough touched it on and Chettle saw his shot go in off a Derby defender.

Two minutes later, however, the Rams were level after Nigel Jemson squandered a good chance to make it 2-0 for Forest. The lively Gary Micklewhite slid in a through pass and Ramage scored a fine goal, clipping his shot over the diving Mark Crossley. Some players might have been tempted to try hammering the ball goalwards, but Ramage used his head and there was no chance that Crossley would block his more measured effort.

It was Ramage's first League goal of the season and Derby's first in the League at home against Forest since 1979.

Nigel Jemson takes evasive action as Mark Wright puts in a challenge.

Rams substitute Craig Ramage wheels away after his equalising goal against Forest.

The Rams now smelled victory and Mark Wright clipped the bar with a header from Nigel Callaghan's free-kick before Crossley made a fine save from Trevor Hebberd, the 'keeper reacting well when Hebberd shot through a crowded penalty area.

On the hour, Derby found their winner and what a classic it proved. Mick Harford rose to win a long free-kick from Mark Wright — again having a fine game — and then Micklewhite, in plenty of space, drove in a perfect centre for Dean Saunders to plant a superb header into the back of the Forest net. It was a magnficient goal, exquisitely created and finished off in style.

At the back, Mark Patterson and Nick Pickering did well at full-back and although Patterson was booked for bringing down Pearce, it simply showed that the Rams defender had no reservations when it came to challenging the fearsome Forest full-back. Ramage, Forsyth, Harford and Laws were also booked, Harford after being painfully caught from behind by Pearce, although

referee Trussell did not consider it a foul.

The win took the Rams up to 17th place but somehow it seemed that the worst thing they could do was beat Forest. This 1990 win was exactly 11 years to the day since they last beat the Reds in the League. Both seasons ended in relegation and both wins heralded disastrous spells. In 1979-80, Derby went 13 games without a win after beating Forest; in 1990-91, after beating Sunderland at Roker Park, the following Saturday, they then had to endure 21 games before winning again. But for all that, a defeat of Forest is always sweet.

Derby County: Shilton; Pickering, Patterson, G.Williams(Ramage), Wright, Forsyth, Micklewhite, Saunders, Harford, Hebberd, Callaghan.
Nottingham Forest: Crossley; Laws, Pearce, Walker, Chettle, Hodge(Starbuck), Crosby, Keane, Clough, Jemson, Parker.
Referee: C.C.Trussell (Liverpool)

Att: 21,729.

Forgotten Gee Stars In Seven-Goal Villa Thriller

Wednesday, 5 February 1992

Derby County 3   **Aston Villa 4**

THIS was the game that had practically everything — seven goals, two missed penalties, a sending off and the most stunning goal by Derby County midfielder Paul Williams. The only blot on a remarkable evening, so far as Rams fans were concerned, was that it was Aston Villa and not Derby who marched into the fifth round of the FA Cup.

The Rams' brief Cup campaign had already had its share of incident in 1992. In the third round, they took a first-minute lead at Fourth Division high-fliers Burnley. The Clarets soon equalised, Derby regained the lead but Burnley levelled the scores again late in the game.

The Baseball Ground replay was memorable but for all the wrong reasons. Fifteen minutes from the end, the Rams were leading 2-0 when fog, which had swirled around the ground all night, caused the game's abandonment. It was a particularly dismal night for young Rams full-back Mark Patterson, who scored a spectacular goal and was then carried off with a serious knee injury. Now the game — and Patterson's goal — counted for nothing.

When the game was finally replayed to a finish, on the Saturday afternoon set aside for the fourth round, Derby again went into a 2-0 lead and this time they were able to hold it.

Now the scene was set for the visit of Ron Atkinson's First Division Villa and a near-full house. Evening games at the Baseball Ground always seem to have that extra bit of atmosphere and this crackling fourth-round tie was no exception.

Long before the start the old ground was buzzing with anticipation and with only five minutes gone, it erupted when the Rams,

Peter Shilton holds a cross under his bar during the FA Cup thriller against Aston Villa.

Phil Gee (9) holds his arms aloft after scoring against Villa. Ted McMinn, the provider, has already started a lap of honour.

attacking the Osmaston End, went ahead. Martyn Chalk had already shot over the bar when he got the ball to Ted McMinn, who cut inside and let go a shot which Les Sealey could not gather. The ball went to Phil Gee and the Rams striker, so desperate for a good performance, hit it over the line.

The Rams could not have hoped for a better start, but 18 minutes later they trailed 3-1 with hopes of a sensational result apparently vanished.

In the ninth minute, Kevin Richardson took a corner and Paul McGrath touched the ball on to Dwight Yorke, who levelled the scores from close range.

Ten minutes later, Derby hearts sank when the Rams went behind, although the goal looked of dubious pedigree. It was another corner, this time from Steve Froggatt, which posed the danger and as Shilton came out for the cross, he appeared to be impeded. The referee would have none of it and Yorke hit home his second goal after 19 minutes.

Four minutes later, the Rams looked to be well on their way out of the Cup when Garry Parker hammered a spectacular shot into the top corner of Shilton's goal. The former England 'keeper appeared to have been caught flat-footed, but in reality there was nothing he could do about it.

Seven minutes before half-time, however, Derby were back in the game. Geraint Williams played the ball out to McMinn and he left McGrath stranded before getting in a cross which Gee headed past Sealey.

It was turning out to be a magnificent night for Gee, who over the previous months had failed miserably to recapture the form which had brought him a hatful of goals when the Rams marched from the Third to the First Division.

This was turning into a remarkable game — and the drama was far from over. Before half-time, Shilton failed to take command of an awkward situation and Coleman felt he had to stop Yorke by fouling him. Shilton

Simon Coleman gets in a tackle on Villa's Dwight Yorke while Paul Williams and Ian Ormondroyd look on.

partially redeemed himself by stopping Yorke's penalty, but the Villa winger hit home the rebound and again Derby were two goals adrift.

Twelve minutes into the second half, Villa were awarded another penalty when Coleman handled Richardson's free-kick. Again Shilton stopped Yorke's spot-kick but this time the Rams' 'keeper held on to the ball.

It was a vital save because within two minutes Derby had pulled back to 4-3 — and what a goal it was. Jason Kavanagh took a quick free-kick and Chalk took the ball forward before centering. There was Paul Williams, off the ground, to volley the most magnificent goal past Sealey.

The crowd now willed Derby on and their cause was helped with 15 minutes to go when Villa's Polish international, Dariusz Kubicki, who had already been booked along with McGrath, body-checked McMinn and was ordered off.

Those closing minutes were real nail-biters. Paul Williams and Gee each had two chances

to level the tie, while Daley hit a Derby post.

At the final whistle, supporters stood to applaud the teams from the pitch. It had been a magnificent Cup tie and for Derby, central defender Andy Comyn, midfielder Geraint Williams and the flying Ted McMinn stood out. The Rams, though, were out of the Cup.

Incidentally, although Phil Gee scored twice against Villa, it was the last time he started a game for the Rams. Eventually he was part of the transfer that took Gee and Ormondroyd to Leicester City and brought Paul Kitson to Derby.

Derby County: Shilton; Kavanagh(Davidson), Forsyth, G.Williams, Coleman, Comyn, Chalk(Stallard), Ormondroyd, Gee, P.Williams, McMinn.
Aston Villa: Sealey; Kubicki, Small, Teale, McGrath, Richardson, Daley, Yorke, Regis, Parker, Froggatt(Carruthers).
Referee: K.Morton (Bury St Edmund's)

Att: 22,452.

So Close To Wembley and the Premier League

Wednesday, 13 May 1992

Derby County 2   Blackburn Rovers 1

THERE can have been few Baseball Ground nights in recent times to match this remarkable evening of passion, as Derby County strove so hard for a place in the Second Division play-off final at Wembley and a chance to go into the new FA Premier League.

Three days after throwing away a 2-0 lead in the first leg of this play-off semi-final at Ewood Park, the Rams battled so hard to close the two-goal gap between themselves and the Second Division's other big spenders, Kenny Dalglish's Blackburn Rovers.

There was even a point on the last day of the regular season when the Rams looked on course for automatic promotion. They were beating Swindon Town, also promotion hopefuls, at the Baseball Ground when the electronic scoreboard announced that every other game affecting promotion was going Derby's way. But in the end, although the Rams won, results around the country conspired to put them in the play-offs against Blackburn.

After 14 minutes of the Ewood game, it seemed that the Rams were on their way. Marco Gabbiadini and Tommy Johnson had given them a 2-0 lead. But by half-time, Blackburn had wiped out that lead and by the end had eased into a 4-2 advantage.

The fact that the Rams had scored two away goals was hugely significant, however. They now had to win by three clear goals in normal time at Derby, or by two clear goals if the second leg went to extra-time.

It was a glorious late spring evening and the Baseball Ground was packed, the atmosphere probably not as intense since the great European nights of the early 1970s, or even since the memorable League Cup win over Chelsea in 1968.

The Rams had two prerequisites — an early goal and clean sheet — and as they began by hammering away at the Blackburn defence in search of the former, the latter was always going to be in danger.

After 23 minutes, the Baseball Ground erupted. Lee Richardson obstructed Paul Williams — and had a kick at him for good measure — and although a Blackburn defender got in the way of Paul Simpson's fierce free-kick, the ball found its way to Simon Coleman, who got it to Johnson. He centred and there was Coleman's central-defensive partner, Andy Comyn, to beat Bobby Mimms with a diving header.

The Rams were right back in it and before half-time, Williams, Coleman and Kitson each might have scored a second, which would have given Derby the edge.

Four minutes into the second half, however, Blackburn equalised. The Rams had conceded some bad goals during the season and this was one of the worst. Scott Sellars pumped over a high corner which Williams could only head up into the air rather than out of the area. Steve Sutton was already well off his line as the ball dropped to Kevin Moran and as Coleman also came in, Moran checked and the ball went into the net off the back of his head.

It was an awful moment and Blackburn might well have been awarded a penalty when David Speedie appeared to be brought down by Sutton as the two went for a Comyn back-pass.

Johnson was now playing alongside Gabbiadini in the middle with Ted McMinn now wide on the right as the Rams tried to reassert themselves in search of more goals.

They might have had one when Kitson put a Johnson cross over the bar — the Rams striker was always stretching for the ball — and in the 74th minute it came from another low centre, this time from Williams. The ball eventually ran to McMinn, who saw his shot deflect off Alan Wright and into the net.

Derby now needed another goal to send the game into extra-time. And if they could take Blackburn into the extra period, then all they needed to do was to hold on.

The Rams certainly strived for that vital breakthrough. Williams shot narrowly wide and then volleyed Simpson's effort across the face of the Blackburn goal as the crowd roared Derby on.

Andy Comyn has just put Derby 1-0 ahead against Blackburn and is congratulated by Marco Gabbiadini and Paul Kitson.

But Rovers defended well and the goal would not come. It was Blackburn who went to Wembley, where they beat Leicester City to win promotion.

It was perhaps ironic, because after leading the table in the early part of the season, Blackburn had faltered and re-entered the play-off positions only on the last day of the season. The Rams, meanwhile, had finished third, four points and three places higher than Blackburn, despite dropping many home points. But they could trace their ultimate downfall to an awful half-hour at Ewood Park the previous Sunday.

A jubilant Kevin Mopran has just deflated the Rams play-off hopes, heading a corner home despite the usual packed Derby penalty area.

At Derby, five players were booked by referee David Elleray, who earlier in the season had sent off Simon Coleman at Molineux. Paul Williams was shown the yellow card after only two minutes and he was followed by Richardson, Speedie, Wright and Moran for Blackburn. After the game, Speedie clashed with a Derby fan on the pitch and both men eventually found themselves in court. The fan was convicted, but Speedie was let off.

Derby County: Sutton; Kavanagh, Forsyth, McMinn, Coleman, Comyn, Johnson, Kitson, Gabbiadini, P.Williams, Simpson.

Blackburn Rovers: Mimms; May, Wright, Cowans, Moran, Hendry, Richardson, Atkins, Speedie, Newell, Sellars.

Referee: D.R.Elleray (Harrow)   Att: 22,920.

Rams Run Riot And Equal A Record

Sunday, 6 December 1992

Swindon Town 2	Derby County 4

AT the beginning of the 1992-93 season, Derby County were everyone's tip for promotion to the FA Premier League. Indeed, one national newspaper even ran the headline, 'Who'll Go Up With Derby?'

But when the season got under way, events proved rather different. Instead of storming to the top of what was now the First Division, Derby faltered. And even the injection of more new — and expensive — blood failed to put right what was becoming an increasingly embarrassing situtation for a club which had just spent some £10 million on buying a promotion side.

The Rams lost their first three games, the second of which was at home to Kevin Keegan's Newcastle United, who were on their way to an explosive start to the season. Derby's first League victory, meanwhile, did not come until their eighth game, against Southend at the end of September. Yet the following week the Rams embarked on an amazing away run which began with a victory at Cambridge and continued with wins at Luton, Wolves, Notts County and Bristol Rovers.

The run was even more remarkable if one counts away wins in the Anglo-Italian Cup, a competition relaunched for clubs in the English First Division — in reality the old Second Division — and the Italian Serie 'B'.

Another aspect of the new-look football set-up was an increase in the number of Sunday games, televised live. Derby, amongst others, were not happy with the pay-off, but on the first Sunday in December they again found themselves having to play out of sequence when they met Glenn Hoddle's talented Swindon side at the County Ground.

And if their home form had been poor, away from the Baseball Ground the Rams were more than unbeatable. So much so that when they travelled to Wiltshire, they were looking for their sixth consecutive League victory which would equal the record set by Brian Clough's side which won the last five away games of the 1968-69 Second Division championship season and the first on their return to Division One.

The omens were good — Derby had not dropped an away point since drawing at West Ham on 20 September — and on a terrible, rainswept afternoon they stormed to a 4-2 victory with a breathtaking display of attacking, utterly efficient football. As Gerald Mortimer said in the *Derby Evening Telegraph*, for once the Rams had done exactly what they had planned.

Derby made two changes to the side which had been beaten at Highbury in a Coca-Cola Cup game the previous Wednesday. Dutchman Richard Goulooze took over at right-back for his first full League game and Paul Williams replaced Ted McMinn in midfield.

There were perhaps two keys to this emphatic victory: Marco Gabbiadini played a more withdrawn role and had a magnificent match, his passing quite superb; and Mark Pembridge never left Micky Hazard's side throughout the 90 minutes.

Yet again there was an early miss from Tommy Johnson, who shot straight at Hammond, but the miss was not costly and after 28 minutes it was Johnson who put Derby ahead, sliding the ball under Hammond's body after good work by Kitson and Gabbiadini.

Then Johnson, Gabbiadini and Williams all went close before the Rams scored a second in the 40th minute. Hoddle fouled Gabbiadini and from the free-kick Johnson over-ran the dead ball, allowing Pembridge to crash home a rocket of a shot.

Although Kitson might have made it 3-0, Swindon came back into the game after half-time and Steve Sutton had to make three good saves before the Rams eventually found that third goal. Goulooze, who looked impressive at right-back, especially with his passing, rolled the ball square and Martin Kuhl hammered home his first goal for Derby after 57 minutes. It was a magnificent strike and wrapped the game up.

There was still time for a frenzied finish,

Tommy Johnson places the ball past Swindon goalkeeper Nicky Hammond to give the Rams the lead.

however, with plenty of chances at either end. In Derby's defence Craig Short, the Rams' £2.5 million centre-half, and Simon Coleman, standing in for the injured Darren Wassall, held Swindon at bay, whilst Gabbiadini (twice) and Forsyth both went near to making it 4-0.

As it turned out, it was Swindon who scored next, when Hoddle took a free-kick and Shaun Taylor slammed the ball back into the danger zone for Hazard to head past Sutton with three minutes remaining.

Derby replied immediately with substitute McMinn knocking the ball over the line at the far post after Kitson had gone clear down the left. It was a gloriously executed goal.

Still the excitement was not over and in the 89th minute, Coleman slipped and Maskell was able to make it 4-2. It should have been 4-3 because in the dying seconds Goulooze fouled Kevin Horlock in the box but Sutton turned Maskell's penalty around the post. It was the last kick of the game and the Rams had equalled a record.

On 20 December they set a new mark, winning at Grimsby — again live on television — to extend their run of successive away wins to a remarkable seven. It came to

Johnson celebrates his 28th-minute goal at the County Ground. Poor Johnson did not have the best of seasons after his six-figure move from Notts County and might have had many more goals with better finishing.

an end with a Boxing Day defeat at Brentford.

Swindon Town: Hammond; Kerslake, Horlock, Hoddle, Calderwood, Taylor, Hazard, Summerbee(Moncur), Maskell, Ling, Mitchell(White).

Derby County: Sutton; Goulooze, Forsyth, Short, Coleman, Pembridge, Johnson(McMinn), Kuhl, Kitson, Gabbiadini, Williams. *Referee: P.Don (Haworth)   Att: 8,924.*

Rams So Near To Cup Glory Over The Owls

Monday, 8 March 1993

Derby County 3　　　Sheffield Wednesday 3

THIS was an evening filled with passion, good football and plenty of incident in a game which see-sawed either way and seemed eventually in Derby County's hands until a converted defender with a phenomenal scoring record struck again to take the Rams back to Hillsborough just when a place in the semi-finals of the FA Cup appeared theirs.

The Rams were twice behind against Premier League side Sheffield Wednesday in this sixth-round tie, but they showed tremendous character to haul themselves back on each occasion and were within six minutes of the semi-finals after scoring three goals of the highest quality.

Yet at half-time it looked as if Derby had surrendered to a side who had proved fearsome Cup opponents in recent seasons. Chris Waddle, the Owls' veteran star, had worried Derby throughout the first 45 minutes and by the interval, with the Rams trailing 2-1 and looking groggy, it was hard to see them figuring in the draw for the last four.

Such is the nature of football these days that the old sixth-round Saturday was no more with games spread over a long weekend to accommodate television, who increasingly call the tune when it comes to when football should be staged. The Rams' tie had been selected by Sky Sport, the satellite channel, although the big Baseball Ground crowd were spared the dancing girls, fireworks and parachutists who had intruded upon the station's Monday night coverage of Premier League football.

There were two surprises in the line-ups: Derby included Martin Kuhl, left thigh heavily strapped and short of match fitness; Wednesday had Danny Wilson back only two weeks after he had broken two ribs. Kuhl's presence was explained by the fact that Arthur Cox obviously felt Derby needed his influ-

ence, although he was hardly the most mobile man on the field.

The game was only 12 minutes old when the Rams went behind from the penalty spot. Warhurst let Waddle's pass through and Mark Patterson, although it appeared that he was trying to avoid contact with Mark Bright, clipped the Wednesday man's heels. John Sheridan put away the penalty even though Martin Taylor guessed correctly and managed to touch the ball.

After 29 minutes the Rams were level with a stunning goal. They were awarded a free-kick and after Anderson and Gabbiadini joined Waddle in the referee's book, Kuhl turned the free-kick to Shane Nicholson on the left and the young full-back, in only his fourth senior game for Derby — although something of a veteran by the time he left Lincoln City — let fly from more than 30 yards. The ball slammed off the crossbar, bounced down and went in off Chris Woods. It came off the 'keeper but it was Nicholson's goal and a great one at that.

Seven minutes later, Wednesday were back in front when Waddle laid on a great pass and Warhurst, converted from centre-half to a striker, beat the advancing Taylor. It was a dispiriting moment for the Rams who were probably glad when the half-time whistle sounded.

But they were level again after 59 minutes with another great goal. Paul Kitson headed the ball on and Marco Gabbiadini turned, went past England defender Carlton Palmer and then held off the Wednesday defence to smash a shot into the roof of the net.

In 74 minutes, the Rams took the lead for the first time — and yet again it was a classic. Mark Pembridge tapped the ball to Nicholson, who curved over a fine centre which Kitson put away with a magnificent header. The Baseball Ground exploded and for the first time, thoughts of a FA Cup Final at Wembley were at the front of the mind.

But if Wednesday lost some of their authority, they were still dangerous and with six minutes remaining, Waddle fed substitute Jemson with a glorious pass. He pulled back a cross and there was stand-in Warhurst to bury his 11th goal in ten games.

Derby had not won at Hillsborough since

Johnson is on hand to help Marco Gabbiadini celebrate his magnificent goal which levelled the scores against Wednesday.

This time it is Paul Kitson's turn to accept the congratulations from Mark Pembridge after Kitson's header put the Rams ahead for the first time in the tie.

1936 and, alas, the replay was not the night they broke that wretched run. But what a night to remember this Baseball Ground had been.

Derby County: Taylor; Patterson, Forsyth, Nicholson, Short, Pembridge, Williams, Kuhl, Kitson, Gabbiadini, Johnson.
Sheffield Wednesday: Woods; Nilsson, Worthington, Palmer, Harkes(Jemson), Anderson, Wilson, Waddle, Warhurst, Bright, Sheridan(Hyde).
Referee: G.R.Ashby (Worcester)   Att: 22,511.

SUBSCRIBERS

PRESENTATION COPIES

1 Derby County Football Club • 2 Brian Fearn Esq
3 Lionel Pickering Esq • 4 Michael Dunford Esq

5 J A Harris
6 David & Tim Dixon
7 Mick Derby
8 C-Stander (Derby County Fanzine)
9 Chris Kendall
10 Chris Kendall Football Programmes
11 Jason Bates
12 Alan Beresford
13 David Horobin
14 Stephen Barnes
15 James Andrew Warren
16 Michael Rickwood
17 Shane Sanghera
18 Mr K C Saunders
19 Daniel Luke Spencer
20 Andrew John Ellis
21 Richard J Coles
22 Thomas & Peggy
23 Peter Rusbridge
24 Joe & Paul Smith
25 Brian Flint
26 Leslie W Campbell
27 Martin Allgood
28 Joan Paginton
29 Stephen Attwood
30 D R G Millward
31 David Rudkin
32 Anthony David Harrison
33 Nigel J Bailey
34 K J Orpe
35 J W Bant
36 Christopher Eaton
37 Gary Roy Clarke
38 Philip Brewin
39 Paul Barlow
40 James R Woolley
41 A J Vanter
42 Mark Ferris
43 Bill Heseltine
44 Mr Jeremy Tonks
45 Neil Oliver
46 Frank Burton
47 Paul Stanley Rowley
48 Pauline A King
49 John Joseph Higgins
50 Richard Latham
51 Neil A Beresford
52 Paul Andrew Sharp
53 Graham M Bolam
54 James Yeomans
55 Christopher Wood
56 Jon Goodall
57 Barrie & Stephen Dunn
58 Pam & Roy Eley
59 Mr Barry Snaith
60 David E H Frost
61 Mr & Mrs H A Stone
62 Paul R Lester

63 Kevin Thomason
64 Robin Watson
65 John Ward
66 Kevin Anthony Griffiths
67 Mr Nathan Blurton
68 David Atkinson
69 Peter J Lockhart
70 Matthew Orme
71 Cyril H Sprenger
72 Andrew Cudworth
73 Terry Doyle
74 Trevor Marsh
75 Gavin R R Claxton
76 Ian Morter
77 B E Cash
78 Mr J B & Miss C A Stevenson
79 David Michael Baggley
80 Ernest Howarth
81 Steven Grant
82 Anna & James Beeson
83 Ray S Brindley
84 Nick Wilson
85 Howard Bettany
86 Leonard Matthews
87 Anthony Nicholas Doleman
88 Carol Jaques
89 Alun Owen
90 Graham J Moore
91 Harry Lewis
92 Anthony Michael Johnson
93 Ziggy Fugiel
94 Andrew David Mitchell
95 Lyndon Brown
96 Chris Neal
97 David L Riley
98 Matt Morris
99 K E Chatterley
100 Deryck Burns
101 P C Robinson
102 Alan Lewis Pewtress
103 Paul Clayton
104 Michael J Yates
105 Dennis Ruston
106 K R Williams
107 P J Gunn
108 D Attenborough
109 Simon Baker
110 Darren Taylor
111 David Phillips
112 Andrew Phillips
113 George Ivor Phillips
114 Guy A Kent
115 Ms Lynne Morgan
116 H Preston
117 Max Bladon
118 David G Sheldon
119 Roger Litherland
120 Judith Margaret Peel
121 H M Shelley
122 Bryan Edward Walton

123 Ralph McSeveney
124 Judy & Harold Draycott
125 Mick Nordemann
126 Jim Wright
127 Andy Pickers
128 Adrian Greenwood
129 David H Eckersley
130 Martin Eckersley
131 Mark Smith
132 G N Draper
133 John S Marshall
134 Gary Bowen
135 Percy Birkinshaw
136 Phillip Cottrill
137 John W Dolman
138 Peter Stephens
139 Colin Grimley
140 Steve Cooke
141 Christopher D Walker
142 Chris Cohen
143 Michael Cohen
144 David Iliffe
145 Alan Cooke
146 Roy A Brelsford
147 Andy & Mandy Garner
148 David Sims
149 Elaine Toon
150 Andrew Brewin
151 Glyn Mellor
152 S Wood
153 Mark Tyrer
154 Barbara Henderson
155 Finn Morten Steen
156 Stephen Hawley
157 Mr Billy Mann
158 Neal Roy Johnson
159 Bob Harris
160 John Anthony Walker
161 Terence Garton
162 Jack Garton
163 Mr K W Oates
164 D Poyser
165 Mr M W Sims
166 David Clowes
167 Ken Guy
168 Richard J Challands
169 David Randall
170 Marsha Limbert
171 Richard Fletcher
172 Douglas Rodgers
173 Andrew Lockley
174 R J Hughes
175 Barbara Osborne
176 A M Winfield
177 Jonathan Styne
178 K & R J Jackson
179 Jonathan Naden
180 David W Slater
181 G N Southall
182 Mr P Church

183 Mr Craig M McLoughlin
184 Christine Gee
185 Martyn Cameron Miller
186 Clery Henderson
187 Jonathan W House
188 Geoffrey K Stone
189 Paul Ashford
190 Michael Lomas
191 David Lomas
192 C S Pritchard
193 David F Heaton
194 Don Curtis
195 Gary Holman
196 Ruth, Edward & Julian Hill
197 David A Quinn
198 Colin J Burford
199 Liam James Clamp
200 Matthew Michael Sanders
201 Phyllis Eleanor Meakin
202 Anthony John Peach
203 A John Newton
204 Stephen Mark Walton
205 Bryan Linden Peach
206 Robert Beeby
207 Mark Thompson
208 Richard S Twells
209 Tony Nicklin
210 Arto Tuominen
211 John Raymond George Sutcliffe
212 Dennis, Joan & Glynn
       Broughton
213 Mark Thompson
214 Ian J R Swift
215 Mrs Thelma Joyce Bolstridge
216 Philip J Kingham
217 Andrew Burton
218 Glyn Hodgetts
219 Kevin G Wedgwood Litting
220 Marcus E Wedgwood Litting
221 Mr Christopher George Boss
222 Stephen Wright
223 Mr R Bradley
224 Andrew J Bell
225 Stewart Osborne
226 Adrian K Mannion
227 Andrew Jarrett
228 Barry Jackson
229 John Priestley
230 T J Whetton
231 Graham Mason
232 P M Riley
233 Mr & Mrs R Shaw
234 Keith James Sims
235 Kevin John Sims
236 Helen Jane Sims
237 Victoria Anne Saunders Sims
238 Tony Bridges
239 Steve Kinsey
240 Kevin Large
241 Craig Fletcher
242 Christine Jennings
243 Rev Gerry Horan
244 Michael G Robinson
245 Ken Hales
246 Gary Keith Shapcott
247 Derek Page
248 John P Dyson
249 John P Dyson
250 Stuart Burnett
251 Dennis P Carman

252 David A J Ahlburg
253 Mr Sheila A Taylor
254 Jonathan N Prime
255 Harry Prime
256 Tony Bosworth
257 Pamela Jones
258 Mrs June Lawrence
259 Mark Llewellyn Jones
260 Allen Wright
261 David Lambert
262 John Timmins
263 Steven McGhee
264 Michael Briggs
265 Stefan Borg
266 Andrew Ian Harris
267 John E Lake
268 Graham Waterall
269 David Hindle
270 Guy Kent
271 John Spencer
272 Stuart Talbot
273 William D Gosling
274 Edwin Annable
275 S M Kelly
276 E Morley
277 Lee Lawrence
278 Martin DuSautoy
279 W Gordon Lee
280 David John Walkup
281 Ian Geary
282 Clare Geary
283 Ronald Hurst
284 Mr Steven Parker
285 Stephen Francis Rowlinson
286 Mr Cliff Hardwick
287 Steven Robert Greenhough
288 Philip Aiken
289 J A Bowler
290 John Middleton
291 Tina Burke & Ian Blythman
292 Inge Harald Haagensen
293 Mrs J M Eason
294 Mr C S K Harpur
295 Paul Wilson
296 Roberto Forchino
297 David Mitchell
298 J W Wharton
299 Colin Walker
300 Pat Thomas
301 Dennis Hawes
302 Simon Wall
303 Christopher Gilbert
304 Ken Walker
305 David Farmer
306 Sue Hyett
307 Dale Allan Jones
308 Anthony Rhodes
309 Arthur Frank Pearson Jnr
310 Mr J Peter Davis
311 Mr Kieran J Mason
312 Charles H B Clark
313 Steven Charles Glaister
314 Anthony John Russell
315 John James Hudson
316 Geoff Webb
317 J Hackman
318 Peter Haslam
319 Paul William Stannard
320 Nigel Wright
321 Gareth Walters

322 Phil & Carol Nicklin
323 Roger Green
324 Paul Green
325 Craig Simpson
326 Duncan Chambers
327 Jason Madeley
328 Anthony K Waterall
329 James Paterson
330 Michael E Holder
331 Roy Woodward
332 Neil Paul Rhodes
333 Peter Seddon
334 Tony Fogg
335 Barry Walker
336 Christopher Taylor
337 Stuart Clarke
338 Jack Statham
339 Darren A England
340 Jeffrey Myring
341 Roger Myring
342 Mick Kerry
343 Sid Slater
344 Fred D Fisher
345 L I Michael Andersson
346 Jonathan J Head
347 Andrew Michael Birch
348 Mark Antony Birch
349 Christopher Robert Dennis
350 Alan William Sellors
351 John R Clarke
352 Graham H Malley
353 Mr Andrew Hallam
354 Tom Noonan
355 Gavin M Collins
356 Andrew J Dawson
357 Raymond Saunders
358 Michael Wilson
359 Michael Wilson
360 David Earnshaw
361 J Ringrose
362 Mr L Dixon
363 Gerald Hill
364 David Keats
365 Jórg-Peter Bartling
366 Peter Pickup
367 Pete Thompson
368 Archways Promotions (Sports
       Booksellers) Edinburgh
369 Andrew Roberts
370 Lyn & Alan Crowther
371 David Cundy
372 Christopher E C Hooker
373 Jeremy Webb
374 David Rigley
375 Mr C Smith
376 Stig Ersvaer
377 Stephen Davis
378 Colin Tustin
379 R Stocken
380 David Gregg
381 John Meredith Williams
382 Mr R Kingman
383 Paul Jerome
384 D Hutt
385 Michael Brett
386 Maurice Curtin